AF560123

Knowledge Transfer and Exchange

Knowledge Transfer and Exchange

Edited by

Dr. S.K. PANNER SELVAM

Assistant Professor, Department of Education

Bharathidasan University, T.N

and

Dr. R.MUTHAIYAN

Assistant Professor, Department of Education

Tamil University

Thanjavur, Tamilnadu

RANDOM PUBLICATIONS

NEW DELHI (INDIA)

Knowledge Transfer and Exchange

ISBN 978-93-5111-896-1

Published in 2016 in India by
RANDOM PUBLICATIONS
4376-A/4B, Gali Murari Lal, Ansari Road
New Delhi-110 002
Phone : +9111-43580356, 011-43142548, 011-23289044
e-mail : sales@randompublications.com
info@randompublications.com
randomexports@gmail.com

Type Setting by : Shah Computer Graphics, Delhi-110094
Printed at: Sanat Printers

Contents

Knowledge Transfer and Exchange

Introduction

Democracy being a group a collective ideology is naturally opposed to the unfettered and unbridled Supremacy of individuals over other individuals. In individuals were to be completely free to do whatever they pleased, as some people think democracy represents, then the physically stronger, the selfish amongst us would acquire ascendancy over those physically weaker, the selfless, the straight forward, the honest and thereby deprive the latter of their political, economic, social freedom and equality. For a democratic nation to be people-welfare oriented it should generate and exchange knowledge and so this paper reflects the role of educational institutions in knowledge exchange. Education always reflects the social culture of which it is a part. It can be established, developed, improved, or completely remade only in terms of the society for which it exists. Education has its basic purpose, always the preservation, and sometimes the improvement of the institutions and culture that constitute society. It is essential, than that a study of our educational program is oriented in a study of our society and our ideals and aspirations for that society. Such a study involves some problems.

The view on knowledge transfer by academic discipline depends on different issues and focuses on specific aspects or stages of the transfer process. Until the early 1980s, the focus of technology transfer research was on international transfers, especially from industrialized nations to Les industrialized countries (Croissant and Smith-Doerr 2007). With the end of the last century, the national research on knowledge transfer gained increasingly in importance. While early studies on business management often dealt with intra-sectoral knowledge transfers and the relationship between technology and business strategy, numerous recent economic studies focus on alliances of companies in the context of development and transfer of knowledge (Bozeman 2000). The study combines ideas about knowledge transfer and knowledge exchange to provide a deep understanding of the nature of knowledge production in educational practices. It advances the literature on knowledge management and organizational learning by exploring organizational knowledge processes at the group level in dispersed settings, and offers a model for effective knowledge exchange processes within other groups with similarly-configured memberships in order to improve the quality of higher education.

Education should make a difference to the learner, it should make a perceptible change in his life; it should matter to him in one way or the other; and should add value to his dreams. It may be knowledge, skill, attitude, behavior, wealth, health, character or learning; it could be anything and in any degree but it should be imparted to a person through education. Collaborative Learning refers to the instruction method in which students at various levels work together in small groups toward a common goal. Collaborative learning shows that school achievements, creations of positive inter group relations and socialization is higher in cooperative settings. Both mainstream and minority students show far greater increases in academic achievement when they participate in collaborative learning projects than when they remain in traditional teacher focused class rooms. Therefore, it is highly advocated as a modern class room technique to provide learner-centered teaching as well as learner participation and contribution in the teaching learning process. The quest for improvement of quality is the central feature of every educational system today. Many progammes have been initiated from time to time based on the emerging needs and analysis of previous experience to achieve national goals. National council of educational research and training (2007) states that innovation is more than having new ideas, it includes the process of successfully introducing them or making things happen in a new way. We all are tired of the traditional method of learning to the stereo typed lecture of various teachers. An exceptional educational environment begins with a vision that the most powerful and meaningful learning when thinking and feeling are fused together. Collaborative learning is a situation in which two or more people learn or attempt to learn something together. Collaborative learning is a technique designed to make learning a lively and successful process.

University is seen as the central source of knowledge, reaching recipients in a one-way relationship. On the other hand, the knowledge interaction through targeted transfer implies critical feedbacks from the recipient, the interaction eventually affecting both partners on their research and transfer activities. Accordingly, the study of untargeted or targeted knowledge flows implies distinctive research tools and methodological approaches. A positivist approach seems appropriate to understand and measure knowledge flows under an explicit form such as patents and other formalized sources. An interpretive or constructivist approach should be more suitable to fully explore knowledge flows occurring through interactions: whereas objective quantitative methods would fall short to capture the tacit component of targeted knowledge flows, a subjective qualitative approach would give the researcher deeper insights about such created knowledge. The global economy is becoming increasingly more competitive and education is one of the key drivers. In order for society to advance the people must be educated. The importance of education is quite clear. One can safely say that a human being is not in the proper sense till he is educated. Education is the knowledge of putting one's potentials to maximum use. It is therefore not an overstatement to say that education and knowledge is the priority for the future. It is an important tool for nation building and development. Knowledge transfer is not only from business to university and vice versa but there is also a big involvement from the government and other knowledge bodies and they should become partners in policy making. Governments of developed nations are actively involved in education and knowledge transfer and this is helping a lot in the transfer of skills to young professionals. It would be of great help if the developing nations can be carried along in some of the projects. This will make a lasting impact on the development of the developing countries. Education and knowledge are important tools for capacity building, food safety, quality and chain management.

A knowledge society is one where growth, development, and innovation are driven by optimal use of information and information products For over a decade now, universities have been aware of the pressures to expand access to higher education.1 The knowledge society needs more graduates, and those graduates will keep returning to study as lifelong learning takes its place in both work and leisure time. These are the positive pressures for expansion. But the knowledge society, fueled by the expanding higher education sector, is in turn generating more knowledge industries, producing additional, competitive pressures for traditional institutions of higher education. Those involved in university teaching in this digital age must cope with the fact that the knowledge industries are creating the means by which individuals can acquire the immediate skills and knowledge those industries need. As a result, many individuals are questioning the true benefit of a university education, given its cost. In this context, this paper refreshes the ways of improving knowledge transfer to improve quality in education. The knowledge society, fueled by the expanding higher education sector, is in turn generating more knowledge industries, producing additional, competitive pressures for traditional institutions of higher education. Those involved in university teaching in this digital age must cope with the fact that the knowledge industries are creating the means by which individuals can acquire the immediate skills and knowledge those industries need. The first purpose testifies to the university's commitment to the long-term personal development of the individual, in contrast with the focus on the short-term employment needs inevitably driving other forms of post-school education, such as corporate training programs.

Twenty-First Centuries included the following concepts relating to relevance that reflect the complexity and extent of the social tasks of contemporary higher education:

1. Relevance in higher education should be assessed in terms of the fit between what society expects of institutions and what they do. This requires ethical standards, political impartiality, critical capacities and, at the same time, a better articulation with the problems of society and the world of work, basing long-term orientations on societal aims and needs, including respect for cultures and environmental protection. The concern is to provide access to both broad general education and targeted, career specific education, often interdisciplinary, focusing on skills and aptitudes, both of which equip individuals to live in a variety of changing settings, and to be able to change occupations.
2. Higher education should reinforce its role of service to society, especially its activities aimed at eliminating poverty, intolerance, violence, illiteracy, hunger, environmental degradation and disease, mainly through an interdisciplinary and trans disciplinary approach in the analysis of problems and issues. Higher education should enhance its contribution to the development of the whole education system, notably through improved teacher education, curriculum development and educational research. Ultimately, higher education should aim at the creation of a new society – non-violent and non-exploitative-consisting of highly cultivated, motivated and integrated individuals, inspired by love for humanity and guided by wisdom."

This means that research on the general issues of the systems and structures of higher education, the relations between higher education and scientific and technological development, and the links between universities, the State, society in general and the productive sectors in particular are evidently priority items on the agenda of the present debate on higher education. It is important to promote a closer and mutually beneficial relationship between the academic and the productive sectors. In several Latin

American countries there is at present a complete break and reciprocal ignorance between these spheres.

The productive and industrial sector generally the theme of university/productive sector relations is very much bound up with the relevance of higher education, namely its capacity to provide a response to the needs of all sectors of society, including the world of work or employment. All these challenges, giving rise to the "new cultures", necessarily lead to transformations that affect the task of higher education. Such changes should be ultimately embodied in a redesigning of curricula, which is a real yardstick for the degree of transformation undergone by any particular academic institution. When all is said and done, a university is its curriculum. While educators who do not have technical backgrounds may consider it to be a daunting task to develop an understanding of technology, it is critical for the successful take-up of technologies that schools and educators drive selection and deployment of technology and are empowered through the process to take ownership of the technology. For effective ICT deployment in education, a holistic approach to professional development should be multi-pronged and should focus on:

1. ICT skills for government officials and change management processes associated with ICT deployment;
2. ICT for leadership in schools;
3. ICT for administration in schools;
4. ICT technical installation, security and maintenance; and
5. ICT for enhancing teaching and learning.

The concept of a 'Knowledge Society' is often confused with that of an 'Information Society'. The latter is, however, considered more limited, as the application of knowledge to data creates information, and information has to be activated or generated by knowledge. The concept of 'knowledge societies' includes a dimension of social, cultural, economical, political, and institutional transformation, and a more pluralistic and developmental perspective. It is regarded as a human process.

UNESCO argues that progression from Information Societies to Knowledge Societies requires that 'use of ICT must be linked to the recognition that knowledge is the principal force of the social, political, cultural and institutional dimensions of development, founded on human rights.

Possible Ways of Knowledge Transfer

Knowledge is power and the same is strengthened or enhanced when it is transferred among the stakeholders of education. The knowledge when it is shared in right perspective with the different sections of the society, the real fruits of the effect of knowledge is realized to the maximum extent. The stakeholders namely industries, business firms, Social welfare Organisation, NGOS and the community should never remain isolated from the educational institutions. The close proximity between these two will result in a real exchange of relevant knowledge which will be more useful for the betterment of the society. The knowledge transfer in a comprehensive way with the necessary collaborations by all possible means is the need of the hour. The phrase "Knowledge is Power" holds lot of truth, Education is the means of building capacity the important factor in determining ones standard of living and income potential. If the knowledge and learning is to be useful it has to be applied to the areas of life where it can make differences. Knowledge transfer also generates a return investment of public funds in the science research base. Communication is very important in knowledge transfer. Examples of knowledge transfer includes, applied and collaborative research, consultancy sponsored students, regional projects. Healthy system of knowledge, transfer should demonstrate considerable diversity, in knowledge transfer approaches and activities, both within and across institutions, and across disciplines and national research priorities.

Stakeholders are "individuals or entities who stand to gain or lose from the success or failure of a system or an organization". There are many stakeholders in education each of whom needs to play his role effectively in order to help all our children learn better and reach their fullest potential. They are the child himself, his parents and family, his teachers, his principal MOEHQ, the community, business and industry, the Alumni Association as well as the school Advisory Management Committee in helping the child learn and grow. The stakeholders in different capacities contribute much to the development of the society. The expertise in every field gets doubled or multiplied when the knowledge is showed among each. Thus the vital role of knowledge transfers.

Expectations of Stakeholders

Core expectations of individual stakeholders seem to vary according to their particular interest or stake in the issue including profitability, financial growth, quality of leadership, adequacy of resources allocated, efficiency of resources used, cost and quality of services.

1. Society wants to educate children in order to ensure that its various economical and cultural institutions are perpetuated and expanded. Its aim is to mould students into the next generations of producers and consumers.
2. Government wants to educate children to ensure a stable productive and powerful nation in keeping with national goals.
3. Religious groups want to educate children in order to bring them in line with their cultural norms.
4. Parent wants their children to have education so that they are equipped with skills that will allow them to leave home and flourish and do them credit.
5. Students expect to be educated, so that they have plenty of choices in ways in which to comfortably realize the autonomy they so envied in their parents.

Knowledge transfer is part of organizational life. It is carried out whether the process is managed or not. It is transmission of knowledge (experience, lessons learned, know-how) and use of transmission of knowledge. It is conveying the knowledge of one source to another source. Merely making knowledge available is not considered to be knowledge sharing, collaboration, and networking. It is access to scare resources, new insights; new expertise crosses fertilization of knowledge, and creating an organizational environment of excellence.

In order to compete in knowledge intense and globalized world institution must continuously acquire, absorb and transfer knowledge. Institutions that are capable of producing a continuous stream of new knowledge are better positioned to achieve a competitive advantage. Institutions cannot create knowledge without the actions and interactions of individuals because knowledge is created by and resides within individuals. New knowledge is created when individuals solve problems by combining and exchanging information and knowhow with others. Knowledge transfer is not merely communicating or sharing information or making it accessible to people who need them.

Knowledge is one of the most important resources of an organization. It is therefore not an overstatement to say that education and knowledge is the priority for the future. It is an important tool for nation building and development. Knowledge transfer is not only from business to university and vice versa but there is also a big involvement from the government and other knowledge bodies and they should become partners in policy-making Governments of developed nations are actively involved in education and knowledge transfer and this is helping a lot in the transfer of skills to young professionals. Education and knowledge are important tools for capacity building food safety quality and chain management.

Knowledge Transformation

Knowledge management theories and frameworks are applied in the public sector is not well understood due to little evidence being published in the literature. When employees view knowledge as a public good belonging to the whole organization, knowledge flows easily. However, even when individuals give the highest priority to the interests of the organization of their community, they tend to away from contributing knowledge for a variety of reasons: To contribute out of fear of criticism, or of misleading the community members. To remove the identified barriers, there is a need for developing various types of trust, ranging from the knowledge 'based to the institution' based trust.

Knowledge management, arguing that its focus on to create a network structure may limit its potential for encouraging knowledge sharing across social communities. In the other, while IT was used to provide a network to encourage sharing, there was also recognition of the importance of face to face interaction for sharing knowledge. The emphasis was on encouraging active networking among dispersed communities, rather than relying on IT networks. Argues for a community 'based model of knowledge management for interactive innovation and contrasts this with the cognitive' based view.

The concepts of knowledge translation, knowledge transfer, knowledge exchange, research utilization, implementation, diffusion, and dissemination. The concept of moving knowledge into action. It also offers a conceptual framework for thinking about the process and integrates the roles of knowledge creation and knowledge application. The implications of knowledge translation for continuing education. On the best available knowledge, the use of educational and other transfer strategies that are known to be effective, and the value of learning about planned-action theories to be better able to understand and influence change in practice settings.

Improving Knowledge Transfer Through Education

At a more basic level, the curriculum would seem to be seriously out of gear with the demands of work in knowledge economies, where new knowledge, skills and attitudes are at a premium the ability to learn how to learn and other met cognitive or 'thinking' skills; the ability to learn on the job and in teams; the ability to cope with ambiguous situations and unpredictable problems; the ability to communicate well verbally, not just in writing; and the ability to be creative, innovative and entrepreneurial. To enable teachers to help students to learn in these ways, and so to organize schools, would indeed be transformation. In the knowledge society teachers must be models of what their students are to become, highly effective and adaptable learners.

Knowledge transfer and exchange is as an interactive process involving the interchange of knowledge between research users and researcher producers. Despite many strategies for it is not clear which ones should be used in which contexts. The synthesis of the Knowledge transfer and exchange for policy. The Dynamic Knowledge Transfer components required for social systems to generate disseminate and use new knowledge to meet their needs of stakeholders. Transformation has recently become the language of educational policymakers in different places. They seem very comfortable with the term, though. When virtually every new development is purposefully transformative, for transformation has to mean more than just continuing improvement if it is to be more than a rhetorical device for selling the latest educational initiative. Transformation implies a profound or fundamental change, a metamorphosis that involves some radical innovation, not just incremental innovation.

Knowledge Creation

The knowledge represents knowledge creation and consists of the major types of knowledge or research that exist and can be used in quality education. As knowledge moves through the education, it becomes more detailed and refined and presumably more useful to stakeholders. Another analogy would be to think of the research being sifted through filters at each phase so that, in the end, only the most valid and useful knowledge is left. For example, the phase of knowledge inquiry represents the unmanageable multitude of quality that is out there and that may or may not be easily accessed. This can be thought of as first-generation knowledge that is in its natural state and largely.

Knowledge synthesis or knowledge represents the aggregation of existing knowledge. The process involves the application of explicit and reproducible methods to the identification, appraisal, and synthesis of studies or information relevant to specific questions. It is done to make sense of all the relevant knowledge. This knowledge often takes the form of systematic reviews, including meta-analysis and meta-synthesis. Knowledge consists of knowledge. Such as practice guidelines, decision aids and rules, and care pathways.

There is conceptual use of knowledge that describes changes in levels of knowledge, understanding, or attitudes; instrumental use that describes changes in behavior or and strategic use that relates to the manipulation of knowledge to attain specific power or profit goals. Monitoring use of the knowledge is necessary to determine how and the extent to which it has diffused throughout the potential-adopter group. It can also be used to determine whether the interventions have been sufficient to bring about the desired change or whether more of the same or new interventions may be required. If the degree of knowledge use is less than expected and desired, it may be useful potential adopters at this stage about their intention to use the knowledge.

Our description of knowledge translation and knowledge transfer demonstrates that, the field of knowledge transformation while not exactly uncharted territory is territory that has differing views on its boundaries and on the nature of the terrain. In order to advance the science of consensus on terms and definitions is essential if knowledge producers and implementers and users are to effectively and meaningfully communicate with each other. The establishment of a common nomenclature is also often an important step in advancing a new field of scientific inquiry and is particularly useful in outlining the research agenda and highlighting its gaps. Ensuring that knowledge to action occurs is complex and challenging. As we have outlined, is about an exchange of knowledge between relevant stakeholders that results in action. To achieve this, appropriate relationships must be cultivated

Knowledge Transfer Process

In recent years, knowledge, the human capital, and learning organizations have become the key determinants of current global progress. Higher educational sector has been faced with globalization and strong competition. Therefore, the need has arisen for professional management structures and more entrepreneurial style of leadership. Organizations have been transformed to learning organizations by the lifelong learning concept, whilc the knowledge management has become the leading tool in building competitive advantages. High education organizations are being pushed forward by competitiveness. That pressure requires continuous improvement emphasizing the need for measuring outcomes and building excellence. The paradigm of stakeholder analysis, applied to specific determinations of the system of higher education institutions, could be a good way for comprehending and predicting interests, needs and requirements of all key players in the environment. The purpose of this paper is to enhance the possibility of understanding the connection between higher education institutions and its environment in context of stakeholder analysis. The paper uses literature as a basis in identifying critical parameters for stakeholder analysis and its implementation to higher education sector. The findings of the paper reveal that the concept of stakeholders is critical and difficult to implement everywhere and to everything. There is a clear attempt of all organizations, especially those that create and encourage knowledge, to understand the actions of all participants and predictions of interests and requirements of the changing environment. During the last ten years numerous publications dealing with knowledge management-related issues have been published in journals ranging from Conservation Biology, Post-Communist Economies, Childhood and European History Quarterly to more business-oriented journals such as Research Policy, Journal of Knowledge Management, Harvard Business Review and KM World. It can be argued that in aiming for efficient Knowledge Management (KM), the search for "correct" choices of methods and steps is crucial. These choices require a well-defined taxonomy with clear concepts and terms. The content and meaning must be clear cut and there should be no ambiguity about the aim when fundamental concepts are used. Although this is undoubtedly a desirable objective, it is hardly the current state of affairs regarding commonly used terminology in KM. In many cases, the authors use central terms interchangeably and without making a distinction between them and sometimes without sufficient explanation of from which perspective the terms are used.

Development of the Terms: Knowledge Transfer and Knowledge Sharing

In the first part of this section, we try to show the emergence, reemergence and development of KT and KS. Figure 1 is an attempt to visualize the different authors use of the terms with regards to their level on an individual-industry scale and the publication year. This is followed by the development of KBs. The emergence and of KT and KS Knowledge, its definition, source and method in which it is acquired has been discussed (at least) since the time of the philosophical debates by Aristotle and Plato. We would, therefore, propose that the initial emergence of the terms comes from these discussions and that the suggestions on how to deal with efficient and effective knowledge transfer and sharing has been ongoing to a varying degree of intensity since then. The second stream is based on the writings of Michael Polanyi and the terms tacit and explicit knowledge. In an influential Harvard Business Review article, Ikujiro Nonaka touches on the issues of KT and KS, even though he does not mention them explicitly. He writes "Explicit knowledge is formal and systematic, for this reason, it can be easily communicated and shared" Later in the same article, he says "This helps create a "common cognitive ground" among employees and thus facilitates the transfer of tacit knowledge."

The knowledge transfer process in education aims to increase the use of research results by potential users (Havelock 1973; Huberman 1983) in order to improve practices, to implement new programs, and to resolve specific problems. As explained earlier, four theoretical frameworks led the study of this concept in the education literature: the RDD models, the problem-solving models, the linkage models, and the social interaction models. The examination of the included studies shows that the three first models have received serious criticisms from the scientific community of researchers on education. In addition to paying all the attention to the university-created knowledge, the RDD models have been criticized to support logic of absence of knowledge exchange and interaction between actors belonging to different disciplines and different fields of expertise (Hargreaves 1999).

In view of the fact that the management is becoming increasingly aware of the role of education and development, it is obvious that the importance and meaning of modern high educational organizations are changing along with the importance of education in general. Individuals, organizations, and entire economies are finding knowledge and investing in education to be a unique opportunity for developing personal, organizational, economic capabilities and potentials in achieving competitive advantage.

The paper shows the complexity of problems in managing higher educational organizations in context of dynamics and its relation to the environment. Organizations in field of higher education also need to build a quality management system that respects the philosophy of Knowledge management, and they have to deal with problems of Human Resource management in relation to appearance and development of knowledge workers. Furthermore, the modality of stakeholders indicates the diversity and multidimensional environment that defines and determines a modern organization. By organizing the model of lifelong learning and respecting the learning organization criteria we should be able to build organizations highly representative in our competitive era.

Higher education in India is undergoing considerable change. With over 600 million people in India under 25 years old, the system is under tremendous pressure to expand. India's young population has a huge appetite for education and, as the growth in the size of the middle classes escalates, millions are increasingly able to pay for it. By 2020, India will have the largest tertiary-age population in the world and will have the second largest graduate talent pipeline globally, following China and ahead of the USA.

The opportunities for the UK to engage with India through education are considerable.

Higher education in India: the context for change The Indian higher education system is facing an unprecedented transformation in the coming decade. This transformation is being driven by economic and demographic change: by 2020, India will be the world's third largest economy, with a correspondingly rapid growth in the size of its middle classes. Currently, over 50% of India's population is under 25 years old; by 2020 India will outpace China as the country with the largest tertiary-age population. Despite significant progress over the last ten years, Indian higher education is faced with four broad challenges:

In the next decade, India will experience enormous growth in its middle classes: from 50 million now, to 500 million by 20257. By 2020, India will be the world's third largest economy. The relationship between economic growth and growth in the tertiary enrolment ratio is particularly strong for economies with lower levels of GDP (purchasing power parity) per capita. As India's economy continues to grow, a huge number of first generation learners will demand access to higher education. In ten years' time, 25 million households across India will have an income equivalent to $15,000 and will be able to pay fees for higher education, an increase of 15 million on today's enrolment rates8.

However, growth will be uneven; India will be challenged by a growing disparity between those who have access to better life chances, and those who do not. Despite huge strides in primary enrolment rates, India still has the largest number of out-of-school children in the world, more than the whole of sub-Saharan Africa, and 69% of India's population still lives on less than $2 a day9. The World Bank categorizes India as "an extreme dual economy"

The World's Biggest Tertiary-age Population

Another significant driver for educational change is population growth and the demographic profile. More than 50% of India's population is under the age of 25. By 2020, India will have one of the youngest populations in the world, with an average age of 29 years10. India will outpace China in the next ten years as the country with the largest tertiary-age population11 and its relative success in boosting primary enrolment, access to secondary education and improved retention rates should see it have the largest growth in tertiary enrolment in the world in 202012.

The interview data and the extensive reforms in higher education in India reveal a system undergoing considerable transformation. There is a sense of urgency in policy makers, institution leaders and faculty to expand the system at a fast enough pace to meet the surge in demand, while increasing quality and ensuring equitable access. There is a great deal of caution about the way reforms will unfold; progress is likely to follow an unpredictable course. The federal government is enabling states and institutions more autonomy to drive through reforms, which is creating greater potential for international engagement. Indian institutions are seeking more international collaboration on their terms and which will address their challenges. These reforms and the needs of the higher education sector have implications for future collaboration with Indian higher education. This section provides some considerations and opportunities for UK institutions as they plan for future strategic engagement with India.

The last decades have been defined by significant social, economic, political and cultural changes, while European higher education sector has been transforming, and above all those important changes affect the conceptualization and functioning of universities. Modern economy, organizations and workers are focused on and are determined by knowledge. Because knowledge is a key resource and a basic asset in this day and age, our society is being transformed by new skills, techniques and paradigms of knowledge, so new generations need 21st century skills: critical thinking, communications, collaboration and creativity. The function of human resources management becomes strategically important when providing organizational purpose in the highly competitive environment. In that context, the managing of high education organizations means understanding the complexity of the environment, investing in capable people, developing research capacity through concept of knowledge management and increasing the competitive advantage from stakeholders perspective.

In view of the fact that the management is becoming increasingly aware of the role of education and development, it is obvious that the importance and meaning of modern high educational organizations are changing along with the importance of education in general. Individuals, organizations, and entire economies are finding knowledge and investing in education to be a unique opportunity for developing personal, organizational, economic capabilities and potentials in achieving competitive advantage. The process of transformation of economy and society in the era of knowledge is inevitably tied to the entire education system, especially to high education organizations. Consequently, a stakeholder analysis could be one of the successful tools when planning and managing such type of organizations in a highly changing environment. The role of knowledge and education in the knowledge society is not the same as it was some time ago. It is dramatically changed, and it will continue to change in the years to come.

Human resource management process involves the acquisition, retention and development of human resources, its basic dimensions are: (i) recruitment/selection, (ii) performance appraisal and (iii) training. Human resource management is important for several reasons. First many studies have concluded that people are the most significant source of competitive advantage, second Human resource Knowledge is important part of organizational strategies and finally, the way organizations treat people has been found to significantly affect organizational performance. In the age of human capital, human resource strategy means – a people centered approach which emphasizes the need to develop to their fullest potential all present and future employees.

Government and Stakeholder Relationship in the Knowledge Management Process

Management process is as four core interrelated phases, each of which has an underlying factual or scientific and social dimension (McAdam and Reid, 2000):

1. Knowledge construction.
2. Knowledge embodiment.
3. Knowledge dissemination.
4. The application of knowledge.

The paper shows the complexity of problems in managing higher educational organizations in context of dynamics and its relation to the environment. Organizations in field of higher education also need to build a quality management system that respects the philosophy of Knowledge management, and they have to deal with problems of Human Resource management in relation to appearance and development of knowledge workers. Furthermore, the modality of stakeholders indicates the diversity and multidimensional environment that defines and determines a modern organization. By organizing the model of lifelong learning and respecting the learning organization criteria we should be able to build organizations highly representative in our competitive era.

Influencing Knowledge

The importance of the family firm in the economy of a country is an indisputable fact, even more if the consequences of their business activities in the integral development of a society are analyzed (Donckels & Fröhlich, 1991; Basco, 2010). Studies in different countries have shown that family businesses play a key role in terms of economic growth and employment generation (Pistrui, Huang, Oksoy, Jing & Welsch, 2001; Anderson & Reeb, 2003). It is estimated that these kinds of companies account for 85 percent of all companies worldwide, 65 percent of the GDP and employment in Europe, and 50 percent of US GDP and 60 percent of its employment.

A very important aspect related to the development of leadership in a succession process is the level of successors' commitment and motivation, which reflects an emotional bond with the organization characterized by the desire to enter and remain in it: as well as predecessors' motivation and commitment (Bracci, 2008; Le Breton-Miller et al., 2004; Sallán, 2006). However, to Cabrera and Martín (2010), in some cases, the incorporation of the successor in the company is related to a sense of obligation and loyalty to the family. These two commitment dimensions, affective and normative respectively, can do that successors have completely different behaviors. So, when commitment is affective, successors will be more committed to the company and will be identify and involve more with business's goals. Nevertheless, when the commitment is normative, successors will not dedicate the maximum effort to the company or will not fully appreciate what they have of it, because they will be on the company by obligation and not by vocation.
Cabrera-Suarez et al. (2001) point that the quality of the inter-generational relationship is important because it can affect the ability of the predecessors to teach and train their offspring, so that it is possible the important knowledge transmission to the company (Bracci, 2008).

Psychological Ownership of the Family Business

Following Chirico (2008), psychological ownership refers to the emotional feeling possessed by family members over the family business, with a strong sense of identity, residence, responsibility and control over it. That is, to invest a lot of energy, time, money and emotions in the family business is part of the identity and culture of the family members that increase their feelings of ownership over the organization. Family ownership reinforces the family members' psychological identification with and the involvement in the family business, stimulating learning and knowledge transfer (Zahra, 2012).

Preparing successors for leadership involves knowing the key aspects of the company, the sector where it operates, developing management skills and gaining knowledge of themselves. So it is necessary that the training process is both before joining the company as once incorporated in it (Cabrera & Martín, 2010). For this, successor must have a significant absorption capacity to understand, embrace and exploit the new knowledge gained through their predecessors (Argote & Ingram, 2000; Zapata et al., 2009).

The predecessor or founder is the main source of knowledge in the family business. He should be motivated and aware of the necessary steps through business succession and the gradual loss of power and activity in the day to day and strategic decisions. So he should work and put effort to support the transfer of knowledge (Le Breton-Miller et al., 2004. The first step to achieving this is the consciousness of this need and the predecessor's motivation and active involvement in the successors' training and development, resulting in effective knowledge transfer, what will facilitate their access to the company. Thus, the predecessor should involve and delegate functions and power to successors, and in turn maintain a supervisory and observation role (Bracci, 2008).

Relationships with Family Business Associations

In some countries there are Regional Associations formed by family businesses in various sectors of activity. These family business associations have four main objectives:

1. improving the legal framework of family businesses,
2. carrying out training and advice activities in order to contribute to the continuity and strengthening of the family business,
3. increasing awareness of family businesses among the public
4. being a meeting point for business people.

We have defined knowledge transfer as the communication process of knowledge from one generation to another or between the same generations. This knowledge concept includes information, experiences, beliefs, values, insights, know-how and skills. Once defined, we have analyzed the factors, aspects or characteristics that make up the knowledge transfer, in terms of relationships between members, commitment, successors' training and experience, predecessor involvement, relationships with associations. This knowledge can be more easily shared and transferred within family businesses because they have special characteristics that differentiate them from non-family firms. In family firms, successors need to acquire knowledge from the previous generation, but also need to add the new knowledge they have acquired through their education and personal experience and share it among their generation and the rest of generations.

Knowledge Transfer Among Stakeholders of Education

Education is a key factor of progress, and investments in education are crucial for "knowledge economy" when referring to people and organizations, well-organized and innovative education system ensures overall economic growth. The organizations in the area of education are in particular need of a good leadership, capable employees, and good quality staff programs and work performance monitoring. Globalization, demographic changes, IT revolution and Knowledge economy are drivers of contemporary changes determining the new knowledge society while simultaneously searching for new skills and knowledge's.

Employers are the only living organizational element and the most valuable asset of this successful organization. Good training (Seminar, Workshop, Orientation programme, Sports meet), development, Monitoring, the opportunity for advancement good reward programmes, are given to develop and encourage the employers. The essential purpose of University is teaching and education, but also research and innovation. The third part of the mission covers the knowledge management, the cooperation between sectors and questions the role and the position of knowledge and high education organization in the contemporary, turbulent times.

Some of the results of this cooperation that take the form of expert advice, policy recommendations, guidance documents, peer review of national policies and awareness raising initiatives. The first step is trying to identify the key stakeholders, their goals and expectations. The second step is trying to fulfill their goals to their utmost satisfaction concurrently accomplishing the organizational mission. Stakeholders are any group or an individual who can affect or is affected by the achievement of the organization objectives. Stakeholder analysis can be used to generate knowledge about relevant actors so as to understand their behavior, intentions, interrelations, agendas, interests and the influence or recourses they have.

Enhancing change agent skills and abilities in managing the change process in teachers, leaders and other educators. Person to person consultation is the preferred means of getting new information. Having an individual at the user end, who understands the needs for and application of reliable information is important. Use of electronic medium to store information and Internet is advisable where available. Researchers should consider the purposes of different media; the identification of media 'routes'; ensuring the message is accessible; the nature of available media; the selection of the right media – printed media, broadcasting media, media for giving and receiving; and improving media practice.

Strategies for Communication and Knowledge Exchange

1. Promote and support community media, knowledge sharing and networking by providing technical expertise to help communities to make their own publications, recordings and programmes and form networks and federations to share experience.
2. Network and undertake knowledge sharing experience with peers by publishing their experience and providing feedback and acknowledgement to those that have provided ideas.
3. Ensure participatory planning and strategy making by encouraging citizens to participate in new development and redevelopment and pay special attention to improving the participation of marginalized groups.
4. Appraise periodically resources and skills available to do the tasks above by monitoring, auditing and improving all aspects of

knowledge transfer ensuring its effectiveness at all levels and in all directions.

Knowledge transfer capacities and skills

The list of related facilitating practices of the Recommendation includes the following:

1. "Sufficient resources and incentives are available to public research organisations and their staff to engage in knowledge transfer activities.
2. Measures are taken to ensure the availability and facilitate the recruitment of trained staff (such as technology transfer officers) by public research organizations.
3. A set of model contracts is made available, as well as a decision-making tool helping the most appropriate model contract to be selected, depending on a number of parameters.
4. The pooling of resources between public research organizations at local or regional level is promoted where these do not have the critical mass of research spending to justify having their own knowledge transfer office or intellectual property manager.
5. Programmes supporting research spin-offs are launched, incorporating entrepreneurship training and featuring strong interaction of public research organizations with local incubators, financiers, business support agencies, etc.
6. Government funding is made available to support knowledge transfer and business engagement at public research organizations, including through hiring experts."

The ultimate goal is the building a model of learning organizations – organizations that have developed the capacity to learn, adapt and change continuously. The world is changing daily, forcing the concept of knowledge and technology to become the key factor of modeling organizations and the entire society. Education institutions are changing and are in need of entrepreneurial style of leadership.

Knowledge Exchange

Knowledge Transfer (KT) is the transfer of knowledge, expertise, skills and capabilities from universities as the academic knowledge base to companies or organizations in need of the knowledge, such as non-government organizations, commercial and industrial sectors, and various non-academic beneficiaries. In the past, it was called technology transfer or simply commercialization, but the new term now encompasses transfer of knowledge and know-how in the Arts, Education, and Humanities etc. The ultimate goal of knowledge transfer is to implement impacts on institution, network, knowledge and personal aspects so as to generate strategic innovations through synergy. Apart from seminars and public talks, knowledge transfer encompasses a very broad range of activities, including:

1. Contract Research /Collaborative Research/ Consultancy / Facilities and Testing.
2. Innovation/IPR/Spinout activity /Regeneration Support/CPD/ Training/Workforce Development/ Student entrepreneurship / Social, Cultural and Community Engagement.

Knowledge exchange (KE) is a process which brings together academic staff, users of research and wider groups and communities to exchange ideas, evidence and expertise. A global Knowledge exchange landscape is swiftly changing, moving towards open innovation. The open innovation paradigm demonstrates the need to exploit internal and external knowledge transfer pathways in order to remain competitive in a market place. The industrial companies are increasingly facing pressure from growing competition, a shortening product life cycle and increased complexity. Assuming that transfer activities between academic and private sectors will contribute to business competitiveness and economic growth, researches have intensively investigated University-Industry relationships. This paper focuses on studying knowledge-transfer collaborations between academia and industry.

Knowledge exchange is a two-way process where social scientists and individuals or organisations share learning, ideas and experiences. We are committed to knowledge exchange and encouraging collaboration between researchers and the private, public and civil society sectors. By creating a dialogue between these communities, knowledge exchange helps research to influence policy and practice. We build partnerships and work collaboratively in a range of ways. Examples of our collaborative activity include:

1. developing strategic partnerships with organisations to ensure we maximize the impact of our activities
2. working with partner organisations to develop and fund major research and capacity building initiatives
3. supporting initiatives to foster direct collaboration between social scientists and other individuals and organisations.

Business, civil society, public service organisations as well as individuals in these organisations can benefit by collaborative working with academic researchers. Through collaboration, partners can learn about each other's expertise, share knowledge and gain an appreciation of different professional cultures. Shared activities can enable partner organisations to engage with academic research to add value, offer insights and influence key issues of concern for policy and practice.

The benefits of such collaborative activities are greatest when considered before the start, and when built into a project, and shouldn't be considered an add-on at the end of a project. Business, civil society and public services can directly benefit through knowledge exchange and collaborative working with researchers by:

1. accessing experts and cutting edge research
2. accessing innovative ideas that could improve policy or practice
3. enhancing organizational creativity, performance and productivity

Exploiting Collaborative Knowledge

There are four critical knowledge management processes used by firms to access and transform knowledge from an alliance context to a partner context: technology sharing; JV-parent interactions; personnel movement; and linkages between parent and alliance strategies. These processes create connections for individual managers through which they can communicate their alliance experiences to others and form the foundation for the integration of knowledge into the parent's collective knowledge base. As individuals interact through the various connections, the interactions become larger in scale and faster in speed as more and more actors in the organization become involved. This process has been described as a "spiral" of organizational knowledge creation.11 In the spiral, knowledge starts at the individual level, moves up to the group level, and then to the firm level. As the knowledge spirals upward in the organization, it may be enriched and extended as individuals interact with each other and with their organizations.

Although the knowledge management processes are not complex or difficult to understand, the lack of complexity should not be associated with a lack of effectiveness. The creation of organizational knowledge requires the sharing and dissemination of individual experiences. Each process provides an avenue for JV parent managers to gain exposure to knowledge and ideas outside their traditional organizational boundaries. The processes deal with both operational and strategic knowledge and taken together, provide a comprehensive view as to how alliance knowledge can cross organizational boundaries and become the basis for knowledge creation in parent firms.

India: A Knowledge Based Society

Knowledge enables an individual to think, to analyse and to understand the existing situation, and the inter-linkages and externalities of each action. It empowers an individual to form his or her own opinion, to act and transform conditions to lead to a better quality of life. The knowledge-based society can offer tremendous potential for reducing social exclusion, both by creating the economic conditions for greater prosperity through higher levels of growth and employment. The Indian education system improvement is required at many levels– from primary schools to higher education and research institutions of national excellence. At all levels, there is a need to improve both access and excellence. Research in the field of the human social sciences plays a fundamental role in understanding and managing the many ways in which society is currently changing. The increasing extent of services in the pace of technological changes, the advanced level of information and knowledge, as well as the size of the industrial and social re-organizations, all give good arguments in favour of the knowledge based society. In a society of the future, education will play an essential role in creating the new way of life specific to knowledge and learning based society. In order to create a world class knowledge society, every one of us has to be knowledge worker. This paper describes the importance of creating a knowledge based society for making India a powerful country.

We are living in a society dominated by change. The technical, economic and social evolution has shaped people's way of living and thinking. The ability of a nation to use and create knowledge capital determines its capacity to empower and enable its citizens by increasing human capabilities. In the words of our Prime Minister, "The time has come to create a second wave of institution building and of excellence in the field of education, research and capability building so that we are better prepared for the 21st century." A successful advanced society is founded on a strong scientific base that has the ability to convert scientific research and knowledge into products and services. The globalized markets, the technical and technological revolutions are transforming the modern economy into a "knowledge based society" in which new ways of organizing the work are governing the world, demanding a perpetual buildup of competences, solid knowledge and increasing responsibilities.

The Terms of Reference of NKC also reflect its overarching aim to transform India into a vibrant knowledge-based society. The Terms of Reference of the NKC are as follows: Build excellence in the educational system to meet the knowledge challenges of the 21st century and increase India's competitive advantage in fields of knowledge. Promote creation of knowledge in Science and Technology laboratories. Improve the management of institutions engaged in Intellectual Property Rights. Promote knowledge applications in Agriculture, Medical, Industry and other sectors. Promote the use of knowledge capabilities in making government an effective, transparent and accountable service provider to the citizen and promote widespread sharing of knowledge to maximize public benefit.

Now, in the early stages of the 21st century changes are happening again. This time it is Knowledge, that will from now on forward function as the bases of society and the economy. It means that buying of wealth and power is no longer linked to land possession, agricultural production, or industrial output. Increasingly more manual labor is now being performed by machines and robots. Power and wealth has become linked to the possession and production of Data, information, scientific discovery and Knowledge.

Recommendations of the National Knowledge Commission

The main recommendations of the National Knowledge Commission (NKC) set up by former Prime Minister Manmohan Singh in 2005 under the chairmanship of Mr. Sam Pitroda: Education for developing a learning society, Setting up a National Commission on libraries, Provide impetus for developing translation as an industry, Central legislation is required to affirm the Right to Education, Teaching of English as a language should be introduced, along with the first language, starting from class I in school, Build a national knowledge network to connect 5,000 nodes across institutions, Place vocational education entirely under the Ministry of Human Resource Development, Change system of regulation for higher education and create more universities, A National Science and Social Science Foundation to be established to suggest policy initiatives. Knowledge is the most powerful engine of production. Knowledge is defined as "information and understanding about a subject which a person has or which all people have." Knowledge can be found in books, information systems, data systems, organizations, in the new media, in social activities, in cognitive structures, in all kind of products and in social systems. Every day we combine, generate, protect, create, transfer, codify and save knowledge. Knowledge based society is a society whose processes and practices are based on the production, distribution, and use of knowledge. The formation of a knowledge-based society is a global process, and elements of a knowledge-based society develop in a country regardless of its capabilities and resources. Knowledge has become a vital commodity to countries, businesses and individuals in the 21st century - age of the knowledge based society.

Education has played and is still playing an important role in forming and training the individual throughout his existence. In these days society, however, enforces some specific traits of the whole educational process that are anchored into the reality of the present. Education as an essential activity in the development of society has seen major transformations, from which the new methods and models of the modern educational system have resulted. The relationship between the individual and society becomes more complex via education, as the individual gains the capability to make his contribution that would balance the benefits of his living among other individuals. Students, universities, colleges and Indian young community are really the knowledge seeker. They want to acquire new knowledge, work with innovations in each and every field.

Few Suggestions for Making the Knowledge-based Society

There are few suggestions for making the knowledge-based society-

1. To improve working conditions and ensure dignity of worker;
2. Transferring knowledge through education and professional training;
3. Empowering citizens and increasing transparency;
4. Disseminating the knowledge by publishing;
5. Utilizing knowledge in the society's best interest, especially through innovation;

6. Building the motivation to learn and adapt to the perpetual learning process in all;
7. Create new interface structures to forge partnerships between academia and industry;
8. Reducing the transaction cost and improving the reach and quality of public services;
9. Adopt more active approach towards increasing the visibility of the library and its services to the society through various social marketing strategies;

Knowledge can be considered as the only resource, which can be reproduced infinitely. The Indian education system improvement is required at many levels – from primary schools to higher education and research institutions of national excellence. Today's policy makers must extend our country's existing strengths through careful investments in education, institutional quality, and relevant technology. They must create enterprises that are knowledgeable enough to recognize new competitive opportunities and skill full enough to convert those opportunities into wealth. Knowledge based society opens new perspectives such as: chance to decrease the gap between developed and developing countries; more chances for individual development; respect to individuals; freedom of self-organization. In a society of the future, education will play an essential role in creating the new way of life specific to knowledge and learning based society. Therefore, the development of the knowledge based society is dependent on the creation of knowledge, on its spreading via education and on its dissemination via communication and on its involvement in technological innovation. In order to create a world class knowledge society, every one of us has to be knowledge worker for making India a knowledge super power.

Knowledgeable Society

An educational institution is a place where people of different ages gain an education, including preschools, childcare, elementary schools, and universities. 'Knowledge is power', but we can hardly affirm that the society we live in is based on the vigor of knowledge. The market price placed on knowledge fails to provide it with the needed qualitative impetus. We may indeed be restoring a sort of enlightened despotism of a technologically neo-positivistic type, a realm of experts whose 'know-how' is but another term for 'doing without knowing'. In a truly democratic sense, the knowledge society is a basic human right. Knowledge is nourished in society.

A knowledge society generates, processes, shares and makes available to all members of the society knowledge that may be used to improve the human condition. A knowledge society differs from an information society in that the former serves to transform information into resources that allow society to take effective action while the latter only creates and disseminates the raw data. The growth of Information and Communication Technology (ICT) has significantly increased the world's capacity for creation of raw data and the speed at which it is produced. The advent of the internet delivered unheard of quantities of information to people. Innovation in digital technologies and mobile devices offers individuals a means to connect anywhere anytime where digital technologies are accessible. Tools of ICT have the potential to transform education, training, employment and access to life-sustaining resources for all members of society.

However, this capacity for individuals to produce and use data on a global scale does not necessarily result in knowledge creation. Contemporary media delivers seemingly endless amounts of information and yet, the information alone does not create knowledge. For knowledge creation to take place, reflection is required to create awareness, meaning and understanding. The improvement of human circumstances requires critical analysis of information to develop the knowledge that assists humankind.

Societal and natural conditions determine the role and the function of education. Within the relationship between education and society, the most salient feature of education is its communal side. The social context is imperative for education to function well. Society and education complete each other. Society cannot carry on without education and vice versa. Education affects not only the person being educated but also the whole community by starting from his/her family. In other words, raising sufficient number of efficient people for more prosperous society is the duty of education and educational institutions which have certain functions in the community. If established a prior and hierarchical sequence, society can be regarded as the objective and the education can be considered as the indispensible means of this objective. In this respect, to research into the functional relationship between education and society and its other institutions is of great importance for community development.

Community development is an overall development. In this respect, educational system and economy are two closely related social institutions. Schools as an important component of educational system provide instruction and personality formation which enables economic progress and community development. Community development and change is particularly related to the education and instruction that social problems are identified and citizens are informed about these matters in a democratic way. Educational facilities are important due to two reasons: First, it is to prevent people from falling behind changing social and economic conditions. Second, it is to develop and change the community by restraining these conditions. The main duty of institutions in almost every community is to sustain the existence and maintenance by regulating the relations.

Education has an economic value as it proposes a certain approach to cognitive problems. Knowledge is not a product or a process that is acquired on one's own. To illustrate, the concept of community beyond industry means that a community is to be better than other communities in terms of following points: **a.** handling the humanistic, social and global foundations by adopting a pedagogic and systematic approach. **b.** Investing a lot upon scientific research. **c.** Organizing and using the produced knowledge to actualize the communal objectives. Moreover, producing knowledge is not enough to become a developed country. In doing so, it is vital to utilize the produced knowledge to reach at political, social and economic objectives. Produced knowledge should not be left on the shelf, yet it is to be used to actualize the social objectives.

Knowledge Exchange Path Collaboration

Education is fundamental to human progress. It plays a prominent role in all-around development of individual as well as society. Education plays a key role in creating patriotic, disciplined and productive manpower. The progress of the nation in the world of today is more than ever dependent upon the quantity and quality of education received by people. Education, if looked at beyond its conventional boundaries, forms the very essence of all our actions. What we do is what we know and have learned, either through instructions or through observation and assimilation. When we are not making an effort to learn, our mind is always processing new information or trying to analyze the similarities as well as the tiny nuances within the context which makes the topic stand out or seem different. As a whole, people can bring about development only when they know where improvement is necessary for the greater good of mankind. Education helps us understand ourselves better; it helps us realize our potential and qualities as a human being. It helps you to tap into latent talent, so that you may be able to sharpen your skills.

Interest Identification: Students completing the 10th standard exam face the question of which stream to choose. Most students choose according to whichever stream their family or friends advice. In most cases, the student later takes a graduate degree which is completely different from their interest. Learning-Based Education: Many students struggle to cope up with their classes, whereas some students have capacities beyond their class level. This is because each student has a unique pace of learning. It is difficult for a teacher to teach the students of mixed calibre. Should she teach for the slowest student or at an average pace? This can affect the quality of education delivered to the class as a whole. Shortage of Efficient Faculty: Even the top schools in India have very high pupil-teacher ratio. In several schools this ratio rises to as high as 100 students per teacher. In such a scenario, a teacher is unable to devote attention to individual students. Since the attraction of higher studies is tilted towards engineering and management courses, students are choosing teacher profession only as an alternative choice. Lack of Value Based Education: The main focus of education is imparting the knowledge and not the values. Children of today are highly educated but they lack their basic values which they ought to possess. Students in those days learnt many values. They were able to excel in their lives. Children of today lack these values. Value based education should be incorporated in the curriculum in order to strengthen their mental ability which in turn would help them to face any challenges boldly in their lives. Need for Value Based Education: Students in those days learnt many values. They were able to excel in their lives. Children of today lack those values. Value based Education should be incorporated in the curriculum in order to strengthen their mental ability which in turn would help them to face any challenges boldly in their lives. Lack of Leadership Opportunity for Girls: Girls were not given leadership and were often denied to showcase their talents. This situation has to be changed and girls should be encouraged to participate in all the extra-curricular activities and develop their leadership qualities. Rote Learning: The education system in India focuses primarily on students scoring high marks in the end-of-year exams. The system forces the students to learn the syllabus by rote and write as such in the exam papers. This kind of learning is usually forgotten by the students by the next academic year. Remembering Our Roots: If you ask any young student what is their ambition in life, they will say engineer, doctor, lawyer etc. These are the professions which are the most lucrative. But if everyone moves towards the urban side, who will feed the next generation? Students with a strong base in our farming traditions will be in shortage in the near future.

Practical Solutions for the Challenges

To help the students identify their preferences right from the young age, a school should involve the students in co-curricular and extra-curricular activities. These may include anything from science camps to dance competitions. This helps the students to get an idea of where their interests lie. Once the student has an interest in a subject, they will automatically shine in it. Summer camps can be conducted for a few weeks during the vacation period. In these camps, children of different ages but approximately the same learning level can be grouped together and coached at the same pace. For example, students who can do multiplication tables only up to 5 can be grouped together and taught the 6-tables. This group can have students from any age group. The obvious solution is the recruitment of more teachers, but this is not feasible. Instead, students can be put in small study groups of 3-4 and made to monitor each other. If a bright student is a part of each group, the student benefits by teaching other students and learning responsibility, while the rest of the group is monitored. In this way the teacher can make sure that all students are up to date in classes. Gardening can be taught to student's right from primary school. This develops a love of nature in them right from a young age. A small child learning to water and nurture plants also learns responsibility and patience while gaining satisfaction of a job well done. If even some of those students go on to study agriculture, the next generation's food requirements will be well taken care of.

Knowledge Exchange through Education

Democracy being a group a collective ideology is naturally opposed to the unfettered and unbridled Supremacy of individuals over other individuals. In individuals were to be completely free to do whatever they pleased, as some people think democracy represents, then the physically stronger, the selfish amongst us would acquire ascendancy over those physically weaker, the selfless, the straight forward, the honest and thereby deprive the latter of their political, economic, social freedom and equality. For a democratic nation to be people-welfare oriented it should generate and exchange knowledge and so this paper reflects the role of educational institutions in knowledge exchange. Education always reflects the social culture of which it is a part. It can be established, developed, improved, or completely remade only in terms of the society for which it exists. Education has its basic purpose, always the preservation, and sometimes the improvement of the institutions and culture that constitute society. It is essential, than that a study of our educational program is oriented in a study of our society and our ideals and aspirations for that society. Such a study involves some problems.

Accompanying man's search for a satisfying way of life in his personal search for a way of life, many of us in India have come to accept, purposefully the belief that satisfying experiences along with poverty are the ultimate goals of life, while a section of our society accepts the belief that happiness and satisfying experiences are the ultimate goals of life, but these can be attained only by developing our potential to the maximum. But these will be enjoyed to the fullest extent only if we have mutual regard for tomorrow because in doing so he will obtain the greatest amount of happiness and satisfaction. The democratic way of life is a faith, a faith in the inherent honesty and ability of society to effect its improvement without serious impairment of the development and happiness of the individual. Democracy as a philosophy of living involves the preservation of the greatest possible personal freedom consistent with the acceptance and performance of the reasonable responsibilities inherent in an adequate society towards the end of maximum happiness and satisfaction for all.

Education Guide to Democracy Way

Such concurrent exercise of 'equal rights' by individuals necessarily entails a reconciling, blending and harmonizing of individual rights and obligations. This process may, and does, involve restraints or sacrifices on the part of the individual in the larger interest of society, of which he is a member and beneficiary. The restraint or sacrifice on his part is in fact self-rewarding. The application of this principle is not just left to individuals or groups to exercise their judgment. For convenience rules, procedures and codes of conduct are formulated and institutions designed, on the basis of rational and scientific thinking, to ensure collective security and collective well-being nationally and globally.

The disregarding of this fundamental feature of an orderly society, would inevitably lead to conflict, discord, anti-social activities, disruption and disintegration of the social fabric be it the relationship between nations in their dealing with one another. It should be open to all citizens, irrespective of their race, caste, colour or creed to participate in the political, economic, social and cultural life of a nation in accordance with their aptitude and be duly tolerant and respectful towards each other's sub-cultures.

Education Make in Peace to Society

Education for peace should not be included as a spate subject in the school curriculum, but its notions should be integrated in the total school curriculum especially in social studies languages moral education and community studies.

The following are the peace notions:

1. Economic and social justice
2. Religions and their basic principles
3. International organizations i.e. U.N. its character on human rights.
4. Peace through country constitutional rights
5. Feeling of universal brotherhood
6. Non aggressive interaction within family, school, community and society.

As we view the problems for a better social order here. We must apply our minds to its national as well as international aspects. So far as first one is concerned problems will differ from country to country but with many common features, there are no great difference in the aim and objectives for which educationists of vision and goodwill are serving in different countries. We conceive of good life not merely in terms of the satisfaction of our material needs but also in terms of our socio-cultural and spiritual needs. I am sure in our discussion we will have an opportunity to discuss the common problems and solution to these problems and we will eventually find that basic human identities are more important than the differences and that a rightly conceived program of peace education can inculcate. Attitudes and values are as applicable as vitally important for the preservation and improvement of our democracy.

At the end I would like to quote what Jesus said and pray that we all remember it while we are struggling to bring peace and goodness in all the societies of the world. "Do your best, add goodness to your faith; to your faith add knowledge; to your knowledge add self-control, to your self-control add endurance to your endurance add Godliness, to your Godliness add brotherly love, to your brotherly love add love. These are the qualities you need and if you love them in abundance they will make you active and effective".

This concept of living is probably the highest expression of the democratic way of life. It is not a life in which every person has the right to do as he pleases and lives solely by the rights, but one in which each person recognizes and meets the responsibilities of group living. It is one in which rights and privileges are the reward for meeting the obligations of democracy, one in which these obligations come first. Democracy is a product, not a discovery. It should not be taken for granted, for it is to be achieved by each generation. One great advantages of a conference like this is the opportunity it affords to view our problems in broader perspective context and with a sense of detachment. We normally think of these problems keeping in our own socio-economic and geographical set up.

Knowledge Transfer and Knowledge Exchange

Increasingly, the creation of new organizational knowledge is becoming a managerial priority. New knowledge provides the basis for organizational renewal and sustainable competitive advantage. A failure to create knowledge and manage it as a critical organizational asset may account for the declining performance of many well-established firms. However, our understanding of the organizational processes surrounding knowledge creation and management is rather limited. By examining knowledge creation through alliance strategies, this article provides insights into how firms manage knowledge. Understanding the process by which new knowledge is created poses a fundamental challenge to the development of a learning organization. Organisationally the system can be divided into three types of units. In-house expertise units – are typically knowledge transfer offices, dealing with contacts with surrounding society for funding, collaborative research, commissioned education etc. Commercial units – are incubators and holding companies, and Cross-border units – are science parks, public private partnerships etc.

Most of the universities have made efforts to gather and centralize different kinds of support, for instance, external relations, commissioned education and research marketing, career services, IPR issues. Still, the assortment of units and their overlapping functions are numerous. The situation seems to be complex and hard to see through, both for internal and external parties. The overall aim for the process is to provide a path for the transfer of research to market. The support is about preparing the participant to be able to introduce his/her service or product to the market, and/or to obtain financing for projects that require more time for commercial take off. A general description of the process is: scouting, screening, IP management, proof-of-concept and commercial development, i.e. a process from action plan to pre-seed to preparation of external financing and exit. Besides the supporting process, the universities also offer courses and competitions and also aim to strengthen the interest in commercialization and entrepreneurship among university staff and students. Most universities target the early stages, until the proof-of-concept step. The main reason is to not intervene with market forces for commercial development. However, it can also be a result from lack of financial resources and competence, and from the fact that the process is rather recent and the kind of support offered has not yet experienced the later phases. Some researchers may consider the commercialization process not relevant to their research field. For example, the innovation policies and the measurable goals for innovation often pick up expressions from the physical sciences (patents, products) making it hard for the social sciences to apply a similar policy on its activities. This in turn, results in difficulties for researchers and students to identify with the strategies and goals. Knowledge creation is a dynamic process involving interactions at various organizational levels and it encompasses a community of individuals that enlarge, amplify, and disseminate their knowledge. It can be haphazard and idiosyncratic and should be viewed as a continuous process, rather than one with identifiable input-output phases. While not all knowledge creation efforts will be successful, some will yield surprisingly important results. Also, not all knowledge creation efforts will have immediate performance payoffs. However, over the long term, successful knowledge creation should strengthen and reinforce a firm's competitive strategy.

Comprehensive models of knowledge transfer so far found little attention in the academic discussion. Decades of scientific work of different disciplines produced abundant literature on various aspects of knowledge and technology transfer from the perspective of different scientific interests. Although the lack of effectiveness or lack of success of knowledge transfer in various regions, countries, industries or forms of cooperation is noted and chosen in a variety of studies as a starting point, the question of the process of knowledge transfer so far has not been of central interest in economic research. The aim of this paper is to know the factors of knowledge production and how it can be developed to improve the quality of higher education. "*Never mistake knowledge for wisdom. One helps you make a living; the other helps you make a life.*" – Sandra Carey.

Knowledge transfer is a major concern in improving educational practices (Huberman 1990; Love 1985; Willmott 1994). "Cooperative efforts among government, industry, and universities have grown in importance as strong contributors to the nation's technological and economic competitiveness in the global environment" (Geisler, 2003). "First, successful technology transfer is an on-going, interactive process where individuals exchange ideas simultaneously and continuously. Feedback is so pervasive that the participants in the transfer process can be viewed as "transceivers", exchanging ideas among the individuals involved." The diagram below outlines the Knowledge Cycle which involves knowledge production, knowledge transfer, knowledge application and knowledge diffusion. Other inputs required include creative inspiration, an intellectual property strategy and entrepreneurial skills and resources, including funding.

Unfortunately, one of the most difficult processes that we encounter, both from a research-borne or industry-borne perspective, is the translation of great ideas into practical solutions and applications. A number of factors contribute to the difficulty in successfully applying knowledge and ideas, and conversion into products and services:

Humans are generally risk averse

Limited availability of early stage risk capital

Access to know-how required to take ideas to market

Scarcity of entrepreneurial skills and experience

Lack of motivation and desire – it is hard work!

Those who seek and acquire knowledge through reading, learning, observation, investigation and experimentation will grow and develop in their specific disciplines. Those who then adopt or apply the knowledge will create significant value for society.

The view on knowledge transfer by academic discipline depends on different issues and focuses on specific aspects or stages of the transfer process. Until the early 1980s, the focus of technology transfer research was on international transfers, especially from industrialized nations to Les industrialized countries (Croissant and Smith-Doerr 2007). With the end of the last century, the national research on knowledge transfer gained increasingly in importance. While early studies on business management often dealt with intra-sectoral knowledge transfers and the relationship between technology and business strategy, numerous recent economic studies focus on alliances of companies in the context of development and transfer of knowledge (Bozeman 2000). The study combines ideas about knowledge transfer and knowledge exchange to provide a deep understanding of the nature of knowledge production in educational practices. It advances the literature on knowledge management and organizational learning by exploring organizational knowledge processes at the group level in dispersed settings, and offers a model for effective knowledge exchange processes within other groups with similarly-configured memberships in order to improve the quality of higher education.

Knowledge Exchange: A Collaborative Path in the 21st Century

Knowledge transfer and exchange issues have captured the attention of a variety of academic disciplines such as health, management, education, marketing, and applied social research. As a result, work in this area employs a variety of terms and concepts such as dissemination, knowledge diffusion, knowledge brokering, knowledge utilization, knowledge transfer, knowledge exchange and knowledge management that are often used interchangeably. Knowledge exchange is the mutual sharing of research and data knowledge, practice and experience based on knowledge, for the purpose of improving practice. Knowledge exchange can take place in person, online, through webinars, as learning collaborative or through resource sharing. A knowledge exchange platform provides people with an opportunity to connect and share their experience with one another to learn and improve their practice. Knowledge exchange platforms can include both in-person and online opportunities.

Principles for Effective Knowledge Exchange

1. ***Design:*** It is important to know what everyone involved hopes to achieve through knowledge exchange and that these aims are built into the environmental project from the beginning.
2. ***Representation:*** The distinction between those who carry out research and those who use its results should be made as early as possible. The input of the two groups should be used to help design both the research and knowledge exchange.

3. ***Engagement:*** Two-way communication and long-term trust should be encouraged between researchers and other stakeholders wherever possible, to facilitate knowledge exchange.
4. ***Facilitate:*** The knowledge exchange process needs to enable those involved to effectively listen to each other, share knowledge and skills, explore new ideas and to learn, adapt and apply the knowledge they gain.
5. ***Generate impact:*** To keep potential users of research engaged with the research process, there should be a focus on creating tangible results as early as possible, and ensuring that the results that will be valued by as many academicians as possible.
6. ***Reflect and sustain:*** Effective knowledge exchange is based around long-term relationships and learning. Monitoring and reflecting to continually improve the process key. Considering ways to sustain knowledge exchange, even after project funding ends, is also important.

Key Elements of Knowledge Exchange

In constructing any message, it is important to focus on the 5Cs (Abernathy, 2001):

1. ***Clear:*** a message is easy to understand,
2. ***Concise:*** a message is easy to read,
3. ***Consistent:*** a message is related to information that is consistent with other existing information,
4. ***Compelling:*** a message offers something that commands attention, and
5. ***Continuous:*** a message has follow-up to make sure it is not forgotten or overlooked.
6. ***Method:*** The choice of method for transferring and exchanging knowledge will depend on the audience and the message.
7. ***Messenger:*** The messenger is the person, group, or organization that delivers the information to the audience.
8. ***Evaluation:*** Evaluation explains the effects that are expected as a result of transferring or exchanging knowledge.

Knowledge Exchange Instruments

1. **Community of Practice:** A community of practice is a group of people who interact regularly on a common topic of shared interest with the goal of learning from one another.
2. **Conferences and Fora:** These events are opportunities for a large number of stakeholders to engage on a specific topic with a high level of interaction among participants.
3. **Dialogues:** An exploration of participants' knowledge on a common subject from which new or stronger understanding, meaning, and possibilities can emerge. Dialogues raise awareness, support consensus building, and encourage informed action.
4. **Expert Visits:** A subject matter expert (or group) goes to a requesting country, city, or organization to impart knowledge in their area of expertise.
5. **Peer Consult Action:** A process by which peers work together in small groups for mutual benefit providing critical, yet supportive and feedback.
6. **Study Tours:** Visits by an individual or a group to one or more countries/areas for knowledge exchange. Study tours provide an opportunity for key stakeholders to learn relevant, good development practice from their peers.
7. **Twinning Arrangements:** A process that pairs an organizational entity in a developing country with a similar but more mature entity in another country.

Knowledge Exchange Activities

1. **Action planning:** An action plan describes how participants will implement the knowledge gained during the exchange. It's a road map for follow up actions. Usually, a facilitator helps the participants create the action plan.
2. **Brainstorming:** Brainstorming is a group problem solving technique used for generating many ideas about a specific topic or issue.

3. **Demonstration:** In a demonstration activity, an expert or presenter shows participants how to perform an activity or procedure or introduces a new process or innovation.

4. **E-Discussion:** This is an online dialogue in which people discuss a topic in an open setting. E-discussions are asynchronous; communication does not have to occur at the same time, so participants can engage when it is convenient for them. E-discussions are managed online through a discussion forum or similar tool.

5. **Group Discussion:** They can be very informal to highly structured and challenging conversations as part of learning and knowledge-sharing events.

6. **Panel of Experts:** A panel of experts is a group of people with specialized knowledge who are invited to discuss a topic/ issue before an audience. It requires a coordinator and moderator.

7. **Presentation:** A presentation is an oral report of information in which the pattern of communication is mainly a one-way transmission from the presenter to participants.

8. **Role Play:** A highly interactive activity in which participants act out situations and problems and then analyse the situation with the help of other participants and observers. Role-play requires an experienced facilitator.

9. **Simulation:** A simulation exercise presents a realistic situation and invites learners to interact in that setting with objects and/ or people.

10. **Survey:** A survey is a way to gather information from participants. Surveys can be used to prompt discussions, surface areas for consensus or stakeholder ownership, and prioritize important next steps from knowledge-exchange activities.

Effective knowledge transfer and exchange efforts treat knowledge as a means to improve practice and situations by having positive impacts, rather than as an end in itself (Williams Group 2003). Given that the overall goal of knowledge transfer and exchange is to reduce the gap between knowledge and practice, the following are some desirable changes that have been discussed in some studies and could be observed when moving towards this goal.

Knowledge Revolution

Education should make a difference to the learner, it should make a perceptible change in his life; it should matter to him in one way or the other; and should add value to his dreams. It may be knowledge, skill, attitude, behavior, wealth, health, character or learning; it could be anything and in any degree but it should be imparted to a person through education. Collaborative Learning refers to the instruction method in which students at various levels work together in small groups toward a common goal. Collaborative learning shows that school achievements, creations of positive inter group relations and socialization is higher in cooperative settings. Both mainstream and minority students show far greater increases in academic achievement when they participate in collaborative learning projects than when they remain in traditional teacher focused class rooms. Therefore, it is highly advocated as a modern class room technique to provide learner-centered teaching as well as learner participation and contribution in the teaching learning process. The quest for improvement of quality is the central feature of every educational system today. Many progammes have been initiated from time to time based on the emerging needs and analysis of previous experience to achieve national goals. National council of educational research and training (2007) states that innovation is more than having new ideas, it includes the process of successfully introducing them or making things happen in a new way. We all are tired of the traditional method of learning to the stereo typed lecture of various teachers. An exceptional educational environment begins with a vision that the most powerful and meaningful learning when thinking and feeling are fused together. Collaborative learning is a situation in which two or more people learn or attempt to learn something together. Collaborative learning is a technique designed to make learning a lively and successful process.

Collaborative Learning

Collaborative learning is 'an instructional method in which students at various performance levels work together in small groups towards a common academic goal'. It is nothing but the grouping and pairing of students, for the purpose of achieving more in their academic achievement. The students are responsible for one another's learning as well as their own. Thus, the success of one student helps other students to be successful (Gokhale, 1995).

Principles of Collaborative Learning

The principles of collaborative learning are:

1. Learning actualized in small groups consists of 2-6 persons.
2. Interaction of students in group is important at learning.
3. Competition between groups is more important than competition among students.
4. Success or failure is belonging to groups more than individuals.
5. Applications of this method concrete students in classroom who have different abilities and characteristics. Also friendship is increased among students.
6. Cognitive, affective and social behaviour of students are improved using this learning application.

Strategies of Collaborative Learning

1. ***Think-Pair-Share:*** The instructor poses a question, preferable one demanding analysis, evaluation, or synthesis, and gives students about a minute to think through an appropriate response.
2. ***Three-Step Interview:*** Common as an ice-breaker or a team-building exercise, this structure can also be used to share information such as hypotheses or reactions to a film or article.
3. ***Simple Jigsaw:*** The faculty member divides an assignment or topic into four parts with all students from each learning team volunteering to become "experts" on one of the parts.

4. ***Numbered Heads Together:*** The instructor calls a specific number and the team members originally designated that number during the count off respond as group spokespersons. Because no one knows which number the teacher will call, all team members have a vested interest in understanding the appropriate response.

Collaborative Class Room

Collaborative classrooms seem to have four general characteristics. This first two capture changing relationships between teachers and students. The third characterizes teacher's new approaches to instruction. The fourth addresses in the composition of a collaborative classroom.

Difference between Collaborative and Traditional Classroom

1. ***Shared knowledge among teachers and students:*** In traditional classrooms, the dominant metaphor for teaching is the teacher as information giver: knowledge flows only one-way from teacher to student. In contrast, the metaphor for collaborative classrooms is shared knowledge. The teachers have vital knowledge about content and skills, and impart information to students. However, collaborative teachers value and build upon teacher's knowledge, personal experiences, language, strategies and culture that students bring to the learning situation.
2. ***Shared Authority among Teachers and Students:*** Collaborative teachers differ in that they invite students to get specific goals within the frame work of what is being taught, provide options for activities and assignments that capture different student interests and goals, and encourage students to assess what they learn
3. ***Teachers as mediators:*** As knowledge and authority are shared among teachers and students, the role of students connect new information to their experiences and to training in other areas, help students figure out what to do when they are tamped and helps then learn how to learn.

4. *Heterogeneous Grouping of students:* The perspectives, experiences and backgrounds of all students are important for enriching learning in the classroom.

Students Roles in a Collaborative Classroom

Students role assume new roles in the collaborative classroom. The major roles are collaborator and active participator. It is useful to think how these new roles influence the processes and activities students conduct before, during and after learning; they assess their performance and plan for future learning. Learning is the most effective when it is multimodal - when the material is presented in multiple forms, and when students have multiple means of accessing and interacting with material and demonstrating their knowledge being evaluated.

1. **Collaborative Networked Learning**: It is a form of collaborative learning for the self-directed adult learner. Youth directed collaboration, another form of self-directed organizing and learning relies on a novel, more radical concept of youth voice.
2. **Computer-supported collaborative learning:** This is relatively a new educational paradigm within collaborative learning which uses technology in a learning environment to help mediate and support group interactions in a collaborative learning context. CSCL systems use technology to control and monitor interactions, to regulate tasks, rules, and roles, and to mediate the acquisition of new knowledge.
3. **Learning Management Systems:** This is a context that gives collaborative learning particular meaning. In this context, collaborative learning refers to a collection of tools which learners can use to assist, or be assisted by others. Such tools include virtual Classrooms, chat, discussion threads and application sharing among many others.
4. **Collaborative Learning Development:** This enables developers of learning systems to work as a network. Specifically relevant to e-learning where developers can share and build knowledge into courses in a collaborative environment. Knowledge of a single

subject can be pulled together from remote locations using software systems.

5. **Collaborative Learning in Virtual Worlds:** Virtual worlds by their nature provide an excellent opportunity for collaborative learning. At first learning in virtual worlds was restricted to classroom meetings and lectures, similar to their counterparts in real life. Now collaborative learning is evolving as companies starting to take advantage of unique features offered by virtual world spaces - such as ability to record and map the flow of ideas use 3D models and virtual worlds mind mapping tools.

Computer Supported Collaborative Learning (CSCL)

Collaborative learning is defined as groups learning together for achieving a common goal. The difference between CSCW and CSCL are that CSCW tends to focus on communication techniques themselves and CSCL focuses on what is being communicated; CWCW is used mainly in the business setting, CSCL is communication and productivity, and the purpose of CSCL is to scaffold or support students in learning together effectively. Collaborative learning method is examined as an alternative learning method for the other methods used in traditional visual arts education to seek for effective and complete learning. In collaboration students improve their skills successfully using constructivist learning model. Students to think clearly and independently is important equally is to think collaboratively. Thinking is an internal and individual process.

A good eLearning course requires the right combination of learning events. A learning event is a simplified description of the student's learning activity. There's an infinite number of learning strategies, but only eight learning events. Derek Stockley defines it is education through by electronic. It isn't necessary to use all the events in the creation of your course. Just get acquainted with each of them to make sure you use the right combination to make your course effective. E-learning has easy to way for higher education. E-learning provides the knowledge explosion of education. We have more knowledge has been delivered to more number of people.

E-learning enables learner to sit in the comfort zone of his home and learn. It has improved the ways of learning and improvised the dissemination of knowledge. E-learning has globalized teaching and learning process. E-learning materials in a variety format to suit different learner styles. E-learning in education was a debatable topic amongst the society. Everyone had their own views on modernizing education and making it technology aided. There were a huge number of positives and negatives to education technology. But, gradually as technology was embraced by the educational institutes, they realized the importance of technology in education. Online learning in many forms is on the rise in schools of all types across the country. Students in many parts of the country now have a long list of choices when it comes to e-learning. The menu of options often includes full-time, for-profit virtual schools; state-sponsored virtual schools; supplemental online learning courses offered by brick-and-mortar schools; and charter schools presenting a hybrid option of digital material coupled with face-to-face instruction.

E-learning is a learning program that makes use of an information network- such as the internet, an intranet (LAN) or extranet (WAN) whether wholly or in part, for course delivery, interaction and/or facilitation. Web-based learning is a subset of e-learning and refers to learning using an internet browser such as the moodle, blackboard or internet explorer.

Increasing access, growing acceptance, and decreasing cost are all helping to make the use of mobile devices a popular and increasing trend within the world of e-learning. Researchers have also found that games and simulations may help students learn by helping them visualize processes they otherwise could not see, such as the flow of an electron or the construction of a city. Games can also promote higher-order thinking skills, such as collaboration, communication, problem-solving, and teamwork

Important of E-learning

With technology, educators, students and parents have a variety of learning tools at their fingertips. Here are some of the ways in which e-learning improves education over time:

1. ***Teachers can collaborate to share their ideas and resources online:*** They can communicate with others across the world in an instant, meet the shortcomings of their work, refine it and provide their students with the best. This approach definitely enhances the practice of teaching.
2. ***Students can develop valuable research skills at a young age:*** Technology gives students immediate access to an abundance of quality information which leads to learning at much quicker rates than before.
3. ***Students and teachers have access to an expanse of material:*** There are plenty of resourceful, credible websites available on the Internet that both teachers and students can utilize. The Internet also provides a variety of knowledge and doesn't limit students to one person's opinion.
4. ***Online learning is now an equally credible option***: Face-to-face interaction is huge, especially in the younger years, but some students work better when they can go at their own pace. Online education is now accredited and has changed the way we view education.
5. ***Learner with Disabilities:*** It's always best to design and e-learning course for accessibility so that all your learners can use it comfortable. For example you may not know that one of your learners is hard of hearing, so adding a text transcript of audio files is a good way to make sure no one misses out on any course content.

Think about more ways of how technology has improved education and how it can positively impact it in the near future. Feel free to share these views, additional knowledge or clarify doubts you may have on the relation of education and technology. I think one of the most exciting aspects of technology in education is its use for designing creativity. We can create so many different types of content **written, audio, video, 2D** and **3D**, they can create music, they can create videos they can create photos, they can create **magazines**, conduct experiments and then after creating this content they can use the technology to present their ideas whether it be online or in person. So in other words technology can be present at every stage of education process from the introduction and the research to the project making to the presentation.

Knowledge Interaction

It is a very broad concept, and there is no single definition for it. Knowledge transfer is when know-how and knowledge are becoming available in a systematic way to those who did not have previous access to it. The concept is still frequently misunderstood and it is very important to communicate the new message. A lot of people still think of it as a sneaky way for universities to make money out of the good ideas of their academics which is rather a narrow and old fashioned viewpoint. That's not to say that research institutions and universities are not going to make money by selling products of their research work It represents a major component of the community's return on public investment in universities and should consequently be valued and actively encouraged across all disciplines and all institutions.

The knowledge created in the academic sphere takes various paths before finally reaching a competitive recipient, from patent and licenses to research publication or consulting. Actually, knowledge is created throughout the three main functions of universities: the education of workers to be, the development and dissemination of research work, and their active participation to social and economic development, which has led to the concept of entrepreneurial universities. This variety of channels leads to a real challenge for researchers interested in the field. Untargeted and targeted knowledge transfers have different but complementary epistemologies. Indeed, knowledge diffusion through publications and patents occurs under a codified, articulated form while the specific relationship built up through targeted transfer allows the sharing of explicit and tacit knowledge. Those different perspectives also suggest a specific meaning of.

Knowledge Transfer Through Collaborative Projects

University is seen as the central source of knowledge, reaching recipients in a one-way relationship. On the other hand, the knowledge interaction through targeted transfer implies critical feedbacks from the recipient, the interaction eventually affecting both partners on their research and transfer activities. Accordingly, the study of untargeted or targeted knowledge flows implies distinctive research tools and methodological approaches. A positivist approach seems appropriate to understand and measure knowledge flows under an explicit form such as patents and other formalized sources. An interpretive or constructivist approach should be more suitable to fully explore knowledge flows occurring through interactions: whereas objective quantitative methods would fall short to capture the tacit component of targeted knowledge flows, a subjective qualitative approach would give the researcher deeper insights about such created knowledge. The global economy is becoming increasingly more competitive and education is one of the key drivers. In order for society to advance the people must be educated. The importance of education is quite clear. One can safely say that a human being is not in the proper sense till he is educated. Education is the knowledge of putting one's potentials to maximum use. It is therefore not an overstatement to say that education and knowledge is the priority for the future. It is an important tool for nation building and development. Knowledge transfer is not only from business to university and vice versa but there is also a big involvement from the government and other knowledge bodies and they should become partners in policy making. Governments of developed nations are actively involved in education and knowledge transfer and this is helping a lot in the transfer of skills to young professionals. It would be of great help if the developing nations can be carried along in some of the projects. This will make a lasting impact on the development of the developing countries. Education and knowledge are important tools for capacity building, food safety, quality and chain management.

Creating Knowledge and Sharing Ideas

In discussing strategies to improve schools academic capacities, and knowledge management is now intensively applied to the education setting, extensive research on knowledge management in journals, seminar papers, book and research papers proved that knowledge management is a vital consideration in maintaining the organizational capabilities and capacities. Knowledge management is defined as an important approach knowledge management highlights new knowledge generated by the substitution from implicit knowledge to the explicit knowledge. Knowledge is often in the eye of the beholder, and one gives meaning to a concept through the way one uses it. As justified true belief, knowledge is a construction of reality rather than something that is true in an objective or universal way. Knowledge is both explicit and tacit and effective knowledge creation depends on three. Knowledge is dynamic, relational, and based on human action; it depends upon the situation and people involved rather than on absolute truth or artifacts.

The definition of innovation includes the concept of novelty, commercialization and/or implementation. In other words, if an idea has not been developed and transformed into a product, process or service, or it has not been commercialized, and then it would not be classified as an innovation. Innovation is never a one-time phenomenon, but a long and cumulative process of a great number of organizational decision-making processes, ranging from the phase of a generation of a new idea to its implementation phase. New idea refers to the perception of a new customer need or a new way to produce. Administrative innovation involves innovations that pertain to the organizational structure and administrative processes. In this case it can be specifically related to strategies, structure, systems, or people in the organization.

Sharing Knowledge is Important

Today, the creation and application of new knowledge is essential to the survival of almost all businesses. There are many reasons. They include: "intangible products- ideas, processes, information are taking a growing share of global trade from the traditional, tangible goods of the manufacturing economy." Increasingly the only sustainable competitive advantage is continuous innovation. People don't take a job for life any more.

When someone leaves an organization their knowledge walks out of the door with them," our problem as an organization is that we don't know what we know." Large global or even small geographically dispersed organizations do not know what they know. Expertise learnt and applied in one part of the organization is not leveraged in another.

We are talking about sharing knowledge and information – not just information. The purpose of knowledge sharing is to help an organization as a whole to meet its business organizational culture. The main contribution of this study is enhanced understanding about knowledge management enablers in transnational projects. There are three main findings of this study. Of the four knowledge management enablers studied in this paper, organizational culture was the most important, but also the trickiest one to realize, a finding in line with several other studies. The essence of organizational culture is to encourage individuals to create and share knowledge as well as to define what knowledge is valuable. We conclude that in a transnational culture. Those who unit, the individuals are invaluable as they from the organizational culture. Those who are appointed, communicate what knowledge is valued and what knowledge must be kept inside the organization for innovativeness not only to the individuals within the transnational project, but also to the permanent organization.

Elements of Knowledge Transfer and Knowledge Exchange

Knowledge grows when it is used and depreciates when it is not. Knowledge is a means to improve practice and situations. It is not an end in itself but has positive impacts. The desirable changes in the user's capacity have increased manifolds by applying knowledge. Integrating knowledge into decision making process, promoting cultural shift and increased collaboration are some of the applications of knowledge transfer and exchange among the knowledge producers and users i.e. the teacher educators, teachers, students and society. Cooperation, collaboration and knowledge sharing should be encouraged. Both knowledge transfer and knowledge exchange can be used in a variety of terms and concepts like dissemination, knowledge difference, knowledge brokering, knowledge utilization and knowledge management interchangeably.

In organizational theory knowledge transfer is also referred to as the practical problem of transferring knowledge from one part of the organization to another. It is otherwise the process of communication. It can also be defined as a set of activities and approaches that are undertaken to move knowledge among those who have interest or needs in it. It can either be a one way process or a two way movement between the researchers and practioners. The purpose of knowledge transfer is to catalyst and facilitate innovation or work based learning projects or hands on learning like school based activities, case study ,action research, sociometry test etc. leading to innovations and generation of new ideas.

Knowledge exchange strategy was first developed in 2009.Knowledge exchange activities are often inter disciplinary involving colleagues across schools and colleges .It is a process which brings together academic staff , research scholars , wider groups and communities to exchange ideas , evidence and expertise. The method used includes collaborative research. It continues to share good practice through exchange programmes and events and provides appropriate training and mentoring .It helps coordinate the support provided by the research centers, schools, colleges to maximize the use of resources.

1. Audience: i.e. the student learner
2. Message should be clear, concise, consistent, compelling, and continuous
3. Teaching methods: choice of method depends on transferring and exchanging knowledge and on the student learner and the subject matter or message.
4. Messenger: the teacher educator or teacher is the person who delivers the information to the student learners.
5. Evaluation: Evaluation of the process explains the effects that are expected as a result of transferring or exchanging knowledge.

The process of academic audit involves three stages - self-study involving understanding the teaching learning process, peer review and evaluation. Funding agencies play an important role in enabling knowledge transfer and exchange. They create incentives for researchers or train them to better communicate their findings. The Institute of knowledge transfer is the body devoted to supporting and promoting the knowledge professionals. Individuals are involved in innovation, enterprise and transfer, exchange, sharing and management of knowledge. Helping students develop holistically will ensure development of soft skills through involvement in social service projects. It would be better if the industry takes an active part in the educational system. We need to ensure that educators and industry work closely together to maximize the social and economic benefits of new ideas. Student exchange programme at school and college levels are the best e.g. for knowledge transfer and knowledge exchange.

Factors Influencing Knowledge Transfer

In a modern society, universities are the generators and repositories of knowledge. At the same time, the universities are not only the birthplace of knowledge and intellectual resources but also have more responsibilities as the Research and Development (R&D) institutions of science and technology for the benefit of society. Transfer of scientific knowledge and products from university to industry plays a vital role in the advancement of society at large. As a typical example, a university will provide ideas and knowledge to an industry, and then, the industry will utilize and transform these ideas and knowledge into practice (Prabhu, 1999). At this juncture, it is important to have strategic knowledge transfer collaboration between university and industry because is not only important to industrial companies but also to the country and its economic development and competitiveness (Brown & O'Brien, 1981). There are number of factors influencing knowledge transfer collaboration between university and industry. This paper is intent to highlights some of the factors on the basis of literatures.

Knowledge is a leading factor in contemporary society. Knowledge transfer is a dynamic process which involves acquisition, communication, application, acceptance and assimilation (Gilbert et al., 1996; Tsai, 2009). Knowledge production and diffusion is widely accepted as a critical factor for economic growth (ConceiÇão et al., 2002). The universities are playing an influential role in developing knowledge-based economy through the process of knowledge transfer collaboration with industries. Dosi (1982) defined knowledge and technology transfer in the context of university-industry collaboration as follows: knowledge and technology transfer between academic institutions and business sectors is understood as any activity aimed at transferring knowledge or technology which may help either the company or academic institute – depending on the direction of transfer – in order to further pursue its activities (Arvanitis et al., 2008).

There are numerous factors influencing knowledge transfer collaboration between universities and industries including employment for university graduates, combined research initiatives, consultancy services, memorandums on patents and publications and laboratories and also regular academic activists including and industrial visits, workshops and conferences.

I. Factors related to University

There are certain factors of universities are considerable to attract an industry to construct collaboration for knowledge transfer. The academic expertises of the university in both general and specialized subjects are important to make collaboration with an industry. The factors including motivation among researchers, availability of technical staff and resources, incentives and reward structure, support of university authorities, strong leadership and previous experiences of the university working with industry are also the important to have collaboration.

II. Factors related to Industry

The factors related to industry to have collaboration with university includes absorptive capacity, ability to integrate technology into value chain, confidence in results, experience of working with academia, senior management support, sufficient resources, change management capacity, effectiveness of internal communication.

III. Factors related to Technical Features

There are number of factors with respect to both university and industry in terms of technical features which includes technology maturity, technical risk, project viability and technical feasibility, well-defined objectives, stakeholders' involvement, application capacity/usefulness and strategic context.

IV. Factors related to Relationship between University and Industry

The relationship between university and industry is most important than all other academic and technical factors. Both university and industry have an equal responsibility in making of good relationship between them. The factors includes mutual confidence, sharing of vision, professional and personal relationship, cultural interface, established planning and coordination, clarity of role and responsibilities, access to information/transparency, flexibility, effective project management and long-term relationship.

University – industry collaboration playing a key role fostering innovation in knowledge fields. The effective cooperation between university and industry promotes knowledge transfer collaboration in research and development activities for the welfare of society. Healthy and adoptable relationship between university and industry is critically important in shaping of new industries. It is needed that holistic approach and usage of variety of mechanism by the universities, industries and other stakeholders in knowledge transfer collaboration for bridging gap between scientific research and its application in industry.

Collaboration for Successful Knowledge

Knowledge transfer and exchange is a dynamic process involving interactions at various organizational levels and it encompasses a community of individuals that enlarge, amplify and disseminate their knowledge to transfer and exchange, which helps to reduce the gap between the knowledge and its practice. Knowledge transfer organizations has to identify research results from multiple sources and promote a culture of information sharing and exchange inside their organizations, as well as with researchers and practitioners. They also have to provide the necessary resources and to set up policies that encourage and promote knowledge transfer activities. Knowledge transfer is described as the "third mission" by the higher education sectors of many advanced economics i.e., apart from teaching and research. It can be said that, knowledge transfer is a two way process. The reason is, not only the community enjoys realizable benefits from institutions, but academic and research would also be enriched by having closers ties with the larger community. The development of collaborative research is one of the most important innovative processes that help to transfer the knowledge. Universities and other research institutions have a critical role to transfer new knowledge, ideas etc from one part of the organization to another.

Knowledge exchange is a process which brings together academic staff, users of research and wider groups and communities to exchange ideas, evidence and expertise. It is a process, that is mutually beneficial to both the institution and the community in a broad range of fields and also contributes to regional and global development to increase the opportunities for staff and students to benefit from the commercialization. The university has been engaging in a wide range of knowledge exchange activities through applied research, educational delivery, knowledge dissemination, expertise sharing and community service to achieve a substantial and measurable increase in the quantity and impact of our knowledge exchange activities. "Knowledge exchange is defined so as to cover the full range of ways in which the higher education sector interest with external organizations and which may affect regional economic development. These interactions include educational and training activities, research publications and patenting, conferences, contracting and consulting activity, internships, joint research and development and licensing and new business formation."

Communication is very important in knowledge transfer. The interaction between different project units through meetings, conference will develop communication channels. Interaction will facilitate the establishment of knowledge networks if it is communicated to the right people in the right way at the right time. By encouraging joint conferences and by conducting collaborative research, knowledge can be spread to large group. Knowledge is effectively transferred when the recipient understand it well enough to use it efficiently and effectively to implement in the public sector So by improving the working relation between important stakeholders, we can promote sustainable development in the society by sharing their knowledge, developments, ideas, views, concepts, expectations etc. Knowledge transfer takes place whenever the discoveries or expertise of academics are disseminated more widely. So teachers and students should be exposed in a systematic way to develop knowledge transfer. The vector of knowledge transfer is people. To perform knowledge transfer activities effectively, research institutions need to have sufficient autonomy to recruit experienced knowledge transfer staff on competitive basis. Increased mobility between the public and private sectors will help the research institutions, researchers and managers to share the knowledge needed for the industry.

Knowledge Exchange

Develop a strong knowledge sharing culture. We have to inculcate our academic staff members, a culture of knowledge sharing with the public. Through newsletters, reports, seminars, conferences and public events, we can improve the communication of knowledge exchange within and outside the university. Encourage all academic staff to link-their academic and research aspirations with advancing the well being of local and regional communities, collaborating with colleagues from other higher educational institutions especially where concerned efforts can bring greater impact. By developing and adopting indicators or a panel to measure the quality and quantity of our knowledge exchange activities that takes place, will help to monitor and assess their impact. This in turn helps to disseminating the professional knowledge from one person to another. By allocating funds for conducting knowledge exchange activities between universities, colleges and society, will results in economics and social development. Certain research institutions have staff that activity pursues links with industry, but who do not interact among themselves. By pooling their knowledge transfer competencies, they can make more widely available throughout the research institutions.

Transfer of knowledge between institutions and the society helps to bring about socio- economic impact and improvements to the community and business. Knowledge transfer within organization and between nations also raises ethical considerations, particularly where there is an imbalance in power relationships or in the levels of relative need for knowledge resources. It initiates collaborative research and development projects to cater the needs of the industries. Knowledge exchange program is intended to improve learning outcomes by fostering relationships that facilitate the exchange of evidence and also promote cultural exchange within and between communities at local, national and international levels.

Knowledge transfer is a major concern in improving educational practices. Now new information's and communication technologies have made it much easier for practitioners to access research results, but still there is large gap between the knowledge produced by researchers and the one used in practice. The reason is, more importance is given to the production of new knowledge than to the dissemination of knowledge. So importance should give to accessibility and its relevance. When the information coming from research is easily available and accessible, this makes the practitioners to use it easier. And also knowledge that could have an important impact on the methods of transfer and its relevance will also helps to enhance the collaboration of knowledge. So, the knowledge transfer between researchers and practitioners should be further encouraged and promoted since, it represents the major viable way to significantly reduce the gap between knowledge creation and knowledge utilization.

Knowledge Management in Higher Education

Every academic institution contributes to knowledge. The generated information and knowledge is to be compiled at central place and disseminated among the society for further growth. It is observed that the generated knowledge in the academic institute is not stored or captured properly It is also observed that many a times generated information or knowledge in the academic institute is not known to any one and remains as grey literature, which might be useful if proper recoding is maintained in the organization. In fact academic environment is treasure of knowledge but it is not organized properly and hence utility is also lacking and cause for the repetitions of the activity. This project is undertaken under Board of University and Colleges, University of Pune for finding importance of KM of past knowledge of an institute. Also study on data capture, data analysis, data categorization, data mining, data mapping, knowledge mapping, concept mapping, indexing, linking and repackaging of knowledge, tools, techniques, strategies and copyright issues in sharing this knowledge through knowledge base. Knowledge management is a new immerging field in the academic environment. Many upcoming conferences and seminars at national and International level are on Knowledge Management. Many International Universities are actively participating in KM related activities and doing research. It is now becoming popular in Education field due to need to disclose the intellectual power available in institution for sharing experiences. It has great potential and should have equal and even greater significance for education sector. Knowledge builds on knowledge and past events helps in generating new knowledge.

They are considered as "Knowledge Houses" where knowledge flows from teachers to students and new knowledge is created. The information generated is covered in different forms and sources like books, journal articles, thesis or dissertations, technical reports, fact finding reports, case studies, patents, development of test methods and standards, different scholarly communications etc. Every academic institution contributes to knowledge. The generated information and knowledge is to be compiled at central place and disseminated among the society for further growth. It is observed that the generated knowledge in the academic institute is not stored or captured properly. Knowledge is an important source for value creation in an organization and needs to be managed carefully-Massa and Testa (2009). It is a vibrant force in the rapidly changing global economy and society. Kidwell (2000) discussed Knowledge, which starts from the basic facts called data, which covers only raw data or facts or numbers, based on these facts information is generated. The information generated is captured in various documents and databases and made it available to use which gets searched by researchers using information technology systems, and information retrieval systems.

Types of Knowledge

There are two types of knowledge viz. explicit knowledge and Tacit Knowledge. Explicit Knowledge: is recorded and well documented information that helps in taking action and also expressed in formal language. It is published and made available for use like primary, secondary information sources and also covers packaged, communicable, transferable, and also easily available. Tacit knowledge: is knowledge people carry around in their head. It is embedded within the head/minds of researchers of the institution or organization or research unit etc. It covers insights, perceptions, expertise views, techniques and skills, which is unique to the person. The process by which new knowledge is created within the organization or institute in the form of new products, services or systems becomes the cornerstone of innovative activity. The key to successful innovation process lies in the mobilization and conversion of tacit knowledge into explicit recorded knowledge. The knowledge is generated in all the organizations, institutions, research centers, educational organizations, industries, and also in academics in different forms like books, projects, papers, dissertations, thesis, etc. But all the knowledge is not made available to public use. The knowledge made available is in explicit form only. The tacit knowledge is hard to get in to reality. Though IPR system now developed to protect the innovative ideas and benefited to the researchers by protecting knowledge in different heads like copy right, patents, trademarks.

Knowledge is made available to take action when user needs it. Knowledge is considered as key to generate breakthrough ideas. The real focus of knowledge management is on "doing the right thing" instead of "doing things right". It provides a framework within which the organization views, processes as knowledge processes and all business processes, which involves creation, dissemination and application of knowledge towards organizational sustenance and survival. Knowledge Management can transform organizational new levels of effectiveness, efficiency, and scope of operation, using advanced technology, data and information are made available to users for effective productivity. Knowledge Management is continually discovering organizational tacit knowledge.

Importance of Km in Educational Institutions

Knowledge is the key for decision making and strategy creation. Knowledge should transfer into an action but unfortunately it does not happen always. In order to sustain in competitive world all educational institutes should implement effective tools for knowledge management. Barbara Friehs (2000) mentioned following assignments for effective KM.

1. Mobilize the hidden implicit/tacit knowledge
2. Integrate knowledge from organization and make it accessible to all
3. Identify the missing knowledge
4. Create new knowledge
5. Make knowledge more accessible and usable
6. Create knowledge sharing culture to experiment and learn

7. Evaluate and reflect learning processes
8. Codify new knowledge.

Knowledge Sharing and Open Access Moment

Knowledge Sharing is defined by Yu et.al.(2010) as "Processes that involve exchanging knowledge between individuals and groups". According to Liaw, et.al (2008) Knowledge sharing is one of important goal of an organization where all individuals' experiences and knowledge can be transferred as an organizational asset and maintained for future learning and creating new knowledge with the help of ICT. The role of knowledge professionals and managers in developing KM in the educational institute is to coordinate the information related activities and clustering the data properly. But the main challenge is to capture tacit knowledge and manage it in developing repository. Copyright issue is also to be taken into consideration while capturing and presenting knowledge. Higher education is a center of knowledge creating, delivering, and learning for society. On international level too knowledge sharing policies between two and more countries are going on. For the development of nation it is must. Discussions and exchange of information is very common among staff, students and scholars now days. Open Access initiative is boon to researchers and if at every organizational level the better management, use and sharing of available resources/knowledge both explicit and tacit occur it leads to overall development of educational system and nation at fast speed. Knowledge plays a crucial role in the progression of institutions.

Mental Health Helps Knowledge Exchange

The tremendous and accelerating advances of modern science and technology have led to unprecedented progress and problems. We see the world changing with incredible rapidity and established customs, traditions and values changing with it. One of the major problems today is the constant conditions and to change itself. For efficient functioning of the individual, he should not only possess sound bodily health but sound mental health also. Mental health hazards significantly increased in number and complexity affected the physical efficiency of individuals. This reveals mental health is now recognized as an important aspect of an individual's total development and the individual's development is important part in school. For efficient functioning of the individual, he should not only possess sound bodily health but sound mental health also. Mental health hazards significantly increased in number and complexity affected the physical efficiency of individuals. This reveals mental health is now recognized as an important aspect of an individual's total development and the individual's development is important part in school. Mental health and education are closely related with each other. For any type of education, sound mental health is the first condition. If children are not in sound mental health, they cannot concentrate in learning and retain the knowledge received in the classroom. Learning is dependent on sound mental health. Mental health strengthens human needs, relieve conflict, frustration and stress from mind and make adjustment among them. Now-a-days every citizen has been becoming educated. Human life is the period from birth to death. Therefore mentally healthy students and teachers creating path collaboration for successful knowledge transfer and knowledge exchange Ever and Every Where.

Mental Health

According to Hadfield, mental health is the full and harmonious functioning of the whole personality. It is the developing capacity of the individual to form harmonious relations with others and contribute constructively to changes in his social and physical environment. A student with a healthy personality normally stands a better chance of engaging in creative and productive activities and approaches learning and problem solving tasks more constructively, as against one who is lacking in this vital aspect of mental functioning. It is obvious that improved adjustment and mental health would definitely enhance the efficiency of learning, and will, therefore lead to more satisfying school accomplishments. Mental health and education are closely related with each other. For any type of education, sound mental health is the first condition. If children are not in sound mental health, they cannot concentrate in learning and retain the knowledge received in the classroom. Learning is dependent on sound mental health. Healthy children have a desire to acquire more and more information and skills that will give them better control over their environment.

The school can adopt the following measures in the preservation and promotion of the mental health of the students:

1. A sound body is said to possess a sound mind. So there should be some provision for regular physical training and medical care of the students in the school.
2. Students should be helped in acquiring balanced emotional development and to exercise control over their emotions.
3. Find out rejected and maladjusted children and help in their adjustment with classmates and others by arranging group activities.
4. Develop pupil's self-respect and self-esteem by compliments for work well-done, a smile or word of recognition.
5. Help the children to set a proper level of aspiration.
6. Students should be helped to develop proper patience and power of tolerance to face failure and frustrations in life.
7. Encourage self-discipline on the democratic lines. Should not accept corporal punishment in maintaining discipline.

Characteristics of Mentally Healthy Student

A mentally healthy individual possesses the following characteristics.

1. A mentally healthy person possesses socially adaptable behaviour.
2. He is emotionally satisfied and possesses a resilient mind.
3. His desires are in harmony with socially approved norms.
4. He possesses good habits and constructive attitudes.
5. He is capable of making decisions, assuming responsibilities in accordance with his capacities.

6. He is self confident, adequate and free from internal conflicts, tensions or inconsistencies in his behaviour.
7. He is able to adapt successfully to the changing needs and demands of the environment.

Mental Health of the Teacher

The behaviour of the teacher is an important factor that influences the mental health of the students. The teacher should take care of the following things about their own behaviour:

1. The teacher must be sympathetic and as impartial as possible.
2. The teacher must not play an authoritarian and dictatorial role. Pupils must get opportunity for talking about their worries and problems without fear of being ridiculed or rebuffed.
3. The teacher should possess consistency in his behaviour. He should maintain emotional balance and his behaviour should not fluctuate depending on his mood.

Personal Characteristics of Mentally Healthy Teachers

The following are the characteristics of an effective teacher who contributes to the mental health of his students and his own:

1. Alertness, enthusiasm and interest in pupils and classroom activities.
2. Ability to maintain natural and pleasant interpersonal relationships, cordiality and friendliness.
3. Recognition of one's own mistakes.
4. Patience, kindness, sympathy, sincerity and fairness in dealing with pupils.
5. Democracy and courtesy in relations with pupils.
6. The ability to use praise for work well done.
7. The ability to help pupils with personal as well as educational problems.
8. Pleasing personal appearance and manner.

9. Good disposition and consistent behaviour.
10. Flexibility in opinion, beliefs and attitudes.
11. A good sense of humour- the ability to enjoy a good joke.
12. Physical fitness and good health status.
13. Wide interests – interest in games, sports, dramatics and other socio-cultural activities.

Professional Characteristics of Mentally Healthy Teachers

The important professional traits of a mentally healthy teacher are the following:

1. Good knowledge of subject matter in which he has specialized.
2. Capacity and willingness to teach effectively and mastery of communication skills.
3. Ability and desire to improve professional skills and achieve competence through the study of professional books and magazines.
4. Ability to work together, to share experiences with other staff members.
5. Ability to assume an attitude of individual responsibility and co-operative functioning.
6. Acceptance and understanding of children.
7. Realistic perception of the social expectations and an understanding of his social role.
8. Respect for oneself and one's profession.

Mental health strengthens human needs, relieve conflict, frustration and stress from mind and make adjustment among them. Now a day every citizen has been becoming educated. Human life is the period from birth to death. Therefore mentally healthy students and teachers creating path collaboration for successful knowledge transfer and knowledge exchange Ever and Every Where.

Knowledge Generating

The knowledge society is a human structured organization based on contemporary developed knowledge and representing new quality of life support systems. It implies the need to fully understand distribution of knowledge, access to information and capability to transfer information into knowledge. The understanding of knowledge is the central challenge when defining a knowledge society. From our present perception of the knowledge society, it is useful to emphasize the role of the knowledge society in the future development of human society. Briefly explaining education at different stages, this paper discusses the role of educational institutions in generating a knowledgeable society. The contemporary society, education is becoming a continuous activity, which focuses on developing the intellectual capacities of the individual, an activity generated and pronounced throughout life by his desire for knowledge and by the practical experiences covered by years. The Knowledge Society provides a thorough international investigation of tertiary education policy across its many facets – governance, funding, quality assurance, equity, research and innovation, academic career, links to the labour market and internationalization. Its specific concern is policies that ensure that capabilities of tertiary education contribute to countries' economic and social objectives. As technologies are deployed to improve global information access, the role of education will continue to grow and change. Education is viewed as a basic human right. For a society where reading and counting are a requisite for daily living, skills in reading, writing, and basic arithmetic are critical for future learning. However, in a knowledge society, education is not restricted to school. Institutions are a part of the social construction of a community, and define the way we interact with each other within society.

Education in India

Education in India is provided by the public sector as well as the private sector, with control and funding coming from three levels: central, state, and local. Under various articles of the Indian Constitution, free and compulsory education is provided as a fundamental right to children between the ages of 6 and 14. The Indian government lays emphasis on primary education, also referred to as elementary education, to children aged 5 to 14 years old. The Indian government has also banned child labor in order to ensure that the children do not enter unsafe working conditions. However, both free education and the ban on child labour are difficult to enforce due to economic disparity and social conditions. 80% of all recognized schools at the elementary stage are government run or supported, making it the largest provider of education in the country.

Secondary education covers children aged 14 to 18, a group comprising 88.5 million children according to the 2001 Census of India. The final two years of secondary is often called Higher Secondary(HS), Senior Secondary, or simply the "+2" stage. The two halves of secondary education are each an important stage for which a pass certificate is needed, and thus are affiliated by central boards of education under HDR ministry, before one can pursue higher education, including college or professional courses. Tertiary education also referred to as third stage, third level, and post-secondary education is the educational level following the completion of a school providing a secondary education.

Higher education, post-secondary education, tertiary education or third level education is an optional final stage of formal learning that occurs after secondary education. Often delivered at universities, academies, colleges, seminaries, and institutes of technology, higher education is also available through certain college-level institutions, including vocational schools, trade schools, and other career colleges that award academic degrees or professional certifications. Tertiary education at non-degree level is sometimes referred to as further education or continuing education as distinct from higher education.

The t erm "technical education" is also understood to include the theoretical and practical scientific knowledge.Vocational education is education within vocational schools that prepares people for a specific trade. It directly develops expertise in techniques related to technology, skill and scientific technique to span all aspects of the trade. Vocational education is classified as using procedural knowledge.

Vocational education is education within vocational schools that prepares people for a specific trade. It directly develops expertise in techniques related to technology, skill and scientific technique to span all aspects of the trade. Vocational education is classified as using procedural. Generally known as career and technical education (CTE) or technical and vocational education and training (TVET) it prepares people for specific trades, crafts and careers at various levels from a trade, a craft, technician, or a high professional practitioner position in career's such as engineering, accountancy, nursing, medicine, architecture, law etc.

Advantages of Education in Current Scenario

1. The community is not where the person is living, but where the person participates, shares experiences and has valued relationships with others.
2. People with high support needs (severe disability, aged etc.) will always need support structures as a part of their lives.
3. The amount of participation in a community (living, education, employment or recreation) is directly related to the skills and resources of the person, and, the skills and resources of the community that the person wishes to participate in.
4. Institutions are going to be around in one form or another whether we like it or not, it is the way that they are used that is the problem.
5. The institutions of a society towards a particular group determine the way the group participates in society.
6. The institutions of a particular government department, organisation, profession or service define the way the person is supported within that society.
7. Facilities that support people with high support needs do not need to be the nursing homes or prisons in the sense that they

are today, but can become warm inviting community places that offer a range of services to the community, as well as be a part of the wider community within that society.

The Purpose and Function of Educational Institutions

Although sociologists have debated the purpose and function of educational institutions, most agree that access to educational opportunities has a profound effect on individual life chances and attainment. We'll consider how specific education policies and practices -like school choice, curriculum differentiation, school finance, and school assignment - shape the range of educational opportunities afforded students. Education has a great social importance especially in the modern, complex industrialized societies. Philosophers of all periods, beginning with ancient stages, devoted to it a great deal of attention.

1. To complete the socialization process

The main social objective of education is to complete the socialization process. The family gets the child, but the modern family tends to leave much undone in the socialization process. The school and other institutions have come into being in place of family to complete the socialization process.

2. To transmit the central heritage:

All societies maintain themselves, by exploitation of a culture. Culture here refers to a set of beliefs and skills, art, literature, philosophy, religion, music etc. that are not carried through the mechanism of heredity.

3. For the formation of social personality

Individual must have personalities shaped or fashioned in ways that fit into the culture. Education everywhere has the function of the formation of social personalities.

The present study revealed through a qualitative research, teachers' perceptions about the role and how to integrate e-learning technologies into classroom current activity. Recognized as tools that could bring a significant contribution to the process of improving students' academic results, e-learning platforms are rarely used in classes and even little integrated within teaching – learning processes. The random use of these systems to explain some phenomena from the different subjects taught is not a method to integrate them and neither to increase the efficiency of the educational services.

Successful Knowledge Creation

THE knowledge-based economy is based on the production, distribution and use of knowledge and information. It is affected by the increasing use of information technologies to increase the competitive advantage in the economy. The main objective of the industry cluster development and supply chain management is to maintain competitiveness of the each industry in the market by using available information/knowledge. Though, industry cluster and supply chain are not the same aspect. Industry cluster is more in the macro-economic level which focuses on collaboration between partners in the same industry. But, Supply chain is more in the micro-economic level which focuses on the information sharing between companies who are in the same production chain. But, there are some focal points between two aspects which will be explained in the next section. On today's global world, generating new knowledge and turning it into new products and services is crucial to maintain and enhance the EU's competitiveness. Even more so, it is a precondition for sustaining the "European Way of Life". Innovation and excellence will positively impact on our lives in very different ways: through improved medicines, more efficient and sustainable energy resources, and with new technological solutions to protect our environment or to guarantee the security of the citizens. Transforming the results of scientific research into new commercial products is, however, a complex process involving a broad range of actors. We need to ensure that researchers and industry work closely together and maximize the social and economic benefits of new ideas. Knowledge creation is a dynamic process involving interactions at various organizational levels and it encompasses a community of individuals that enlarge, amplify, and disseminate their knowledge.

This paper examines interim knowledge transfers within strategic alliances. Using a new measure of changes in alliance partners' technological capabilities, based on the citation patterns of their patent portfolios, we analyze changes in the extent to which partner firms' technological resources 'overlap' as a result of alliance participation.

Creating Path Collaborative Knowledge

There are four critical knowledge management processes used by firms to access and transform knowledge from an alliance context to a partner context: technology sharing; JV-parent interactions; personnel movement; and linkages between parent and alliance strategies. These processes create connections for individual managers through which they can communicate their alliance experiences to others and form the foundation for the integration of knowledge into the parent's collective knowledge base. As individuals interact through the various connections, the interactions become larger in scale and faster in speed as more and more actors in the organization become involved. This process has been described as a "spiral" of organizational knowledge creation.11 In the spiral, knowledge starts at the individual level, moves up to the group level, and then to the firm level. As the knowledge spirals upward in the organization, it may be enriched and extended as individuals interact with each other and with their organizations. Although the knowledge management processes are not complex or difficult to understand, the lack of complexity should not be associated with a lack of effectiveness. The creation of organizational knowledge requires the sharing and dissemination of individual experiences. Each process provides an avenue for JV parent managers to gain exposure to knowledge and ideas outside their traditional organizational boundaries. The processes deal with both operational and strategic knowledge and taken together, provide a comprehensive view as to how alliance knowledge can cross organizational boundaries and become the basis for knowledge creation. Successful knowledge creation through alliances depends on two main elements. First, there are the organizational processes that firms can use to access and transform knowledge from an alliance context to a parent firm context. While these knowledge management processes are not complex, there was substantial variance in the extent to which firms in this study were actively seeking to exploit the knowledge potential.

Organizational knowledge creation involves a continuous interplay between tacit and explicit knowledge.12 Tacit knowledge is hard to formalize, making it difficult to communicate or share with others. Tacit knowledge involves intangible factors embedded in personal beliefs, experiences, and values. Explicit knowledge is systematic and easily communicated in the form of hard data or codified procedures. Often there will be a strong tacit dimension associated with how to use and implement explicit knowledge. Table 1 shows the four knowledge management processes and the primary types of knowledge associated with each process. The table also provides examples to help clarify the tacit and explicit dimensions. Two of the knowledge management processes, JV-parent interactions and linkages between parent and alliance strategies, create the potential for both explicit and tacit knowledge to be created. Technology sharing provides access primarily to explicit knowledge. Personnel movement, while it could be associated with explicit knowledge, will be most effective as a means of gaining access to tacit knowledge.

Creating path collaboration for successful knowledge transfer and knowledge exchange the most advanced and specialized forms of education and training available in modern societies. Their purpose can be defined in terms of providing society with the capacity for carrying out high quality research, and in terms of providing highly-qualified graduates with the skills and options to engage in their chosen careers. In both respects, social and individual requirements are changing. Today's attention to collaborative creating path collaboration for successful knowledge transfer and knowledge exchange education is one manifestation of these changes. A main objective of the project has been to build constructive dialogue with and among stakeholders engaged in collaborative education. By these means, the project aimed to expand the available knowledge of the range of issues involved, the nature and extent of collaborative programmes, employability perspectives and their relation to so-called transferable skills, and the role of institutional tracking.

Increasingly the creation of new organizational knowledge is becoming a managerial priority .New knowledge provides basis for organizational renewal and sustainable competitive advantage. The primary obstacle to success is a failure to execute the specific organizational processes necessary to access, assimilate, and disseminate alliance knowledge. Successful firms exploit learning opportunities by acquiring knowledge through "Grafting," a process of internalizing knowledge not previously available within the organization. Global cooperative ventures have tended to focus on governance forms and task structures. This study highlights the importance of knowledge structures and work systems in influencing the success of collaborative ventures.

Universities are an important source of new knowledge creation and dissemination, which is a fundamental element for the promotion of regional development. The transfer of technologies from universities to enterprises is considered to boost competitiveness, stimulate economic growth and increase prosperity ,whereas the benefits of knowledge exchange between universities and enterprises have been documented in various cases, there is still a long way to go considering the identification of the best-suited policy framework for the enhancement of this process, on national and regional levels .In recent years, a number of contributions have been developed considering the models that describe the process of university to industry knowledge transfer , as well as the relative importance of the different channels for its diffusion . In literature, the transfer of technology has been met as a linear sequence of steps but also, in the framework of informal interpersonal networks and established relationships that promote knowledge sharing and learning.

Organizational learning is a systems-level concept that can become useful only when its component parts are thoroughly understood and brought down to an operational level. Unless individual knowledge is shared throughout the organization, the knowledge will have a limited impact on organizational effectiveness. Thus, organizational knowledge creation represents a process whereby the knowledge held by individuals is amplified and internalized as part of an organization's knowledge.

Effective Knowledge

Effective knowledge creation through alliances depends on two main elements. First, there are the organizational processes that firms can use to access and transform knowledge from an alliance context to a parent firm context. While these knowledge management processes are not complex, there was substantial variance in the extent to which firms in this study were actively seeking to exploit the knowledge potential. Studies of teachers working together have exposed the capricious nature of collaborative activity: sometimes it seems to work well; at other times collaboration actually works against improvement. Success in collaborative relationships is best understood through an appreciation of how teachers form and use knowledge. The teachers' knowledge perspective is used in this paper to interpret qualitative data from two successful collaborative relationships in schools. Evidence supports the contention that personal qualities, underscored by mutual trust and respect for knowledge, form the basis for successful relationships in teaching, operating in different ways, for different purposes, for different people. Providing that teachers are approached with respect, collaboration holds promise as a slow (but powerful) path towards educational change.

'Collaboration' is a broadly used term which serves to describe a wide variety of behaviours. In the most general sense, collaboration is said to have occurred when more than one person works on a single task. For our purposes, however, it is helpful and in fact necessary, to draw some specific parameters around what we refer to as collaboration. The following definition delineates the kind of behavior. Collaboration is a coordinated, synchronous activity that is the result of a continued attempt to construct and maintain a shared conception of a problem. We make a distinction between 'collaborative' versus 'cooperative' problem solving. Cooperative work is accomplished by the division of labour among participants, as an activity where each person is responsible for a portion of the problem solving. We focus on collaboration as the mutual engagement of participants in a coordinated effort to solve the problem together. We further distinguish between synchronous and asynchronous activity. Although we do not propose that collaboration cannot occur in asynchronous activity, we focus on face-to-face interactions, which can only occur as a synchronous activity.

Knowledge transfer is the practical problem of transferring knowledge from one part of the organization to another. Like knowledge management, knowledge transfer seeks to organize, create, capture or distribute knowledge and ensure its availability for future users. It is considered to be more than just a communication problem. If it were merely that, then a memorandum, an e-mail or a meeting would accomplish the knowledge transfer. Knowledge transfer is more complex because (1) knowledge resides in organizational members, tools, tasks, and their sub networks and (2) much knowledge in organizations is tacit or hard to articulate.

There are many factors that complicate knowledge transfer including:

1. The inability to recognize & articulate "compiled" or highly intuitive competencies—tacit knowledge idea
2. Limitations of Information and Communication Technologies (ICTs)
3. Lack of a shared/super ordinate social identity
4. Areas of expertise
5. Internal conflicts
6. Generational differences

7. Motivational issues
8. Lack of trust
9. Capability

Knowledge exchange is a two-way process where social scientists and individuals or organizations share learning, ideas and experiences. Knowledge exchange encourages collaboration between researchers and the private, public and civil society sectors. Knowledge exchange (KE) is a process which brings together academic staff, users of research and wider groups and communities to exchange ideas, evidence and expertise. Within the College of Humanities and Social Science (CHSS), Industry, Policy, Practice and Public represent our main target groups for activity and the overall aim is to contribute to economic, social, cultural and environmental benefits to society. In practice, a lot of knowledge exchange engages across these audiences. Through mutual exchange and collaboration, the process also benefits academic teaching and research. Detailed investigations of collaboration can contribute to future investigations of computer-supported collaborative learning in at least two ways. First, this type of analysis can be viewed as a methodology for coming to a deeper understanding of how the benefits of collaboration are realized. Second, this type of analysis can lead to better development of the kinds of supporting resources that computers can provide for collaborative learning. Clearer understanding of the collaboration as a process of constructing and maintaining a shared conception of the task can be beneficial for future designs of collaborative learning environments. Knowledge exchange between academic institutions and enterprises is a complex activity that involves high risk and is build upon trust. The benefits as well as the direction of the knowledge transfer are often reciprocal, with the academic institutions benefiting from market knowledge.

Impact of Knowledge Transfer and Exchange

It is very broad concept, and there is no single definition for it. Knowledge transfer is when know-how and knowledge are becoming available in a systematic way to those who did not have previous access to it. The concept is still frequently misunderstood and it is very important to communicate the new message. A lot of people still think of it as a sneaky way for universities to make money out of the good ideas of their academics which is rather a narrow and old fashioned viewpoint. That's not to say that research institutions and universities are not going to make money by selling products of their research work. Above all it's about creativity, without which knowledge transfer will be a non-starter. The effective transfer and exchange of knowledge is a crucial capacity for nonprofit organizations. It can provide the foundation for any activity that attempts to influence practices, policies or behaviors including:

1. Delivering programs and services to clients and members
2. Making the case for support to funders and donors
3. Engaging in collaborative efforts with other organizations.

Knowledge transfer and exchange issues have captured the attention of a variety of academic disciplines such as health, management, education, marketing, and applied social research. As a result, work in this area employs a variety of terms and concepts such as dissemination, knowledge diffusion, knowledge brokering, knowledge utilization, knowledge transfer, knowledge exchange and knowledge management that are often used interchangeably. Effective knowledge transfer and exchange efforts treat knowledge as a means to improve practice and situations by having positive impacts, rather than as an end in itself (Williams Group 2003). Given that the overall goal of knowledge transfer and exchange is to reduce the gap between knowledge and practice, the following are some desirable changes that have been discussed in some studies and could be observed when moving towards this goal.

Enablers for Knowledge Transfer and Exchange

What are the factors that enable knowledge transfer and exchange in an organization? Besides the five key elements of effective knowledge transfer and exchange that should be considered in planning, what can facilitate the process of our work? These can include such things as, having funders establish supportive practices and policies, creating a positive organizational culture in which knowledge are used, establishing partnerships between knowledge producers and users, and having ongoing dialogue among parties interested in knowledge.

A successful knowledge-sharing effort requires a focus on more than simply the transfer of the specific knowledge. Instead, many of the activities to be undertaken need to focus on structuring and implementing the arrangement in a way that bridges both existing and potential relationship issues, and examining the form and location of the knowledge to ensure its complete transfer. In other words, while the activities used to share knowledge, such as document exchanges, presentations, job rotations, etc., are important, overcoming the factors that can impede, complicate and even harm knowledge internalization are equally important in determining the ultimate results of a knowledge-sharing effort. Accordingly, any evaluations of the Bank's knowledge-sharing efforts need to incorporate assessments of its use of activities related to understanding the form and embeddedness of the knowledge, establishing and managing appropriate administrative structures, and facilitating the transfer of the knowledge.

Development of the Knowledge Transfer

Higher education organizations are being pushed forward by competitiveness. That pressure requires continuous improvement emphasizing the need for measuring outcomes and building excellence. The paradigm of stakeholder analysis, applied to specific determinations of the system of higher educational institutions, could be a good way for comprehending and predicting interests, needs and requirements of all key players in the environment. The purpose of this paper is to enhance the possibility of understanding the connection between higher education institutions and its environment in context of stakeholder analysis. There is a clear attempt of all organizations, especially those that create and encourage knowledge, to understand the actions of all participants and predictions of interests and requirements of the changing environment.

Every individual has a right to education. It is universally recognized that the main objective of education is to provide quality education to all children. This draws global attention to the fact that *"Education for All"* is a fundamental human right which cannot be realized without enabling. All people who have improving knowledge transfer among stakeholders of education. This is to enable them attain their full potential and be able to meaningfully contribute and participate in their society throughout their lives. Making such people access knowledge transfer is important for human capital development. It prepares those who were most likely to be dependents to become self-reliant. Therefore this paper attempts to give certain important inputs in knowledge transfer among stakeholders of education.

Knowledge Sharing

In the first part of this section, we try to show the emergence, reemergence and development of knowledge transfer and knowledge sharing. It is an attempt to visualize the different authors use of the terms with regards to their level on an individual-industry scale and the publication year. The emergence of Knowledge, source and method in which it is acquired has been discussed (at least) since the time of the philosophical debates by Aristotle and Plato. We would, therefore, propose that the initial emergence of the terms comes from these discussions and that the suggestions on how to deal with efficient and effective knowledge transfer and sharing has been ongoing to a varying degree of intensity since then. The main stream is based on the writings of Michael Polanyi and the terms tacit and explicit knowledge. He writes "Explicit knowledge is formal and systematic. For this reason, it can be easily communicated and shared.

The knowledge transfer process in education aims to increase the use of research results by potential users (Havelock 1973; Huberman 1983) in order to improve practices, to implement new programs, and to resolve specific problems. As explained earlier, four theoretical frameworks led the study of this concept in the education literature. The examination of the included studies shows that the three first models have received serious criticisms from the scientific community of researchers on education. In addition to paying all the attention to the university-created knowledge, This linear approach to knowledge creation and diffusion process, stresses much more the knowledge production phase and practically ignores the users' context (Neville and Warren 1986).

In view of the fact that the management is becoming increasingly aware of the role of education and development, it is obvious that the importance and meaning of modern high educational organizations are changing along with the importance of education in general.

1. Individuals, organizations, and entire economies are finding knowledge and investing in education to be a unique opportunity for developing personal, organizational, economic capabilities and potentials in achieving competitive advantage.
2. The process of transformation of economy and society in the era of knowledge is inevitably tied to the entire education system, especially to high education organizations. Consequently, a stakeholder analysis could be one of the successful tools when planning and managing such type of organizations in a highly changing environment.
3. A dramatic shift of social, technological and economic values arriving in 21st century is transforming organizations through long life learning model.

These changes are also mirrored in the field of education, and are especially true for high education organizations involving business perspective of thinking and operating. Organizations in field of higher education also need to build a quality management system that respects the philosophy of Knowledge management, and they have to deal with problems of Human Resource management in relation to appearance and development of knowledge workers. Furthermore, the modality of stakeholders indicates the diversity and multidimensional environment that defines and determines a modern organization. By organizing the model of lifelong learning and respecting the learning organization criteria we should be able to build organizations highly representative in our competitive era.

Knowledge Management in Universities

The Knowledge and information became the key factors of competitive advantage. Knowledge management (KM) system" is a phrase that is used to describe the creation of knowledge repositories, improvement of knowledge access and sharing as well as communication through collaboration, enhancing the knowledge environment and managing knowledge as an asset for Universities. A complete knowledge management system must contain four elements. They are knowledge creation and capture, knowledge sharing and enrichment, information storage and retrieval, and knowledge dissemination.

1. ***Knowledge Creation and Capture:*** Knowledge is continually being created in any group, since the very interaction among educators/learner generates knowledge. One of the primary aims of knowledge management is to capture the knowledge that is produced during such interactions. The two factors have become of utmost importance in determining competitiveness – creativity and innovation. The creation of new knowledge will not be possible without creativity and innovation. These are the two most important traits or skills needed to make the Universities more productive and competitive. So Universities encourage creativity and innovations.

2. ***Knowledge Sharing and Enrichment:*** Knowledge can be shared by the University with its faculty members (e.g., through memos and instructions) and sharing of knowledge can occur between faculty members of the University (e.g., through group discussions and internal meetings) as well as with people outside of the Universities (e.g., through attending seminars and workshops). Additionally, when staff members attend outside seminars, workshops and meetings further knowledge sharing and enrichment take place.

3. ***Information Storage and Retrieval:*** This can be done by storing information in a centralized location with sufficient provisions for easy retrieval. The documents and information in databases could then be retrieved through the Internet or the University's intranet websites. There are four main options for storing the information that are captured or shared. These are: (a) file system storage (local and network directories and folders); (b) databases; (c) e-mail; and (d) websites (intranet and external).In order to facilitate retrieval, a two-step process has to be implemented: first, the information should be divided into manageable units; and second, each unit should be categorized. Once the repository of information is created, the next step will be to provide various means for users to have access to the information needed. This involves designing and providing information retrieval pathways. These pathways should be designed with the user community in mind and made as user-friendly as possible.

4. ***Knowledge Dissemination:*** Unless knowledge is effectively disseminated, the development impact of knowledge will remain limited. For knowledge dissemination to be effective it will require the transformation of highly individualized tacit knowledge into explicit knowledge that can be more widely shared. Publications, presentations, websites and libraries are the most obvious forms of dissemination of knowledge. Participation in external networks, establishing partnerships with other Universities, and creation of knowledge centres are also effective means to disseminate knowledge.

Knowledge management is based on the fundamental concept that one of the most valuable assets of University is the experience and expertise that reside in the heads of its officers, administrators and faculty members. In order to derive the maximum benefit from this intellectual capital, ways and means must be devised to manage this knowledge, capture it and share it with others, particularly the co-workers. If executed and implemented in a proper manner, knowledge management is expected to create a more collaborative environment, cut down on duplication of effort and encourage knowledge sharing. In the process, there will be considerable savings in terms of time and money. So many educational aspirants are benefited.

Knowledge Management in educational institution makes good sense and a good combination of intellectual output of the academic organization if preserved well using technology. The KM efforts could be monitored by the libraries and disclose it along explicit knowledge to the users, but tacit knowledge compilation is difficult as it is preserved at individual level. But librarian could make better efforts in making available such kind of knowledge with the support of the knowledge developers using technology to capture tacit knowledge generated in the organization. In this role of each and every staff and student is very important as its not sole responsibility of Librarian. Rashtriya Ucchatar Shikshan Abhiyan (RUSA) is giving importance to employability of the students. The new goal for educational institutions today is to develop such knowledge base of student's knowledge (both tacit and explicit) including their capabilities and skills with the help of latest technologies. It will help to students to pick up their capabilities, talents, prior knowledge and experience and work on that to enlarge and adapt this knowledge more effectively and easier to cope up with present environment Teachers, more than anyone, are expected to build learning communities, create the knowledge society, and develop the capacities for innovation, flexibility and commitment to change that are essential to economic prosperity. At the same time, teachers are also expected to mitigate and counteract many of the immense problems that knowledge societies create, such as excessive consumerism, loss of community, and widening gaps between rich and poor. The teaching profession is a key mediating agency for society as it endeavors to cope with social change and upheaval. But the teaching profession must be trained and equipped so that it will have the capacity to cope with the many changes and challenges which lie ahead. In Universities research work goes on and on haphazardly without any specific direction and coordination. Collaboration with industries gives specific direction to research speedily and takes.

Creating the Conditions for Successful Knowledge Transfer

It has been recognized that the involvement of business in the governance of research institu-tions can help to orient research and education activities towards the needs of society, bring ex-pertise to support knowledge transfer activities, and signal willingness to introduce innovation-ori-ented approaches in all activities. Such interac-tion has helped to facilitate inter-sect oral mobility, namely through temporary staff exchanges as well as through the hiring of young graduates by industry.

Knowledge Sharing Behavior

Previous studies Ismail and Yusuf (2008) and Alarm, Abdullah, Ishim, and Zane (2009), indicated that there are several factors that could influence individual readiness for knowledge sharing. These factors range from physical objects, such as tools and technologies to abstract concepts, such as motivations and providing incentives to encourage knowledge sharing, organizational culture, personal values, and self identity , national culture , trust , organizational resources such as time and space , awareness , altruism , personality ,leadership , and access to knowledgeable people in an organization . These factors are associated with a number of theories and models such as theory of Planned Behavior (TPB) and Technology Acceptance Model (TAM). TPB are adopted through this work in order to propose the new conceptual model. The purpose of the proposed model is to enhance knowledge sharing behavior among stakeholders in Jordanian hospitals using social networks.

In this first notion, the relationship between knowledge and practice is that in which knowledge serves to organize practice, so that greater knowledge (subject matter, educational theory, instructional strategies) leads more or less directly to increased effectiveness in practice. Knowledge for teaching is formal knowledge, derived from university research, and is what theoreticians refer to when they say that teaching has generated a body of knowledge different to common knowledge. Practice, from this standpoint, is about the application of formal knowledge to practical Situations.

The emphasis in research on learning to teach has been the search foreknowledge in action. It has been estimated that what teachers know is implicit in practice, in the reflection on practice, in the investigation of practice, and in the narrative of that practice. This assumes that teaching is an erratic and spontaneous activity, contextualized and built as a response to the particularities of everyday life in the school and classroom. Knowledge is located in the actions, decisions, and judgments of the teachers. It is acquired by experience and deliberation, and teachers learn when they have the opportunity to reflect on what they do.

This last trend is included in the qualitative research line, but close to what is termed *teacher as researcher*. The root idea is that in teaching it is nonsense to speak of one knowledge that is formal and another that is practical, rather that knowledge is built collectively within local communities, formed by teachers working in school development projects, training, or co-operative research (Cochran-Smith and Lytle, 1999).Interactions between the public research base and industry have been gradually increasing over the past decade. These can vary from contractual research to collaborative research or even to structured partnerships Most of these interactions involve the transfer of knowledge between the stakeholders concerned, and enhance the socio-economic impact of publicly-funded research, e.g. by creating new useful products, new jobs and sometimes new companies.

Strategizing and Redefining Educational Perspectives

To become a competitive and dynamic knowledge based economy, one of recommendations made for achieving it is to improve education by recognizing the changing role of teachers in a knowledge society and preparing teachers to play this role effectively. A knowledge society, which India aspires to be, also looks up to its teachers, since the onus lies on schools to develop future knowledge workers with grounding in practices like reflection, innovation and collaboration· Quality of teacher education programs and the ability and/or willingness of universities to provide innovative programs that will produce better-prepared teachers are being questioned. Schools of education are being blamed for mediocrity in preparing teachers for the 21st century classrooms and have been urged to make radical changes in the teacher–training programmes they offer[12]. Though many aspects of pre-service teacher education need to be redefined but only one aspect, the instructional strategy adopted in pre-service teacher education programmes has been considered in the present paper. It has been argued that the current practice of delivering lectures needs to be substituted by those appropriate for nurturing the competencies needed by teachers of the knowledge society, who can in turn prepare knowledge workers.

Teaching methods using transmission with lectures, books and marked assignments dominate in most of the educational institutions. Digital technologies are also used in increasing frequency for supporting this model. However, this kind of use of technology fails to tap the potential of technology for interactive and collaborative learning. Teaching aims to fill minds with information and test reproductive learning. But in the knowledge age, education needs to overcome such 'mind-as-container' metaphor and acknowledge the capability of mind of sustaining knowledgeable, intelligent behavior. Didactic practices are in vogue in teacher education institutions and teacher educators are expected to teach rather than facilitate educational processes promoting ICT and redefining the traditional lecture based transmission of knowledge is a most urgent dimension to be focused upon.

Learning and teaching are two different aspects. One can learn if the proper environment is provided. Learners should create abilities for self-learning, critical thinking, collaborating, communicating, information processing, problem solving and the like leading to cognition as well as metacognition. Fostering learner autonomy by putting into practice the concept of 'engaged learning.' Engaged learning demands self-regulated learners who explore and collaborate to complete tasks that are closely related to real world problems with the intend to build knowledge based communities.

In this age of knowledge building through collaboration involves innovation which has a strong yet complex relation with innovative approaches. Globalization and the changing world economy are driving a transition to knowledge based economies. In particular, developing countries need knowledge based economies not only to build more efficient domestic economies, but to take advantage of economic opportunities outside their own borders. In the social sphere, the knowledge society brings greater access to information, innovations with new forms of social interaction and cultural expression. Individuals therefore have more opportunities to participate in and influence the development of their societies. Innovation is seen as the means of support for development and economic functioning.

Knowledge Society and Information Society

The concept of a 'Knowledge Society' is often confused with that of an 'Information Society'. The latter is, however, considered more limited, as the application of knowledge to data creates information, and information has to be activated or generated by knowledge. The concept of 'knowledge societies' includes a dimension of social, cultural, economical, political, and institutional transformation, and a more pluralistic and developmental perspective. It is regarded as a human process. Knowledge society requires abilities to reflect, act with autonomy but work collaboratively for creating knowledge and be lifelong learners. In response to these demands of the knowledge society and the teaching profession, teachers need to be prepared suitably. The paradigm suggested for this is based on the dimensions that call for teacher educators to facilitate engaged learning with scope for autonomy, problem solving and collaboration especially through ICTs. The present paper has clearly made an attempt to focus on the role of education and educational institution in collaborating successful knowledge transfer and knowledge exchange.

The key elements of knowledge transfer and exchange include audience, message, method, messenger and evaluation. As for impact of knowledge transfer and exchange concerned, the following four areas play eminent role. They are, increased capacity to use knowledge, integrating evidence into decision-making, cultural shift and collaboration. Whereas, enablers for knowledge transfer and exchange depend on four important aspects. They are, funding agencies, organizational culture, partnership in the knowledge development process and ongoing dialogue.

Knowledge transfer and exchange issues have captured the attention of a variety of academic disciplines such as health, management, education, marketing, and applied social research. As a result, work in this area employs a variety of terms and concepts such as dissemination, knowledge diffusion, knowledge brokering, knowledge utilization, knowledge transfer, knowledge exchange and knowledge management that are often used interchangeably. For the purpose of this framework, we use the term knowledge transfer and exchange, which is defined as a set of activities and approaches that are undertaken to move knowledge among those who have interests or needs in it. This movement may involve primarily a one-way flow of knowledge from researchers to practitioners (i.e., knowledge transfer), or can involve the two-way movement of knowledge among researchers and practitioners recognizing that knowledge creation is not the sole domain of any one actor in a system.

Before undertaking a knowledge transfer and exchange activity it is useful to consider the various elements that are involved and the potential outcomes that one wants to achieve. It is also worthwhile to consider some of the enabling factors that can further support and facilitate the planning and delivery of effective knowledge transfer and exchange. Collaboration is a means and an end to knowledge development, transfer and exchange. Knowledge transfer and exchange happens in the context of relationships (Norman & Huerta 2006). Measuring the level of collaboration created through knowledge transfer and exchange is important. A collaborative environment also embraces the continuity of knowledge exchange among those involved and results in stronger links among groups necessary for knowledge transfer (CHSRF, 2005).

In order to foster knowledge transfer and exchange, it is important to have an organizational culture that is open to change and promotes sharing and learning. It is therefore important for organizations to encourage cooperation, collaboration, and knowledge sharing. It is also important for organizations to be openly committed to finding and using high quality evidence and to developing the skills and tools needed to interpret the knowledge and put it into practice (CHSRF, 2005).

Partnership between researchers and practitioners or decision-makers allows opportunities for all parties to better understand each other's perspectives and needs. One way to encourage it is to involve the end users early in the research process (Pyra, 2003). Fostering an ongoing knowledge exchange dialogue between knowledge producers and users is another way to produce an atmosphere in which both groups will better understand each other's perspectives, experiences, and needs. This dialogue, for example, can help policy makers ask questions that are answerable by research and obtain latest skills and tools they need to integrate knowledge into their practices (CHSRF, 2005). There are various activities through which one can make knowledge accessible to those who need it. In these activities, users are relied upon to search through your website or library, come to your booth, or contact you by phone or email and find the information they need. Your main responsibility, as the knowledge producer or sender, is to create a robust collection of knowledge and make it accessible in various ways. You also need to widely promote the knowledge and the ways through which they are available. The focus of this method is on the process of sending the developed knowledge rather than receiving it.

Evaluate Distribution and Accessibility

We need two parallel mechanisms to evaluate two aspects of these activities. One mechanism should focus on the promotion and accessibility of knowledge to confirm that a large number of organizations and the public are aware of the knowledge and how to reach it. An activity log and website tracking software are good tools to collect enough information or inquiries to indicate the effectiveness of the ways through which the knowledge is accessible. Another mechanism should focus on users' satisfaction. Website usability test, user satisfaction survey, casual conversations with users, and anecdotal reports are helpful to receive feedback from the users. This section explains a variety of knowledge transfer and exchange activities that are initially organized to bring a group of people together for various purposes such as discussion, presentation or networking. These people are assumed to have some common interests, experiences, knowledge, skills, or expertise. During these activities, the role of the knowledge producer/sender and the knowledge receiver/user may change/shift various opportunities are provided for all participants to exchange their knowledge or just transfer it.

A workshop is a setting that is planned for interaction, sharing information, and active learning. By having a limited number of people who are highly interested in a topic, a workshop encourages participants to learn from each other or to adopt an innovation into practice. A workshop facilitator has a crucial role in making the workshop more interactive by planning various activities and organizing an agenda that allows participants to get to know each other and to share experiences. Through a workshop, the knowledge producer/sender and the knowledge receiver/user should have equal levels of control and feel supported to exchange their knowledge and experiences.

This section explains a group of knowledge transfer and exchange activities that are designed to help people share information and ideas in a structured environment. The scope of these activities can go beyond the exchange or transfer of knowledge. These activities can generate new ideas, find solutions to a problem, build relationships, and create opportunities for innovations. In these settings, there is no boundary between knowledge producer/sender and knowledge receiver/user and both parties can benefit from the experience. The advantage of these knowledge transfer and exchange activities is that they can create an opportunity in which the knowledge will not only flow among participants but it will grow. The challenge, however, is to make sure that the participants bring diversified experiences, perspectives, opinions, and ideas to the table, and that they are willing to communicate and examine their ideas. Efforts should be taken to ensure that everyone has an opportunity to participate and that all voices are heard.

Theories of Knowledge Transfer

In order to understand human thinking and problem solving in complex and novel situations we need to have a general theory for how people use and adapt their prior knowledge to solve new problems. Aspirations towards such a goal have traditionally been discussed in terms of transfer, or how knowledge acquired from one task or situation can be applied to a different situation (Bransford & Schwartz, 1999; Detterman & Sternberg, 1993; Salomon & Perkins, 1989). Work in cognitive science over the past thirty years has progressed towards this goal by investigating separate strands of transfer phenomena that occur in particular learning and problem solving situations. Although this research strategy has proven successful in developing local, independent explanations of knowledge transfer for particular experimental scenarios (e.g., analogical transfer and transfer appropriate processing), it has done little to bring us closer to a *general theory of transfer*. It is time to begin to weave these separate strands of investigation into a more complete theory that incorporates each strand in principled ways.

It is this charge of theoretical synthesis that motivates the two hypotheses under investigation in the current study. First, it is proposed that there is no single knowledge transfer mechanism, but multiple ones. These mechanisms include (but are not limited to) analogy, knowledge compilation, and error correction. Second, the particular transfer mechanism used depends on both (a) the knowledge actually present and how it is represented, and (b) the processing demands of the transfer task. Below I summarize some of the prior work on transfer that is relevant to the investigation of these two hypotheses.

Mechanisms of Knowledge Transfer

The first mechanism of interest is *analogical transfer* (Gentner, Holyoak, & Kokinov, 2001) . Analogical transfer is composed of three sub processes: retrieving a prior knowledge structure, creating a mapping between it and the current problem or situation, and then using that mapping to generate new knowledge structures relevant to the application context. The transferred knowledge is typically assumed to be a declarative representation, but it can also include procedural attachments (Chen, 2002). The empirical evidence for analogical mapping is extensive (Catrambone & Holyoak, 1989; Gentner & Toupin, 1986). However, the evidence also shows that although people are capable of mapping deep relational structures, the retrieval of an analogue is heavily dependent upon matches between the surface features of the current problem and prior problem solving experiences (Catrambone, 2002; Ross & Kilbane, 1997). Therefore, analogy is perhaps a better explanation for near transfer than for far transfer. The second transfer mechanism of interest is knowledge compilation proposed by John R. Anderson and co-workers (Anderson, 1983; Neves & Anderson, 1981). Knowledge compilation was specifically proposed to explain how declarative knowledge is brought to bear on problem solving in the context of the ACT-R theory. This computational mechanism operates through the deliberate and explicit, step-by-step interpretation of a declarative statement that generates new production rules as a side effect. Those rules are then optimized via rule composition and the result is a procedural representation of the content of the declarative knowledge given a specific goal.

The knowledge compilation mechanism can be viewed as a translation device that translates or interprets declarative knowledge (e.g., advice, instructions, and strategies) into a set of procedures and actions that can be used to solve problems. Since knowledge compilation operates on declarative knowledge it can be used in a wide variety of application contexts because the knowledge has yet to be proceduralized, or tied to the goals of a particular problem solving context. This mechanism embodies a tradeoff between applicability and efficiency in that it has wide applicability across many contexts but requires a complicated and lengthy application process to translate the declarative knowledge into a set of actions. There is some empirical support for knowledge compilation but the evidence is not extensive (Anderson, Greeno, Kline, & Neves, 1981; Neves & Anderson, 1981). The third transfer mechanism of interest is Ohlsson's (1996) error correction mechanism. Ohlsson and co-workers (Ohlsson, 1996; Ohlsson & Rees, 1991) have proposed that the role of declarative knowledge is primarily to help a learner identify and correct his or her own errors. The constraint violation theory has both declarative and procedural components that operate in parallel, and the function of declarative knowledge is to constrain possible problem solutions. When incomplete or faulty procedural knowledge generates undesirable outcomes, these are recognized as violations of those constraints and the responsible rules are revised accordingly.

The power of declarative knowledge is that it can help the learner pinpoint the cause of an error, and transfer is the process by which errors are identified and remedied. This mechanism has wide applicability in that the constraints can be applied to a variety of problems that may require *different* strategies or sequences of actions to produce the correct solution. The constraint violation theory has been shown to generate power law learning curves (Ohlsson, 1996) and to support the design of successful tutoring systems (Mitrovic & Ohlsson, 1999).

In addition to each transfer mechanism using different cognitive processes, each mechanism has also been hypothesized to operate on specific types of prior *knowledge structures*. Analogy uses exemplar knowledge that consists of a declarative representation that may also have procedural attachments (Gentner, 1983). Knowledge compilation uses declarative knowledge such as instructions, advice, or tactical knowledge (Anderson, 1983). Error correction uses declarative knowledge of the constraints for a particular problem domain (Ohlsson, 1996). In summary, researchers have proposed multiple alternative transfer processes including analogy, knowledge compilation, and error correction. Each mechanism has been associated with a particular kind of transfer scenario that specifies the conditions necessary for transfer (i.e., type of prior knowledge and application context). The purpose of the current study is to test the predictions of each transfer theory, and ask whether we can predict what transfer mechanism will be triggered for a given set of transfer scenarios.

The Present Study

In order to test these theories I implemented a between-groups training study in which subjects were given one of three training scenarios (exemplar, tactics, or constraints) and then were tested on a common set of problem solving tasks. Each training scenario was designed to facilitate the construction of one of the three of the aforementioned knowledge structures associated with each transfer mechanism (i.e., exemplars for analogy, tactics for knowledge compilation, and constraints for error correction). In the exemplar training condition participants solve problems similar to those used in the transfer phase. In the tactical training condition participants learn instructional tactics for solving the transfer problems. In the constraints training condition participants learn the constraints associated with the problem solving task domain. The transfer task is Thurstone's *letter extrapolation task* (Thurstone & Thurstone, 1941). In this task subjects are given a sequence of letters containing a pattern and their task is to find the pattern and continue it. Here is a simple example, A B M C D M . . . the correct continuation is E F M G H M. An important aspect of these problems for the current purposes is that prior declarative and procedural knowledge can make them easier to solve.

Although letter extrapolation is an invented task, it has several elements in common with many real world tasks including: a prior knowledge base (e.g., the alphabet), conceptual content (e.g., the pattern), materials to study (e.g., tactics), and generativity (e.g., one has to generate a sequence of coordinated actions).

Three different extrapolation problems were used in the transfer phase. Each problem was constructed with different properties or affordances, to elicit quantitative (accuracy, solution time, self-corrected errors) and qualitative (solution type) differences in performance from each training group.

The first transfer problem was designed to have a similar surface and deep pattern structure as that used in the exemplar training problems. This problem can also be solved by applying either tactical or constraint knowledge. The second transfer problem is open-ended and depending on how the given sequence is interpreted, different solution types are expected. This problem shares the same deep structure as the exemplar problems. However, the surface similar characteristics are misaligned and suggest a different interpretation. If the given sequence is interpreted as similar to the *surface sequence* one solution is expected. If it is interpreted as a *deep analogy* a second solution is expected. Tactical knowledge can also be used to solve this problem and biases one towards the second solution. Constraint knowledge can be applied as well and does not provide an a-priori bias towards any one of the correct solutions. The third transfer problem has neither surface nor deep structure similarity to the exemplar problems. The tactics are also not directly applicable. However, the constraints can be applied to find a unique solution. In addition to comparing task performance across training groups, each training group was compared to a *no-training* control group for a measure of transfer relative to baseline performance.

Exemplar Training: If participants in this training condition use exemplar knowledge and analogy to solve the first transfer problem they are expected to show high accuracy and fast solution times with few error-correcting behaviors as compared to the no-training group. They should show fast solution times for this problem because there is both surface and deep similarity to the training exemplars (i.e., fast memory access). They should show few error-correcting behaviors because they can transfer both declarative and procedural knowledge from the exemplars. For transfer problem 2 participants are expected to show high accuracy with slower solution times and few self-corrected errors. In addition, they should show a bias for the surface similar problem solution. For transfer problem 3 they should show similar performance to no-training participants.

Tactical Training: If participants in this training condition use tactical knowledge and knowledge compilation to solve the first two transfer problems they should show high accuracy but similar solution times and error-correcting behaviors to that of the no-training group. In addition, for transfer problem 2 they should show a bias for the tactics relevant solution. For transfer problem 3 they should show similar performance to that of the no-training participants.

We are living in a society dominated by change. The technical, economical and social evolution has shaped people's way of living and thinking. The globalized markets, the technical and technological revolutions are transforming the modern economy into a "*knowledge based society*" in which new ways of organizing the work are governing the world, demanding a perpetual build up of competences, a rapid spread of high performance technologies, solid knowledge and increasing responsibilities. In the society of the future, education will play the key part in the way of life specific to this education and knowledge-based society. Introducing in the educational system of new learning and teaching techniques is a prerequisite of national cultural success, as much as it is also a prerequisite of economic competitiveness. The educational system is responsible for the state of the nation, and this state is conditioned by the quality of the educational system, as well as the obvious truth that the apex of high quality education today is more demanding than just forming the capacity to generate new competences. Given the economic crisis, the educational system has a major problem due to lowering financial resources, which can lead to the drop of quality and performance in the educational system and a diminished role of education in the knowledge based society.

Innovative Practices in Educational System

New Technologies have the role of transforming the education by rethinking the purpose and functionality of the educational system in society. Expectations for students and school systems continue to rise while many states face the toughest financial challenges of recent history. These dual realities mean that policy makers and practitioners must do more with the resources they have during these difficult budget times. Though this "new normal" is certainly a steep challenge, it is one that presents opportunities for states, districts, and schools to innovate, increase efficiency and effectiveness, and accelerate reform. Tertiary education policy is increasingly important on national agendas. The widespread recognition that tertiary education is a major driver of economic competitiveness in an increasingly knowledge-driven global economy has made high- quality tertiary education more important than ever before. The imperative for countries is to raise higher-level employment skills, to sustain a globally competitive research base and to improve knowledge dissemination to the benefit of society. Tertiary education contributes to social and economic development through four major missions:

1. The formation of human capital (primarily through teaching);
2. The building of knowledge bases (primarily through research and knowledge development);
3. The dissemination and use of knowledge (primarily through interactions with knowledge users); and
4. The maintenance of knowledge (inter-generational storage and transmission of knowledge).

To conclude the article, throughout the world, the roles of education and of its multiple benefits to the economic and social environment are well known, as education is recognized as being "*the single most important path to development and to limiting poverty*". The increasing extent of services in the economy, the pace of technological changes, the advanced level of information and knowledge, as well as the size of the industrial and social re-organizations, all give good arguments in favor of the knowledge based society. The main component of economic and social development becomes knowledge. In the knowledge-based society the mission of the educational system becomes a key component of change.

Recently, the Educational institutions are equipped for classrooms with audio-visual systems that allow display of videocassettes, paper documents, Internet pages, and interaction with commonly used software such as Microsoft Office. These classrooms are called "smart classrooms," multimedia lecture halls, or electronic classrooms. Their purpose is to create new opportunities in teaching and learning by integrating computer, multimedia, and network technologies. However, it is not clear that using this new technology will automatically result in more effective teaching and learning. After all, extravagant claims were made for the blackboard when it was introduced. This paper focuses on students' comparisons of instruction that uses the smart classroom to the instructional style associated with traditional classrooms. The comparison is limited to the usage of the classroom for presentation of information, and does not address issues such as the relative advantages of the two types of classroom for active and cooperative learning. In the twenty first century classroom fully equipped with the tools and materials is more likely to achieve success than is a poorly resourced one.

Important Resources

1. Interactive whiteboards
2. Classroom desktop computers
3. Pods of laptops for one to one programs
4. PDA's, iPods and cell phones
5. Educationally focused software
6. Learning and content management systems
7. Video and audio conferencing
8. Cameras, videos, tripods, microphones, speakers, headphones and
9. Media production facilities

Students and educators today must have Information and Communications Technology (ICT) literacy and use technology in the context of teaching and learning. The skills they need include such life skills as leadership, ethics, accountability, personal responsibility and more. In addition, an understanding of how to use 21st century assessments, specifically authentic assessments that measure all areas of learning, is key. The Partnership's Framework is a unified, collective vision for 21st century learning. Among its elements are the standards, curriculum, environment, and assessments must implement.

Many instructors use smart classrooms to present information in the form of prewritten visual displays such as Power point slides, PDF documents, graphics, and so forth. They may post handouts for these presentations on a web site, so that students may bring copies of them to class. Using this strategy, instructors do not need to spend any time writing on the blackboard. Instructors who do not use the special equipment use the blackboard to support presenting information. They may write the bulk of the lecture on the board, write down only key concepts and overarching ideas, or use the board to map out class discussions.

Traditional teaching is concerned with the educator being the controller of the learning environment. Power and responsibility are held by the teacher and they play the role of educators and decision maker. They regard students as having knowledge holes that need to be filled with information. In short, the traditional teacher views that it is the teacher that causes learning to occur. Learning is chiefly associated within the classroom and is often competitive. The lessons content and delivery are considered to be most important and student's master knowledge through drill and practice content need not be learned in context. Smart Class, is the combination of various digital media types such as text, images, audio and video, into an integrated multi-sensory interactive application or presentation to convey information to the students. Traditional educational approaches have resulted in a mismatch between what is taught to the students and what the industry.

Benefits of Smart Technology

1. Take notes on a variety of digital mediums.
2. Save your notes for your future reference.
3. After you have saved your notes you can organize them with ease on your own computer.
4. You can provide exact class notes to an absent student or a student looking for extra help – via the internet
5. You can begin the creation of online courses!

From the above information, it can be concluded that a combination of blackboard and smart classroom technology should be used, and that instructors should always remember that students have widely heterogeneous needs and learning styles. The combination of Smart Class Teaching and Black Board is the best way of teaching. Black Board Teaching allows for more interaction between the educator and the students, and the ability to more dynamically solve problems with the guidance of the professor. In a sense, really see the mental process that the professor goes through to solve a problem. Thus, the students are more involved in learning the material. However, it is critical that an Educator be very comfortable with the material and periphery subjects if Black Board Teaching is used since the discussion may shift across multiple subject areas in order to reach the teaching objectives.

Relationship between Education and Society

India's Destiny is being shaped in Four Walls" is the first sentence in education report submitted to the central government by the education commission in 1966 under the chairmanship of Dr.D.S.Kothari. Four walls are the walls of class rooms of educational institutes where the students and the teachers are expected to work together to develop good human resource for the welfare of mankind. However the present scenario is "India's destiny is being shaped both in four walls and outside the walls". There has been the great belief and confidence of not only the educationists but also by the common people that education has a great impact on the society as a whole. Educational institutions happen to be the centers of human resource development and the learners who come out of these centers are expected to go the society and take up some responsibility including business. Good human resource with ethical and moral values will develop good business and good business will ultimately give good service to the society. Thus the business and the society are interrelated and interdependent. Good educational institutes need to take the responsibility of shaping the future of Business and Society by developing good.

Education is a major institution in most societies. Indeed, it is difficult to imagine any industrialized or industrializing society without a system of schools. Sociologists of education examine many parts of educational systems interaction, classrooms and peer groups, school organizations and national and international systems of education. Sociologists see education as one of the major institutions that constitute society; they place the study of education in a larger framework of institutions found in every society. These institutions include family, religion, politics, economics and health, in addition to education. Society may be viewed as a system of interrelated mutually dependent parts which cooperate (more or less) to preserve a recognizable whole and to satisfy some purpose or goal. Social system refers to the orderly arrangement of parts of society and plurality of individuals interacting with each other. Social system presupposes a social structure consisting of different parts which are interrelated in such a way as to perform its functions. To perform its functions every society sets up various institutions. Five major complexes of institutions are identified familial institutions, religious institutions, educational institutions, economic institutions and political institutions. These institutions form sub-systems within social system or larger society.

Education as a Sub-System

Education is a sub-system of the society. It is related to other sub-systems. Various institutions or sub-systems are a social system because they are interrelated. Education as a sub-system performs certain functions for the society as whole. There are also functional relations between education and other sub-systems. For example, Education trains the individuals in skills that are required by economy. Similarly education is conditioned by the economic institutions. The effectiveness of organized activities of a society depends on the interaction and inters relationships of these institutions which constitute the whole. Now we will examine the role of education for the society and the relationship between education and other sub-system of society in terms of functionalist perspective. The functionalist view of education tends to focus on the positive contributions made by education to the maintenance of social system.

Education in particular the teaching of history, provides this link between the individual and society. If the history of his society is brought alive to the child, he will come to see that he is a part of something larger than himself, he will develop a sense of commitment to the social group.

The submission is reproduced by a number of ideological State Apparatuses", such as mass media, law, religion and education. Ideological State Apparatus transmit ruling class ideology thereby creating false class consciousness. Education not only transmits a general ruling class ideology which justifies and legitimates the capitalist system. It also reproduces the attitudes and behaviour required by the major groups in the division of labour. It teaches workers to accept and submit to their exploitation, it teaches the agents of 'exploitation and repression', the managers, administrators and politicians, how to practice their crafts and rule the work force as agents of ruling class. It can be stated here that education performs certain role for the society. At the same time education is also conditioned by the social structure. Society crates educational institutions such as schools, colleges and universities to perform certain functions in accomplishing its end. The educational system may be viewed as a part of the total social system. It reflects and influences the social and cultural order of which it is a part. The class system, the cultural values, the power structure, the balance between individual freedom and social control, the degree of urbanization and industrialization all these factors exercise a profound influence on school system of any society.

Functional Relationships between Education and other Sub-Systems

What are the functional relationships between education and other sub-systems of society? Many functionalists have argued that there is functional relationship between different sub-systems. For example there is a functional relationship between education and economic system. Skills and values learned in education are directly related to the way in which the economy and the occupational structure operate. Education trains the individuals in skills that are required by the economy. Similarly, education is also influenced by economy.

In a changing society the interdependence of social institutions has a good deal of significance, to quote Ogburn and Nimkoff, for a change in one institution may affect other institutions". For example, when a country changes its Constitution, the change is never confined to its political institutions. Corresponding changes take place in economic relationships, in the educational system, in the class structure and so on. All the social institutions would be in balance, each being adjusted to other, forming a single unified scheme.

Education is a social concern. It is a social process. Its objective is to develop and awaken in the child those physical, intellectual and moral states which are acquired of the individual by his society as a whole and the milieu for which he is specially destined. It is the significant means of socialization. The function of education is to socialize the young by imparting to them norms and values, culture and heritage, and to provide them with skills and placement. This is traditionally, the accepted role of education.

In the West, for long, literacy was not considered essential for all. It remained confined to the priests, ruling classes and to commercial class. The education imparted was literary and religious. The valuation of education was not very high. In the

Indian social milieu, education has been traditionally given significant importance. The modern industrial society with its advance technology, division of labour, job differentiation, assumes a general standard of literacy. It cannot carry on with handful of education and mass illiteracy. The technological advancement has necessitated the re-orientation of education.

The environmental effect of the education of child is now given special stress and attention. J.W.B. Douglas, in The Home and the School has specially developed this aspect of child education. "The advantages which first children have over latter siblings in Douglas's study, are best understood in terms of the greater degree of attention and responsibility which most first children are likely to receive from their parents as well as the greater responsibilities they have to shoulder. Likewise, children from smaller families generally have higher educational attainment, since they are also likely to receive more parental attention than children in large families."

"Focussing on parental attention in this way helps us understand why apparently unconnected factors all tend to work in the same direction. They also affect the child's behaviour at school as well as within the home. The amount and quality of child-adult interactions influence the development of the child's linguistic capacity, e.g., the range of his vocabulary. Likewise, the child's own interest in schooling, as distinct from that of these parents, and his sense of being at ease when at school, are affected both directly and indirectly by his awareness of the importance and value his parents explicitly and implicitly place on schooling. "The family itself thus constitutes a learning situation for the child. Nor is the child simply 'moulded' by the family environment. He or she is an active agent who has to learn to interpret that environment... Consequently, when considering the effects of the home on educational attainment. It is not enough to see this simply as the result of the occupation and education of the parents. Family insecurity, for example, is not only produced by poverty but also results when professional parents with busy lives spend little time with their children. Resentments built up through such family interactions may undermine the good intentions of parents to help their children perform well in school".

In the traditional society, teacher was taken to symbolise the best in social values. He was accepted as a moral authority. But this position has now undergone a distinct change. Teacher in an educated society is not the only person who can be said to have intellectual competence and school too is not the only institution to impart education. The normative aspect of education is not attended to. In fact it has remained neglected. The emphasis in learning is on the accumulation of knowledge or acquiring a qualification, vocational or otherwise.

Equality of Educational Opportunity

The equalization of educational opportunities is essentially linked with the notion of equality in the social system. In a social system if all the individuals are treated as equal, they get equal opportunities for advancement. Since education is one of the most important means of upward mobility, it is through an exposure to education one can aspire to achieve higher status, position and emoluments. But for getting education he must have equal opportunities like other members of the society. In case educational opportunities are unequally distributed, the inequalities in the social structure continue to be perpetuated, it is in this light the quality of educational opportunity has been visualized.

A society which hold high promise of "Equality of status and of opportunity" for all and assures" the dignity of individual and the unity and integrity of the Nations", has to attend to the mass spreading of learning much in the interest of creating the appropriate ground work for the social advancement. Education is supposed to eliminate social and economic inequality. The relationship between education and inequality is a result of the historical particulars of the educational system. There are two factors in this (1) the available opportunities which structure individual choices and (2) the social and economic process which structure individual choices while the above factors point out that the educational system is a product of the social structure it must be remembered that it is not a one-way process because the educational system itself and the values it stands for influences individual decisions.

Educational Inequality

The major problem with respect to the equality of educational opportunity is the perpetuation of inequalities through education. It is through a system of education in which elite control is predominant that the inequalities are perpetuated. In an elite controlled system the schools practice segregation. This segregation may be on the basis of caste, colour or class etc. In South Africa schools practice segregation on the basis of colour. Equality of educational opportunity is more talked about, than really believed. In all modern industrially advanced countries there is the total inequality of educational opportunity. Educational opportunities for a child are determined by his family, class, neighbourhood consideration. The size of the family and the parental attitude makes a lot of difference to the educational career of a child. The educated parents give due attention to the education of the children. The family influence determines the educational goal of the children.

Inequality of educational opportunity also occurs due to the poverty of a large section of the population and the relative affluence of small minority. The poor cannot pay the fees and their children do not find chances of continuing in schools. Children from the families that cannot provide the economic support and other perquisite, suffer badly. From this group, there is the maximum number of dropouts. Education and social status have close connection. Social class position includes income, occupation and life style. These have impact on the upbringing of the child. The attitude of the teacher has much to do with education of the children. The very real measurable differences between middle class and lower class children in tests, as well as the differences between white and Negro children, are to be accounted for, not by innate differences in ability, but by differences of cultural exposure and bearing opportunities.

The children in rural areas studying in poorly equipped schools have to compete with the children in urban areas where there are well-equipped schools and more informative environment for getting admission to the schools for higher bearing on professional colleges. In Indian situation educational inequality due to sex is also very much visible. Girls' education at all stages of education is not given the same encouragement as boys. The social customs and taboos hinder the progress of girls' education. They are given inferior position in the family and their education is neglected. Educational inequality is due to the system itself and also on account of conditions prevailing in society. It is multi-sided affair and is continuing both in developed and developing societies. In many societies it finds expression in the form of public schools. Some of the societies including our own, run public schools which provide much better education than the type of education provided by State run and controlled educational institutions. The education in the former institutions being much costly as compared with the latter and admission obviously open to only few privileged. This creates educational inequality in its own way.

The Equity Action Plans

The following information regarding equity should be provided in the Institution Development Proposals submitted under window 1.1: the particulars of the Nodal Officer responsible for the implementation of EAP (item 1.1, p. 193 of the *PIP*); numbers of SC, ST, OBC and women students, and transition rate of students from 1st to 2nd year (by social categories) (item 1.4, p. 194). Item 2.5 (p. 195) is the specific Action Plan for improving the academic performance of SC/ST/OBC/academically weak students through innovative methods, while items 2.2 (SWOT Analysis), 2.3 (Objectives of the proposal), 2.4 (a) and (b) (Action Plans for improving employability of graduates and learning outcomes of students) are related as they also need to encompass academically weak students. In the proposed Institutional Project Budget (item 2.12, p. 196) the allocation to Academic Support for Weak Students has to be given year-wise and over project life. Finally, the institutional targets for transition from 1st to 2nd year for SC,

ST, OBC and women students also need to be specified (item 2.14, p. 197). This indicator is very important as it is among the monitoring and evaluation indicators of the project as a whole. In TEQIP-II, data on the transition rate between 1st and 2nd year will be obtained from the participating institutions. Some such data already obtained from a small number of institutions indicate that this transition rate is usually higher among girls than boys; and often *but not always* lower among SC/ST students compared with the General category, but *usually* not lower among OBC students. However, the gaps vary considerably among institutions, indicating that the issues of dropout, failure or weak performance are institution-dependent – in addition to the caliber of students that enroll in an institution, its management, teaching force, and actions to remedy students' difficulties clearly have a bearing on the performance of students. The institutions in the above 'sample' indicated that they could bring about 10 to 40 percent improvements in their transition rates over each of three years of 1 Based on the study conducted in sample engineering institutions in Gujarat, Karnataka, Maharashtra, and Uttar Pradesh by World Bank during 2009-10.2 effort under TEQIP-II. Given the shortage of good technical/engineering skills in India and their importance for national growth and development, it is paramount for TEQIP-II institutions to reduce wastage, improve the quality of their graduates, and ensure their employability.

The purpose of this is to identify and describe some interventions that TEQIP-II institutions could make to improve the performance of weak students in undergraduate engineering programs. Although TEQIP-II will include competitively select engineering institutions in the country, even these have some students who are weak at entry and/or perform poorly during their college years. Some students may take several extra years to complete their course; some may fail to secure employment at the end of their degree program because of overall low performance or inadequate skills at the completion of the course. This brief is aimed at reducing these forms of wastage of educational resources and, equally important, of human resources. As equity in the outcomes achieved by students is an important goal of TEQIP-II, the participating institutions must ensure that all students perform well academically and achieve their 'post-college' goals, securing good jobs or enter postgraduate courses, according to their choice, suited to their capabilities, and in line with the education they have received. In this brief we first discuss who weak students are, and then identify several interventions that are being implemented to help them by the institutions such as those that will be in TEQIP-II, describing in some detail a few that could be implemented widely and effectively with relative ease.

The Equity Study

This brief is based on a study of fourteen engineering institutions carried out in Gujarat, Karnataka, Maharashtra, and Uttar Pradesh during 2009-2010, including government, aided and private unaided colleges, and some autonomous institutions. At all these colleges Principals, Deans, some founders and top administrators were interviewed; group discussions were held with Heads of Department and cross-sections of faculty; a survey was administered to Final Year students and group discussions held with them; and in-depth interviews were carried out with students who were considered weak by the institute and/or by themselves. This multiple-method approach and wide coverage has enabled both a broad and deep understanding of the subject. In addition, this brief builds on an extensive literature review, a rapid equity assessment carried out in 2009 in Maharashtra and Uttar Pradesh, and practical knowledge accumulated during six years of implementation of the first TEQIP project in 13 States and 127 institutions. An important lesson from these various efforts is that every institution faces a different situation e.g., student body, teacher force and institutional setting. Hence, this brief recognizes that 'one size does not fit all,' and aims to provide guidance to the institutions trying to evolve their particular solutions to the problem of weak student performance.

Who are Weak Students?

The institutes visited for the Equity study classified as 'weak' students those who had a 3rd class, had failed more than 40 or 50 percent of their subjects in a given year, and/or had lost a year or more. These students were generally believed not to have attended classes regularly. Some – but not all – had entered with low marks through either the reservations or management quota. Falling back by a year or more are known by several names within and across states – for example, in Karnataka the students are known as "back years" while in Maharashtra they are known as "year downs." The existence of such names is itself an indication of the poor treatment of such students.

In general, poor performance is found to arise from a complex of factors in the individual student's college experience, only some of which exist prior to entry. The most important among student factors is reported to be a lack of self-confidence, confidence in the medium of instruction, or application due to lack of interest in the course. These students perhaps do not communicate, do not seek help, and/or have difficulty adjusting to the college environment. The characteristic of 'weak' students that was mentioned most widely was their lack of self-confidence, arising partly from inadequate language or communications skills, as well as *leading* to poor communication and participation in the classroom and other academic activities (and extra-curricular activities also in many cases). An explanation sometimes given by faculty and even students for weak performance was 'distraction,' i.e., some students lacked discipline, fell into bad habits, or viewed college mainly as a time to have fun. Among these were possibly some students who, by their own admission, were disinterested in their studies. It is significant that the factors that produce weak students even among those who enter college with good marks are more psycho-social in nature than socio-economic. They are thus amenable to improvement during the years. As disused below, a number of 'college factors' also underlie poor performance

College Factors: (i) poor teaching either because of poor domain knowledge, or poor pedagogy including a lack of interaction and creativity in the classroom; (ii) improper sequencing or unevenness of curricula or syllabi and related issues; (iii) inadequate exposure of students to 'real world' situations before graduation, such as visits to industries; and (iv) inadequacy of discussion on performance, counseling and mentoring, to name a few. As it is the combination of factors that ultimately results in 'educational wastage,' there is a significant onus on institutions to address both student and institutional issues that cause students – ranging from 10 to 25 percent in the final year - to perform poorly.

Disadvantaged Groups: In general, data gathered on final year students in the private colleges did not show that performance was related directly to the student's sex, caste or tribe status, or religion. In both states, as well as others we have visited in recent years, female students did not have significant academic disadvantage. Many out-performed boys, while the weak performers had some other handicap - social background, language, or self-esteem (discussed above). 'Weak' students were not invariably from disadvantaged social groups. In all colleges, there were good-performing students from Scheduled Caste (SC) categories, from rural backgrounds, poor families, first-generation college goers, and first-generation English speakers. Conversely, among the poor performers there were upper caste/class students, well-to-do students from urban areas, and good English speakers. In the Karnataka colleges, we met very few Scheduled Tribe (ST) students. In Gujarat, most government colleges give high priority to intra-state candidates, including ST students. These students were considered the weakest, because they entered with low marks; but this was not stated about SC students who also enter on reservations quotas as their entry marks were higher. It was also stated that SC students get into private colleges on merit (and pay the higher fees). ST students were 'overrepresented among the weak performers interviewed. There were similar nuanced differences among rural students. In Karnataka, rural students did well – perhaps even better than urban students – apparently because their success in securing seats in the top colleges encouraged them to work hard and make the best of their opportunity. Some also felt pressure to do well *because* they hailed from rural backgrounds would eventually have to support their families, and/or pay back educational loans. In Gujarat, there were many more rural students in the government colleges (than in the private Karnataka ones), and many weak performers among them. As the government colleges charged low fees there were many poor students as well. In the private Karnataka colleges, SC and ST students are charged lower fees but these are still substantial. Some get the fees reimbursed by the government scholarship system, but others who enter on management quotas may take loans to meet their expenses.

Inadequate knowledge of English: As engineering textbooks and materials are predominantly in English, inadequate knowledge of English can be a handicap. However, in the Karnataka colleges we found that poor English did not always mean poor performance – some students who had done their schooling entirely in Kannada language worked hard to learn English and were able to cope by the second year. Students who came from other linguistic communities (e.g., Hindi, Telugu) and had poor.

English were at a greater disadvantage as the teachers, who spoke Kannada and English, could not explain in other languages. The level of English among students in the government colleges in Gujarat was generally poorer and more strongly related to performance, as teachers also were unable to communicate well in English.

Weakness in mathematics was reported among students who entered directly into second year with a Polytechnic diploma. These students have not studied maths beyond Class 10, nor during their three-year course, so they at a considerable handicap when they enter second-year engineering which is, even for 'good' students, a tough year.

Timing of Remedial Courses and Repeat Exams: An important difference that emerged between institutions in the Equity study that partly explains why some colleges have a large backlog of students in the final year is the timing of the repeat exams that can be taken by students who fail in several subjects.

In the better situation, make-up exams are held within a month or so of the original exams, while in the other colleges they are held a semester or a year later. This has two important negative fall-outs – the students have a heavy load as they must take exams simultaneously for both the new semester's subjects as well as for the subjects they fail; and they cannot attend classes in the subjects they have failed as either the syllabi or the college do not allow this. Thus, they do not get any

Additional teaching in the subjects in which they are weak unless they resort to coaching classes or other private means. This may in turn result in cumulative failures, leading some students to take six, seven or even more years to complete the four-year engineering course. In the better situation, on the other hand, remedial classes are provided by the college during the month before the repeat exams, which is usually during vacation, and the combination of the additional teaching and exams immediately thereafter enables the students to go on to the next year without a burdensome backlog. Against this background, we found several practices adopted by institutions to improve the performance of weak students. Broadly, they fall into three categories: (i) student-centered strategies; (ii) strategies to improve teacher effectiveness to deal with weak students; and (iii) strategies beyond the teacher implemented by the college or affiliating university. The strategies are recommended to other institutions and described below to facilitate adoption.

Student-Centered Strategies to Improve Performance

Appointment of Active Student Advisers, Mentors or Proctors: The institution can appoint one faculty member for every 10-15 students entering in the first year. This Faculty Adviser/ Mentor/Proctor establishes a close relationship with each student, orients them to college practices, follows their progress regularly (e.g., with at least fortnightly/monthly meetings) and guides them throughout the four-year course. First-year students are important because the transition from school to college and/or from home to hostel is often uncomfortable. However, contrary to the belief that only 'first years' require counseling and mentoring, students in all four years need this as different problems develop at different times. While the Faculty Adviser (FA) gives academic as well as personal advice, s/he is not necessarily able to address all problems – but plays a role in guiding the student, putting the student in touch with the appropriate assistance, and so on. For example, if a student faces financial difficulties, the FA could help him/her seek a loan from the college administration; if someone has adjustment problems, the help of a Counselor may be sought. The relationship is more informal than formal, allowing students to ask for help when they need it and share their problems without fear. The FA discusses student performance, finds out whether there are non-academic reasons for a student's weak or declining performance, and advises on appropriate study or other measures to be taken. The FA might also mediate between a student and other faculty member if necessary, or seek help from a higher-level person (HOD, Dean, Principal). Although students may not be for this next suggestion – the FA may also keep in touch with parents and talk to them when a relevant problem arises. Faculty may be given some professional training in mentoring and counseling to play this role.

Strengthening State Counseling Centers

An important finding in Karnataka was that many weak students were not interested in studying engineering from the start of their college careers. During the interviews and discussions, many said that they had been 'forced' by their parents to take up engineering, or that they had taken admission in the engineering college though neither they nor their parents really understood what engineering studies entail. The counseling centers at which they opted for their choice of colleges and courses did not provide any counseling. In some cases, they did not get the course they wanted and were disinterested in the one in which they enrolled. Some students and faculty in Karnataka estimated that 30 to 50 percent of students in these top-ranked colleges were studying engineering against their wishes, and that this included the majority of weak students. In contrast, although parental pressure and a lack of counseling were also present in

Gujarat, 'disinterest' was less of a problem – the vast majority of students (including weak ones) wanted to be engineers, though some did not get their choice of course. Thirty to 40 percent even said that they might continue on to post-graduate studies in management.5Although improving counseling at the centers is are commendation to state governments, colleges that find this problem gravely affecting the performance of students could take up the matter with their state government.

Diagnosing and Tracking Student Performance and Attendance: Some colleges start with an initial diagnostic test, supplementing their knowledge of the marks with which students enter the college (Class XII and common entrance test results). Properly devised tests provide information about areas or specific topics in which a particular student is weak, and therefore what additional coaching s/he requires. These colleges also gave information about which topics need to be emphasized by the subject teacher for the student group more widely. It is helpful to carry out such tests particularly before 'tough' subjects begin each semester. The performance of weak students is reviewed by the teacher during the semester, and efforts made to strengthen teaching, and/or provide extra teaching as needed. Reviewing student attendance in connection with performance, and advising students about attending classes, making up classes missed, and getting additional help is also useful. A 'report card' system can be used for each student, and carried through for the four college years.

Improving Academic Performance: Efforts to help students deal with specific academic weaknesses (e.g., in maths) can involve improvements in teacher practices in the classroom – of which many examples are given in the next section, and/or be focused on the weak students. Many colleges offer remedial classes either during the semester (say, in the evenings, on weekends or during periods of preparatory leave) or vacations. Another approach is to provide a two-week period (in addition to preparation leave) when no classes are held but teachers are available to help students address their weaknesses. Extra inputs could also be provided in more innovative ways, such as:

1. Tutorial classes where additional problems are solved and students interact with each other in addition to a faculty member or senior post-graduate student.
2. Where there are a large number of weak students who cannot be handled individually, a 'Student Academic Support Program' could systematically provide extra classes, extra notes and extra guidance.
3. Student and faculty collaborations on projects (which may be integrated in the curriculum) where teachers are available to students formally and informally and focus attention on weak members of the group.

Enhancing English and Communication and Presentation Skills: A college can set up English Language lab where students can listen to tapes and use workbooks to improve their English, particularly spoken English in which they are weakest. Alternatively, holding regular English tutorials which cover both technical and everyday English, and offer the potential of a tutor explaining inadequately understood concepts, can be helpful. Such tutorials can also help students to gain confidence, for example, by asking questions. Another way of improving English language skills as well as communication and presentation skills is by ensuring that students have opportunities right from the first year to develop and make presentations in the classroom. Weak students need to be given special chances and such opportunities should not be confined to brighter students, as they often are. Since this approach is time consuming, and the syllabi already extensive, teachers need to assess where it can be used to good effect and without running the risk of having to "rush at the end of the semester" which is a common complaint. Students feel that language and soft-skill development should be provided throughout their education (not only in the last two or three semesters, as is commonly done for students to do well in job interviews). The programs need to be interactive and oriented to confidence-building, rather than 'exam-oriented,' 'job-oriented,' and 'one-off.' Peer learning groups encourage and help students to develop as they find that others have similar problems and get a chance to discuss their academic problems and other issues. Although students feel that they already work a full day, and have to 'run to catch the bus' in the case of those who are not in hostels, they also agree that they like to study in groups and it is effective. An organized approach to this involves forming groups of 10-12 students - good and weak mixed, who learn jointly. They can revise lessons after class or on weekends, before exams, etc. and undertake group projects also. Good students can help weak ones – the act of tutoring also helps good students. Peer groups can also help each other. There can be 'vertical' integration, i.e., senior students can work with juniors, and student-faculty interactions can also be enhanced, with faculty members being available as resource persons to the student learning groups and even interacting informally with them. A variation of this is the 'buddy system' where good and weak students (or senior and junior students) are paired and work together.

Enhancing Classroom and Teacher Effectiveness

Students including 'weak' ones - appreciate good teaching skills and good domain knowledge among faculty, but often point to the difficulties they face with faculty who have less (or outdated) knowledge, and those who are not able to impart what they know because of inadequate teaching skill or experience. Several suggestions emerged from our discussions with students, faculty and administrators in the engineering colleges with regard to improving the effectiveness of teaching to help weak students (as well as others).

Improving Classroom Practices: One of the most critical needs is to ensure classroom sizes in which teachers can give adequate attention to the students and involve them in the daily lesson. To enhance class's teachers could adopt one or more of the following approaches.

1. Start by asking students what they know and build their knowledge and confidence by teaching some familiar material and gradually moving to a new or difficult topic.

2. Explain the importance of a topic being taught and its relevance to the 'real world,' industry, etc.
3. Give practical examples particularly when explaining difficult concepts. Balancing theory and practice is an important request from students – which also means giving more time to lab work, projects, industrial visits, internships and apprenticeships.
4. Organize lectures by points, including adequate examples in each, using materials beyond the textbook!
5. Move around the classroom and interact with students while they solve problems or read texts, or even while just giving the lecture.
6. Speak clearly and audibly.
7. Use media beyond 'chalk and board,' OHPs and Power-points - classrooms can be equipped with charts, models, projectors and videos to make instruction more visual and tactile.
8. Give feedback to students on their performance and how to improve it. Weak students (and others) say they rarely get constructive feedback; in some instances, they get no feedback at all. Besides making such feedback part of teachers' responsibilities, they need to be trained in how to provide it.
9. Be open to questions and to feedback from students about the teaching contents and style.
10. Be available for formal and informal contact after class.

Increasing Student Participation in the Classroom: Both faculty and students agree that student participation in the classroom must be encouraged because it engages students more, builds their confidence, and helps clear their doubts. There are many ideas for teachers to increase student participation, enjoyment and effectiveness.

1. Ask students questions at the beginning of each class about the previous lesson, thereby helping them to revise the earlier material and providing continuity.

2. Ask students what they have understood in a class after 20-30 minutes, and ask them to summarize the main points at the end of a class.
3. Give students a problem at the end of a class to solve and present in the next class.
4. Ask students to solve problems on the board or on paper individually or in groups.
5. Divide students into groups and ask each group to research a topic from the syllabus and present a seminar on it. Mixing students of different abilities, or varying language skills, is useful. The groups' topics may be different or the same – in the latter students present for 10-15 minutes each, showing how an issue can be looked at from different perspectives or different evidence can be collected, etc. Having one group of students present and another ask questions is a good way to get students to interact, think and discuss. This can be extended to solving a problem or doing a more substantial project, and even a multi-disciplinary project. Preparation of project reports by students and their 'defence' before the class is also successful.
6. Encourage students to ask questions in class, giving extra chances to weak students.
7. Increase the amount of 'hands-on' work in labs, workshops, and projects (which could involve faculty also). Increase team assignments, encourage and reward teamwork, especially where 'mixed' teams (peer groups) have helped weak students improve.
8. Give assignments; ask the students to prepare charts and review these collectively with the students, selecting the most useful to display in the classroom. On-line assignments are also useful, as well as other on-line materials including movie clips, simulations, and lab demonstrations.
9. Move 'back-benchers' to the front, helping to get less confident, bored or disruptive students engaged.
10. Undertake continuous assessment, ensuring that these results count in the final grade/marks.

Improving Teacher Effectiveness

Updating Domain Knowledge: The need for having robust and up-to-date domain knowledge is well understood in the engineering sector given the rapid development of technologies, new areas and even concepts. Traditional methods such as sending faculty on exchange programs, to attend conferences, or to do PhDs in cutting-edge institutions are essential but cover relatively few. Some colleges pay all expenses for faculty to present papers at national or international conferences. Some give faculty members leave without pay with liens on their job, while some even provide full paid leave for upgrading qualifications. The best colleges earmark a proportion of their budget for faculty development activities. Improving domain knowledge can also be done for larger numbers of faculty in several ways. Regular faculty seminars on new topics (which could also include senior students); library corners with compilations of recent journal articles, books, textbooks, etc.; seminars and workshops organized jointly with other colleges are some ideas. Industry interactions on campus and joint industry-institute projects can reach more faculties and include students as well. There is considerable scope to innovate and develop broader-based activities that constantly encourage and help faculty (both the young and more senior) to update themselves.

Training in Pedagogy is also recognized as being needed widely for new teachers as well as some senior ones. Under TEQIP-II all teachers in the selected institutions would have at least one week of such training, providing an excellent overview or introduction to the subject. However, much more may be needed, and institutes could devise ways to deepen pedagogical training especially for teachers who really need to improve their teaching skills, and other who are really interested in achieving excellence in teaching, motivated by a desire to develop the young minds for whom they are responsible, to innovate, and so on. International studies suggest that recruiting teachers who are enthusiastic about teaching and passionate about their subject is the best way to produce quality outcomes. One could add: if institutions have not been able to recruit such teachers, they must enthuse the ones they have recruited. "Joyful learning" is as important in tertiary – and engineering – education as it is in primary schooling, particularly in these times when youth are hyper-stimulated through television, the Internet, other forms of media, the marketplace and changing social mores. Training in pedagogy must be designed to deal with weak students. For example, the methods most sought by weak students are 'interactive methods' such as those discussed above. Some colleges have used videography for teachers to 'see' themselves teach, and obtain feedback from trainers or other teachers.

Fostering Positive Teacher Behaviors: A third important area for improvement of teacher performance is their behavior toward students (especially weak ones). Students report that some teachers not only do not like questions being asked in the classroom, but are also rude about it and, even if approached after class, humiliate or punish the student (e.g., by giving lower marks etc.). Several approaches are used to improve such behaviors, including Faculty Appraisal, discussed below. An important 'first resort' is to counsel teachers who show bad behaviors, help and guide them. Besides having a formal Counselor, some colleges form senior-junior pairs of teachers – the better teacher can help the weaker one; the more 'expert' can help the other improve their knowledge, etc. These pairs can sit in on each other's classes, interact with the other's students, and provide 'real time' feedback and advice.

Faculty Appraisal System: Faculty appraisal can start with a self-assessment form which is rigorously reviewed by the HOD, Deans, Faculty Committee etc. It can usefully include student evaluations. While some institutes are reluctant to consider student evaluations because they feel that students 'give lenient teachers high marks and strict teachers low marks,' others give 'incentive marks,' for example, to teachers who work diligently and are appreciated by students. Institutes may find their own way of taking student evaluations of teacher performance and behavior seriously if weak students (who are often the most difficult to handle) are to be helped. In the Faculty Appraisal marks can be given for a teacher's participation in a range of activities such as:

1. Improving students' examination scores or ensuring 'no failures'
2. E-enabling courses by making materials, manuals, questions and answers available to students
3. Helping to improve the library, labs or other teaching facilities
4. Helping students to get internships and placement
5. Helping to make their department a centre of excellence
6. Teaching new courses
7. Participating in peer teaching (where faculty give feedback on the teaching style of their peers)
8. Using training opportunities provided to them
9. Improving their qualifications
10. Going to rural high schools and inviting students to the campus to interest them in applying
11. Filing for patents

Teachers could be given incentive pay for scoring above a certain level or for specific 'rare' achievements such as 'first publication in a peer-reviewed journal', obtaining a patent, etc. However, kindly note that such incentives pay cannot be funded out of TEQIP-II funds.

Beyond the Teacher

Several other efforts involving the institution more broadly could help weak students.

Improvement of Course Curriculum and Conten: While significant curriculum revision may have been a lengthy and distant affair in the past, it has been made easier with autonomy as each institution can assess student difficulties within its own context (e.g., availability of faculty, numbers and expertise) and make suitable adjustments. Many steps can be taken to assist weak students.

1. Include students in the assessment and revision of curriculum – not only good students but average and weak ones so that their needs can also be taken into account.
2. Properly sequence curriculum and syllabi – going from the simple to the more complex, and ironing out unevenness. For example, students in some states consider the first-year curriculum to be easy and the second year very hard - covering some second-year concepts in the first year would leave more time in the second year to go over difficult material again. (In other states, students feel that the first year is quite difficult; this difference points to the need for solutions to be contextual.)
3. Develop learning objectives. Faculty of a department can get together to design the learning objectives of individual subjects and the overall curriculum. If students are told the necessary learning outcomes in advance, they have a goal to work towards.
4. Integrate theory and practicals. Students and faculty feel that time in labs needs to be increased, more project and group work done, and more practical exposure gained (see below). This is not only helpful but essential for weak students.
5. Identify appropriate methods and provide the relevant technology for teaching different course contents, particularly to balance theory and practice.
6. As discussed above, schedule repeat exams within a few weeks of the original ones, and provide extra classes in the interim to students who must repeat the exams.
7. Include members from industry and other institutes in departmental Boards of Studies. They can assess the curriculum and make necessary changes in keeping with new requirements in the industry.

An important suggestion concerns the “Training, Counseling and Placement Cell”. Students advocate that this be more interactive – a place where they can interact with an active placement officer, “trained friendly counselors,” other faculty, fellow students, even alumni and industry representatives to get advice on future careers and how they are preparing for them throughout their four years of college and not just "at the tail end". This would provide guidance, support and motivation. A database on students, present and past, would help them make contacts not only with prospective employers but with others who took up jobs in particular industries, companies, areas, etc. They can also follow progress in job placement of their cohort. This renovated or innovative placement cell could have several important roles in addition to organizing job interviews and securing job placements: organizing industry visits in at least the 3rd and 4th years which could make a substantial difference to student learning and attitudes; getting good guest lecturers; obtaining 'real live' projects from industries; and securing internships for students in the summers.

A **knowledge society** generates, processes, shares and makes available to all members of the society knowledge that may be used to improve the human condition. A knowledge society differs from an information society in that the former serves to transform information into resources that allow society to take effective action while the latter only creates and disseminates the raw data. The capacity to gather and analyze information has existed throughout human history. However, the idea of the present-day knowledge society is based on the vast increase in data creation and information dissemination that results from the innovation of information technologies. The UNESCO World Report addresses the definition, content and future of knowledge societies.

The growth of Information and communication technology (ICT) has significantly increased the world's capacity for creation of raw data and the speed at which it is produced. The advent of the internet delivered unheard of quantities of information to people. The evolution of the internet from Web 1.0 to Web 2.0 offered individuals tools to connect with each other worldwide as well as become content users and producers. Innovation in digital technologies and mobile devices offers individuals a means to connect anywhere anytime where digital technologies are accessible. Tools of ICT have the potential to transform education, training, employment and access to life-sustaining resources for all members of society.

Social Theory

The social theory of a knowledge society explains how knowledge is fundamental to the politics, economics, and culture of modern society. Associated ideas include the knowledge economy created by economists and the learning society created by educators. Knowledge is a commodity to be traded for economic prosperity. In a knowledge society, individuals, communities, and organizations produce knowledge-intensive work. Peter Drucker viewed knowledge as a key economic resource and coined the term knowledge worker in 1969. Fast forward to present-day, and in this knowledge-intensive environment, knowledge begets knowledge, new competencies develop, and the result is innovation.

A knowledge society promotes human rights and offers equal, inclusive, and universal access to all knowledge creation. The UNESCO World Report establishes four principles that are essential for development of an equitable knowledge society:

1. Cultural diversity
2. Equal access to education
3. Universal access to information (in the public domain)
4. Freedom of expression

Politics

To reduce the span of the digital divide, leaders and policymakers worldwide must first develop and understanding of knowledge societies and second, create and deploy initiatives that will universally benefit all populations. The public expects politicians and public institutions to act rationally and rely on relevant knowledge for decision-making. Yet, in many cases, there are no definitive answers for some of the issues that impact humankind. Science is no longer viewed as the provider of unquestionable knowledge and sometimes raises more uncertainty in its search for knowledge. The very advancement of knowledge creates the existence of increased ignorance or non-knowledge. This means that public policy must learn to manage doubt, probability, risk and uncertainty while making the best decisions possible.

Education

As technologies are deployed to improve global information access, the role of education will continue to grow and change. Education is viewed as a basic human right. For a society where reading and counting are a requisite for daily living, skills in reading, writing, and basic arithmetic are critical for future learning. However, in a knowledge society, education is not restricted to school. The advent of ICT allows learners to seek information and develop knowledge at any time and any place where access is available and unrestricted. In these circumstances, the skill of learning to learn is one of the most important tools to help people acquire formal and informal education. In a knowledge society supported by ICT, the ability to locate, classify and sort information is essential. Equipped with this skill, the use of ICT becomes an active versus a passive endeavor and integral to literacy and lifelong learning.

Rationale and Background of the Project

Juan Manuel Moreno World Bank (HDNED) Teacher training, professional development of teachers and education reform has traditionally been quite divorced processes. All the way from the times of "teacher proof" curriculum design and educational materials to contemporary politics and discourses of educational reform, teachers and teacher education have marginal role. In recent times, with reform agendas emphasizing decentralization, restructuring of school systems and external evaluation and quality assurance systems, one could even argue that teachers have been implicitly seen more as a liability than as an asset for reform efforts. Pre-service teacher education is, almost everywhere, one of the most obsolete pieces of education systems. This is even more so as far as the training of secondary school teachers is concerned, since it realize almost exclusively on specialized knowledge training at universities, with very little, if any, practical training on teaching and learning processes. This results in secondary teachers having to be responsible for their own training and professional development once they start teaching in schools. In such context, it becomes an extraordinary challenge to design policies which enable developing countries to select and train teachers to help students acquire the new competencies that are now demanded by society and required by labor markets. These new competencies overtly require for teachers to behave in classrooms in very different ways as the ones they were taught to. The central answer to the challenge lies in the system of teacher education and professional development.

Online Collaboration tools enabling people to connect and interact virtually, showing signs of rating global economic impact in productivity. Social technologies, frequently called collaboration tools, can provide a growth opportunity across the value chain for development and maturity in enterprise social networks. But it is not about snapping on social tools to our operational processes and expecting organizational change to happen on its own.

Collaboration Tools

The majority of Online Collaboration tools for generating knowledgeable society resemble one of five tools. They are,

1. Project Collaboration Tools
2. Social Software Tools
3. Innovation Management Tools
4. Web Conferencing Tools
5. Wiki Tools

Project Collaboration Tools to Facilitate Learning Collaboration Skills

Project collaboration tools will become natural breeding grounds for project teams to learn collaboration skills. Team members are engaged on a daily basis through shared workspaces and activities. Individuals are responsible for sharing content, performing tasks with dependencies on each other and collectively will be rewarded for positive outcomes of their projects. Individuals can learn to collaborate as the emphasis shifts to the team goals. In selecting project collaboration tools we should consider those that can serve an enterprise and implement by department, group, and project basis.

Social software is the integration of communication and collaboration technologies, both traditional and contemporary to facilitate productivity. Social software design is conceived the way organizations desire a flexible collaborative environment in business, social networking, and community—that is accomplished by coupling these specific technologies. Traditional social software technologies will include email, wikis, blogs, and knowledge sharing functions such as collaborative editing and document management. Contemporary social tools will integrate real-time features, including IM and web conferencing with voice and video. Micro blogging, most often referred to as “status updates” has become an anchor of social software. Use cases, the way people use the system, like knowledge base creation or idea generation, may predicate access, devices, and computing platforms. However, the essence of social software is the design to scale an entire organization so people can communicate and collaborate under one roof.

Innovation management tools provide the impetus for crowd sourcing ideas and collaborative exchange of expertise for co-creating products and services. The innovation processes are managed through presentation of challenges that create business value within an organization. Extending challenges to external users through customer specific community sites and discussion forums can offer unique insights for creating new or improved products and features. Cloud-based innovation tools, typically software as a service (SaaS), provide end-to-end innovation with business process integration, project management, and ROI analysis. Innovation management has become an integral part of manufacturing, packaged goods, and other large scale product development organizations.

Enterprise social networking platforms are evolving with new innovation management technologies to foster unleashing of ideas that create business value. Innovation management is defined as the collection and collaboration of ideas and the processes involved in advancing development. To accomplish innovation, these social innovation tools use crowd sourcing, either in small or large groups, to drive new engagement levels through participation and accountability. Social gaming concepts are also used that involve behavioral techniques to gauge acceptance and promotion of ideas. The psychological dynamics of stakes and prizes come into play to increase motivation. In a similar way, teaching methods are successfully employing gaming techniques in learning and development programs to leverage employee performance.

Enterprise collaboration is inevitably managed through web conferencing tools. Despite the aversion to meetings nowadays, web conferencing tools provide instant connection for virtual meetings when individuals or groups are positioned to initiate collaboration to achieve business results. Web conferencing tools are integral social technologies for communication and collaboration across enterprise social networks near or far. Regional offices in geographically dispersed locations are bridged easily with voice and video, as well as cloud based file storage for use in conducting presentations, webinars, and sales meetings. Global Meet is one particular example among others offering enterprise-class collaboration tools. Online meetings serve as a collaboration tool for daily productive use on project teams, recruiting interviews, and face-to-face client meetings. Higher levels of engagement in online seminars and virtual classrooms are now possible because web conferencing tools have helped advance communication and collaboration capabilities. Educators, corporate trainers, and event managers have many more web conferencing options available than ever before to enrich skills training through social learning. These web conferencing tools among others provide a full range of webinar, eLearning, and online meeting platforms to create, assemble, and deliver programs anywhere on any device in real-time or on-demand.

Knowledge-Sharing Work Processes

Wiki tools are practical for building knowledge bases and

maintaining documents. Enterprise wide access may support collaborative knowledge systems that can integrate ongoing marketing, sales, and technical support activities. Wikis may help to manage decision support systems to update and distribute service and support to a global customer base. For enterprise social networks, wiki tools are practical for building knowledge bases and maintaining documents. Enterprise wide access may support collaborative knowledge systems that can integrate ongoing marketing, sales, and technical support activities. Wikis may help to manage decision support systems to update and distribute service and support to a global customer base. Wikis are typically integrated in social technology toolsets, including team workspaces that will show business benefits for ongoing collaborative work activities. Among a host of tools, wikis are a low-cost enterprise solution. Online Collaboration tools are apt to specific types of technologies that can increase collaborative behavior across the society, which will help people to share interests and activities in achieving knowledge goals. These five types of collaborative tools can demonstrate directly productive activities across the society.

The express growing in the accessibility of computers and others technologies in schools contain through momentous changes in the edification or ganization. Equipment the generate opportunities for students to effort collectively. At similar occasion the teachers' skills in using the equipment is the major factor in improving students learning with technology. With today's technology advancement teacher become a coach or guide as well as or teacher by means of the technology, inventive teaching is apparent to every teacher at the velocity which they keep informed themselves and presentation concentration in perceptive expertise advancements and inventive methods to accomplishment.

Necessitate the Innovative Education

Fundamentally education is required to comprise two most important mechanisms in distribution and getting in sequence. Eventually education tried most excellent to communicate acquaintance as the technique he unstated it. So any communication methods that serve this rationale without destroying the objective could be considered as innovative methods of learning teaching is a high that's shows the mankind the right direction to surge. The purposes of education are not just construction a student knowledgeable but add rationale accepted wisdom knowledge ability, and self satisfactory. In today's' era, information and knowledge position out as extremely significant and critical input for growth and survival. Rather than looking at education simply as a means of achieving societal upliftment they society must view education also as an engine of progression in an information era propelled by its wheels of knowledge and research leading to development. So this is possible only if the teacher attracts and inspires the students by his innovative approach in teaching. Present education system provides knowledge to student's mostly from books only. An innovative teaching skills teacher easily delivered the knowledge and develops creativity among students by technology oriented approach. So it's necessary to reach with innovative techniques in students to improve their skills as well as creativity in this digital age.

constant despite the information that an assortment of instruction methods are enabled in teaching still there is a breach between teaching and students concentration are learning, while assessing the accomplishment of students the success of the above understood teaching methods does not so that to a large extent good organization in teaching. Consequently innovative education teaching techniques in needed to create attention in the middle of student's creative and reflective learning. Nowadays without the help expertise advancements, like media new education is not potential.

Most of the teachers are not operational with the technological skills they experience are essential to control equipment based preparation apparatus. Revolutionize is rarely welcome and many in positions to do so may be reluctant to change obtainable methods of teachers without the knowledge of management technological instruments, it's not possible to establish innovative teaching in classrooms. Most of the school teachers especially government school teachers are not provide with technological are not have the facility are avail technological assistance even they are willing to introduce innovative teaching. This makes them to continue teaching in conventional methods. In some school result oriented approach is followed. In such schools innovative teaching are not practiced and they concentrate only to promote bookish knowledge to attain full result lack of interest and assistance shown by the management shown enhance innovative teaching may reduce the spirit of a teacher in innovative teaching sometimes availability of technology and economics requirements are big barrier to innovative teaching. Teacher cooperation is must in teaching innovative techniques in teaching for society and schools.

An inventive teacher must have creativity and ideas about innovative teaching. Teacher should be mastery in his subject and have the ability to select the teaching techniques which suitably promotes the knowledge to the level of the learners. Teacher should be able to create his own teacher component and programmed with the help of multimedia resources. Management variety of technological instruments is an essential quality for an innovative teacher. Teacher should promote innovative teaching through various modes of technology advancements. Psychological approach to the students and the quality to accept feedback from students is necessary for an innovative teacher. Discussing with other subject teachers and students may create new awareness for innovative ideas. Not only with technology, may other teaching methods also be used for innovative teaching by introducing new ideas in traditional teaching methods in classroom level and also social level.

Innovative teachings consist of resourcefulness new technological thoughts science and equipment knowledge of the teacher and their ability to work with the technology. Recent day's teachers are standing by to use the suitable technology in educational and they aspiration to revolutionize them as techniques based teachers. Most of the teachers are aware of the new technology in teaching and they can without difficulty teach with innovative techniques in the class room. Not only with the technology, have recent trended new innovative strategies thoughts and methods of education in various forms may be entertained and the conclusion be supposed to be monitored personalized if any equipment for best conception of acquaintance society.

Knowledge Transfer and Knowledge Exchange

Increasingly the creation of new organizational knowledge is becoming a managerial priority. New knowledge provides basis for organizational renewal and sustainable competitive advantage. The primary obstacle to success is a failure to execute the specific organizational processes necessary to access, assimilate, and disseminate alliance knowledge. Successful firms exploit learning opportunities by acquiring knowledge through "Grafting," a process of internalizing knowledge not previously available within the organization. Global cooperative ventures have tended to focus on governance forms and task structures. This study highlights the importance of knowledge structures and work systems in influencing the success of collaborative ventures.

Universities are an important source of new knowledge creation and dissemination, which is a fundamental element for the promotion of regional development. The transfer of technologies from universities to enterprises is considered to boost competitiveness, stimulate economic growth and increase prosperity whereas the benefits of knowledge exchange between universities and enterprises have been documented in various cases, there is still a long way to go considering the identification of the best-suited policy framework for the enhancement of this process, on national and regional levels. In recent years, a number of contributions have been developed considering the models that describe the process of university to industry knowledge transfer, as well as the relative importance of the different channels for its diffusion. In literature, the transfer of technology has been met as a linear sequence of steps but also, in the framework of informal interpersonal networks and established relationships that promote knowledge sharing and learning. Organizational learning is a systems-level concept that can become useful only when its component parts are thoroughly understood and brought down to an operational level. Unless individual knowledge is shared throughout the organization, the knowledge will have a limited impact on organizational effectiveness. Thus, organizational knowledge creation represents a process whereby the knowledge held by individuals is amplified and internalized as part of an organization's knowledge.

Effective Knowledge

Effective knowledge creation through alliances depends on two main elements. First, there are the organizational processes that firms can use to access and transform knowledge from an alliance context to a parent firm context. While these knowledge management processes are not complex, there was substantial variance in the extent to which firms in this study were actively seeking to exploit the knowledge potential. Studies of teachers working together have exposed the capricious nature of collaborative activity: sometimes it seems to work well; at other times collaboration actually works against improvement. Success in collaborative relationships is best understood through an appreciation of how teachers form and use knowledge. The teachers' knowledge perspective is used in this paper to interpret qualitative data from two successful collaborative relationships in schools. Evidence supports the contention that personal qualities, underscored by mutual trust and respect for knowledge, form the basis for successful relationships in teaching, operating in different ways, for different purposes, for different people. Providing that teachers are approached with respect, collaboration holds promise as a slow (but powerful) path towards educational change.

'Collaboration' is a broadly used term which serves to describe a wide variety of behaviours. In the most general sense, collaboration is said to have occurred when more than one person works on a single task. For our purposes, however, it is helpful and in fact necessary, to draw some specific parameters around what we refer to as collaboration. The following definition delineates the kind of behavior. Collaboration is a coordinated, synchronous activity that is the result of a continued attempt to construct and maintain a shared conception of a problem. We make a distinction between 'collaborative' versus 'cooperative' problem solving. Cooperative work is accomplished by the division of labour among participants, as an activity where each person is responsible for a portion of the problem solving. We focus on collaboration as the mutual engagement of participants in a coordinated effort to solve the problem together. We further distinguish between synchronous and asynchronous activity. Although we do not propose that collaboration cannot occur in asynchronous activity, we focus on face-to-face interactions, which can only occur as a synchronous activity.

Knowledge transfer is the practical problem of transferring knowledge from one part of the organization to another. Like knowledge management, knowledge transfer seeks to organize, create, capture or distribute knowledge and ensure its availability for future users. It is considered to be more than just a communication problem. If it were merely that, then a memorandum, an e-mail or a meeting would accomplish the knowledge transfer. Knowledge transfer is more complex because (1) knowledge resides in organizational members, tools, tasks, and their sub networks and (2) much knowledge in organizations is tacit or hard to articulate.

Types of knowledge

Knowledge is a dominant feature in our post-industrial society, and knowledge workers comprise an enterprise. If knowledge is the basis for all that we do these days, then gaining an understanding of what types of knowledge exist within an organization may allow us to foster internal social structures that will facilitate and support learning in all organizational domains.

Embrowned knowledge is that which is dependent on conceptual skills and cognitive abilities. We could consider this to be practical, high-level knowledge, where objectives are met through perpetual recognition and revamping. Tacit knowledge may also be embrowned, even though it is mainly subconscious.

Embodied knowledge is action oriented and consists of contextual practices. It is more of a social acquisition; as how individuals interact in and interpret their environment creates this non-explicit type of knowledge.

Uncultured knowledge is the process of achieving shared understandings through socialization and acculturation. Language and negotiation become the discourse of this type of knowledge in an enterprise.

Embedded knowledge is tacit and resides within systematic routines. It relates to the relationships between roles, technologies, formal procedures and emergent routines within a complex system. In order to initiate any specific line of business knowledge transition helps a lot.

Encoded knowledge is information that is conveyed in signs and symbols (books, manuals, data bases, etc.) and de-contextualized into codes of practice. Rather than being a specific type of knowledge, it deals more with the transmission, storage and interrogation of knowledge.

Challenges

There are many factors, that complicates knowledge transfer including

1. The inability to recognize & articulate "compiled" or highly intuitive competencies—tacit knowledge idea
2. Limitations of Information and Communication Technologies (ICTs)
3. Lack of a shared/super ordinate social identity
4. Areas of expertise
5. Internal conflicts
6. Generational differences
7. Motivational issues
8. Lack of trust
9. Capability

Knowledge exchange is a two-way process where social scientists and individuals or organizations share learning, ideas and experiences. Knowledge exchange encourages collaboration between researchers and the private, public and civil society sectors. Knowledge exchange (KE) is a process which brings together academic staff, users of research and wider groups and communities to exchange ideas, evidence and expertise. Within the College of Humanities and Social Science (CHSS), Industry, Policy, Practice and Public represent our main target groups for activity and the overall aim is to contribute to economic, social, cultural and environmental benefits to society. In practice, a lot of knowledge exchange engages across these audiences. Through mutual exchange and collaboration, the process also benefits academic teaching and research. These methods used include:

1. consultancy services and commissioned research
2. collaborative research and other projects
3. placement positions
4. training and continuing professional development (CPD)
5. licensing technologies, tools or training material
6. briefings and other ways of communicating research
7. events with external audiences

The Notable Quotes about Knowledge

All our knowledge begins with the senses, proceeds then to the understanding, and ends with reason. There is nothing higher than reason. Detailed investigations of collaboration can contribute to future investigations of computer-supported collaborative laming in at least two ways. First, this type of analysis can be viewed as a methodology for coming to a deeper understanding of how the benefits of collaboration are realized. Second, this type of analysis can lead to better development of the kinds of supporting resources that computers can provide for collaborative learning. Clearer understanding of the collaboration as a process of constructing and maintaining a shared conception of the task can be beneficial for future designs of collaborative learning environments. Knowledge exchange between academic institutions and enterprises is a complex activity that involves high risk and is build upon trust. The benefits as well as the direction of the knowledge transfer are often reciprocal, with the academic institutions benefiting from market knowledge.

The quality of a teacher is utmost importance to nourish the valuable standards of learning. Values can be imbibed by teacher educator through their ethics and talk and walk approach. In the present paper the teacher education and its stages have been elaborated. To inculcate values the necessary curriculum and skills required for a teacher educator have also been discussed. The proper assimilation of these values by a teacher educator can be done through their positive role and prescribed means. Education is a process of all round development of an individual-physical, intellectual, emotional, social, moral and spiritual. The teacher is expected to function not only as facilitator for attainment of knowledge but also as inculcator of values and transformer of inner being. Teacher Education refers to the policies and procedures designed to equip perspective teachers with the knowledge, attitudes, behaviours and skills they require to perform their tasks effectively. Values are the basis for the social, intellectual, emotional, spiritual and more development of an individual. Value education is not a sphere of activity distinct from other activities. Values are regarded as abstract beliefs that transcend specific situations, objects and issues and they function as standards of conduct as compared to attributes which are evaluative judgements related to specific issues and situations. Values are more central constructs and relate more closely to basic human needs and societal demands. Value acquisition goes on constantly in the school through various activities like instruction, relationship between pupils, co-curricular activities etc. So education has a major role in inculcating basic values of humanism, socialism and national integration among the children and it presents a challenging task before the teacher and taught.

Teacher education refers to the policies and procedures designed to equip prospective teachers with the knowledge, attitude, behaviours and skills they require to perform their tasks effectively in the classroom, school and wider community. Teacher Education is divided into following stages: i) Initial Teacher Education: A pre-service course before entering the classroom as a fully responsible teacher. ii) Induction: The process of providing training and support during the first few years of teaching. iii) Teacher Development: An in-service process for practicing teachers.

Teacher Education and Curriculum

Teacher Education curricula can be broken into areas:

1. Foundational Knowledge in Education: Related aspects of philosophy, history, sociology and psychology of education.
2. Skills in assessing student learning and using technology to improve teaching and learning.
3. Content area and methods- Emphasis is placed upon “transversal” or “horizontal skills”.

Different Approaches to Value Education

Supreka (1976) outlined seven different approaches to value education, which are stated as follows:

1. Evocation Approach: The students are encouraged to make spontaneously free, non rational choices, without thought or hesitation. It provides an environment which allows maximum freedom for students.

2. Awareness Approach: In this approach the teacher presents value laden situations or dilemmas through readings, Films, Role playing, small group discussions and simulation.

3. Inculcation Approach: A positive and negative reinforcement by the teacher helps value inculcation. This can be done by a teacher’s natural actions and responses.

4. Moral Reasoning Approach: Kohlberg’s theory of six stages of moral development is the framework most frequently used in this approach. The teachers set up learning experiences which facilitate moral development. It consists of the students discussing a dilemma and by reasoning they attain a higher level of knowledge.

5. Analysis approach: The group or individuals are encouraged to study the social value problems. They are encouraged to determine the truth and evidence of purported facts and arrive at purported facts and arrive at value decision, applying analogous cases and testing value principles underlying the decision.

6. Commitment approach: It enables the students to perceive themselves not merely as passive reactors or as free individuals but as inner relative members of a social group and system.

7. The Union Approach: The purpose is to help students to perceive themselves and act not as separate egos but as part of a larger inter related whole.

Role of Teacher Educators in Value Education

The role of teacher educator is of supreme the following are the ways by which values can be imbibed among teacher trainees during classroom teaching and learning process:

1. Basic human values need to be encouraged in the classroom teaching. Teacher educators should inculcate in the minds of teacher trainees that a child is born with values, a teacher need to uncover them. Sharma's (1984) study identified a positive correlation between teaching aptitude, intellectual level and morality of prospective teachers.
2. Teacher educator must be clear about the values that he wishes to emphasise. A set of universal values will emerge that may include: honesty, peace, humility, freedom, cooperation, care, love, unity, respect, tolerance, courage, friendship, patience, quality and thoughtfulness.
3. Values cannot be taught in isolation but the teacher can provide experiences and situations in which students can consider and reflect about values and translate this reflection into action.

4. Teacher educator can involve students in active games in the classroom to inculcate the values of fair play, honesty, courage, cooperation; respect and love are best learnt through interaction with peers having diverse cultural, ethnic and personality traits among teacher trainees.
5. Value education should be a process of developing the spirit of rational enquiry and self discovery.
6. Human values need to be cultured for the sake of the mind and the body in the students.
7. Learning how to focus attention and to actively listen while sitting still are other skills that promote reflective learning and good interpersonal skills.
8. Teacher educators should make teacher trainees need to know human nature. With loving attention and care one can bring out the positive human values in child.
9. In order to create a positive school ethos there must be commitment by the whole staff that value based education is central to the school's mission.
10. Celebrating current good practices is the key to encourage students to develop value based education.
11. Teacher educators must develop competencies in teacher trainees to teach on the basis of the accepted principles of teaching and learning.

In nutshell it can be said that a teacher educator is the teacher of future teachers which means a lot-a double responsibility. First of all the teacher educators must have his own standard of quality and values which is to be imbibed by the teacher trainees and to the young youth of the nation. Time to time various introspective and retrospective measures must be taken to assess the quality of value education at all levels. The grassroots level of our objective must be strong enough to fulfill our dreams. Values have been overlooked and finally dropped plunging humanity into chaos and danger. The remedy is to rein duct them. This can be done at curriculum planning stage. There is need of value education in teacher education curriculum which involves 'educating the heart as well head'. Learning to live together becomes the most essential pillar of education. It promotes the values (for example: peace, tolerance, human rights, democracy, justice, equality etc.) for teachers, teacher educators, education planners and administrators. This is major issues which needs utmost attention and follow up to enhance and save the quality of our education system.

Modern Educational Institutions

Education is one of the integrated features of society providing the identity and functionality to an individual and to a community. Education is not a static phenomenon which starts at a particular age and ends at a formal age but is a lifelong process. Society recourses to diversified ways of imparting education such as through the formal, informal and non formal means and thus creates functional necessities of life and reality. Education serves in defining and redefining the life and outlook of an individual and of a society. Socialization, commonsensical knowledge and normative are some of the essential characteristics of education in addition to providing nuanced skill and technical prowess and academic acumen to the individual. Education is heuristic and teleological in the sense that it seeks to enlighten the individual by helping him or her to realize the individual skills and sufficiently provides the wherewithal and the analytical mindset in solving problems and resulting in the growth and development of the individual and of the society.

Education in sundry times is associated with the religious institutions which sought to instill values, hope and norms of the society. It thus sought to refine a person according to moral and ethical understandings. The character building and essential grooming of the individual to overcome the innate selfish and animal tendencies is one of the aims of education. But education in the modern period is understood not only as enhancement of the character and values but primarily an arena which results in the growth and development of the individual psyche and personality that seeks to maximize the potentials of the individual with necessary skills and abilities to face the issues and concerns of life and reality.

Educational Institutions play a formidable role in defining and redefining an individual because of the longevity and durability an individual spends at the lawns of the educational institutions from kinder care to portals of higher learning. The continuous impartation of skills, information and technical abilities shapes the individuals perception and cognitive process and helps him to advance in life in terms of outlook and skills. The educational institutions may be modern in character and outlook but the essential feature of training and development is ancient and fundamental. Modern character of educational institutions is its tendency to be public, secular, inclusive in intent and purpose and emancipative in vision and mission. This essential feature had helped many societies to traverse from its primal and backward states into a progressive path. The impervious influence of science and technology in the society of what a modern educational institution has done to our life and reality and continues to provide the perspectives of life and reality to one and all. There are very few who can be away from such mighty influence of the modern means of educational institutions. The plethora of goods, instruments and the mechanized tools and gadgets helps us to live our lives with ease and convenience. Has education and the portals of educational institutions served in bettering human lives? Or in other words is the form of education offered by modern educational apparatus made us more humane and just. This is the objective and the concern of the present paper which critically analyses the role of modern educational institutions and the lack it has over the society.

Indian society which is ancient and traditional had its own ways of socializing, educating an individual by following the precincts and practices of dharma. Following one's own dharma remained the cardinal feature of Indian society which therein defines an individual according to the paradigms and practices of society. The caste based learning and living both helped in division of labor in the society and also in augmenting the society in rigid patterns. The regimentation remained one of the central characteristic of the Indian society and education followed the conventional methods of learning the essential traits and values according to the caste beliefs and practices. This layered learning of skills and traits provided the necessary base and vitality for the Indian society which continued to define suiting to the essential conditioning of the dharma. The caste based society defined learning on the basis of birth and there is little change or alteration permissible as society tried to follow it meticulously and religiously. Any deviation and discrepancy is scornfully detested and all forms of change or improvisation are desisted fiercely. This has induced a state of obduracy in the life and character of the society. Thus there existed less progress and the role of educational institutions is to continue with the existing things and following it orthodoxically. This resulted in Indian society succumbing to all illogical and unscientific dispositions and conditions signaling a process of decay and redundancy. The advent of modernity in the Indian soil through the mechanism of colonialism and of its agencies is at first opposed later on remained as panacea of all evils of the Indian society. The Indian psyche embraced the western education as a savior and redeemer of its despicable conditions and forthrightly followed it to see it emerge from its precarious state. This adulation of western paradigms of knowledge by the Indian masses and also by western educated Indian elites was scorned by some Indian thinkers and reformers was never taken seriously and the country followed the modern educational enterprise in an undetached manner resulting in some sort of material growth and prospects in the country.

Modern or Morbid

The advent of modernity and science and technology resulted in accelerated life style. Humanity progresses at great speeds in the hope of seeing a better world. The democratization of society made education available and accessible to all people in particular to the vulnerable sections of Indian society. Modern Educational Institutions provided the needed professional, academic and conceptual clarities and skills and resulted in the furtherance of science and technological means and methods. It seemingly remained as the essential tool of change and development. The world wars had helped to humanity to veritably know the evil and pernicious influence of the modern educational institutions which has not salvaged the animal and brutal character of human beings. In other words people felt the need to have an education that seeks not only material well bring and mechanized gadgets and conveniences but a holistic perception to life and learning. Defining human being as modern should not be the essential aspect of education but making him more humane and that is possible only with the moral laced scientific and technological education.

The modern educational institutions have produced many graduates and professionally competent individuals who are trained and educated with the *know-how's* of life and reality but do not have holistic perception of life. The modern educational institutions have enhanced the greed and appetite of the human beings for material well being and less for the spiritual well being. Materiality and consumerism remained as the essential output of the modern educational institutions as it defines success and growth in terms of the possessions and material well being.

Modern educational institutions seek to make human beings more individualistic and narrow in their outlook. They are less driven by the common welfare and good and often consider life and reality from the individual point of view. Modern educational institutions are less other focused and more geared towards interiority. Indian society is perplexed at the advent of consumerism and materiality exhibited by the highly educated Indian young people. The pinnacle of success and growth and the state of apathy by the techno-centric individuals towards the marginalized and the vulnerable questions the ethos and values of the educational institutions which provided them with the essential training and skills.

The modern educational institutions barring the premier institutions and portals of learning have not provided the Indian youth with sufficient skill set and often makes them lag behind the others in the market. The rise of unemployment and the non availability of suitable jobs highlight the lacunae of these institutions of learning. While these modern educational institutions have laced human life with technological skills and features but it had not imbibed them with the necessary psychological tools and skills to handle pressure. The modern Educational Institutions in India have a tendency to import ideas and knowledge of the West. The indigenous and native knowledge is often derided when compared with the best of the things offered by the West. Modern Educational Institutions in India have a greater responsibility to serve the legitimate interests of the country and of its people. Rather than bludgeoning with the materiality and information centric methods and means the role and purpose of education at all times is to better the individual personality and it is possible only with character defining moral and spiritual education. Changing the outer contours and features will not sufficiently alter the inner course and perspective of individuals. This lack should be addressed by the pundits and the learned academics belonging to the modern educational institutions by following wisdom that is native and indigenous.

Any institution should impart futuristic technological education and instill remarkable discipline through their dedicated staff. These staffs shoulder a great responsibility of creating global standards and molding their students technologically superior and ethically strong. As a result the trained students shall enhance the quality of life of future generation.

Bridging the Gap

Ancient method of imparting knowledge by a teacher to his students was entirely different from modern methodology of teaching. Once the teacher was regarded as Guru and a student as a disciple. Gradually the word Guru was replaced by the word (student) teacher and the world disciple was replaced by the word student. Old methodology of teaching was given a good bye and a new methodology of teaching emerged (i.e.). Once the teacher was an actor and the student was a passive spectator. Today students have become almost independent in learning by adhering to modern technologies like computer, Internet and other modern devices. The teachers too hence given up the old monotonous method of teaching. They are banking on advanced technologies like multimedia. The explosion of technologies has brought a great change in the life style of students. The field of I.T and software era has brought a tremendous influence over the thinking of student community. This is one of the innovations which our society enjoys.

Younger generation (youths) is our wealth of future India. In I.T field they have greater exposure and enlightenment. But at the sometime the student community has great distraction and diversion. How to harness their minds? Here lies the greatest responsibility on a teacher who has to harness their minds and souls together and enhance their academic knowledge with communication skills. So that they could face the challenges of life with courage. This is the need of the hour to create a dynamic and competent society in order to make our nation the knowledge of superpower. Today building innovation for creating disciplined and sensible society is the most important factor as it helps the nation to create a lot of job opportunities to eradicate poverty in order to build a rich nation. A nation's progress depends on the employability. No nation can peacefully run the government if there is an unrest regarding unemployment. So innovation is absolutely necessary for the creation of healthy and wealthy society which can offer jobs to lakhs of people. In many countries the unrest due to unemployment problem is prevalent.

How to make a student talented? One should equip himself thoroughly if he wants to land into lucrative jobs that offer handsome salary. What are the minimum requirements one should have apart from his U.G. or P.G Degree? One should possess at least four skills called Reading, Writing, Listening and speaking. Without these skills one can't make his entry into multinational companies. Hard working students of today may become Billgates of tomorrow. So presentation of skills before an interview board is very much required for a job-seeker. He should excel in both oral and written test. For example a student after the completion of his degree attends an interview. He should know the caliber of interviewers and what type of questions would be asked. He must be in a position to answer any question asked by the interviewer. Similarly when a teacher delivers a speech, he should understand the caliber of the audience. He should keep it in mind about their intelligence, their level of education and their practical as well as theoretical knowledge. Then only he can become a successful teacher.

Trend Towards Learning

All of us have dreams but only a few of us are able to convert our dreams into reality. What are the features of reality? Not only intelligence and diligence are required but novelty also is required for creating a new healthy society. That is reality nowadays getting a job is a Herculean task. As far as employment is concerned India seems to be facing paradoxical situation. Why in the job market millions of educated youths are not getting employed. They may have knowledge but they don't have innovative methods either to write or to speak or facing interviews. Since they lack innovative knowledge they are not able to succeed. What they need is personality development. If they undergo a systematic training in self-skills they can make themselves globally employable.

> Coming together is a beginning
> Keeping together is progress.
> Working together is success.
>
> -Hendry Ford

The above words will become true and invaluable if we follow them sincerely. So let us create a new society by working together using innovative methods helping our new generation to become employable globally. If any student knows how to convert a problem into challenge that will work wonders in life. When a person faces problem he loses his balance. Whereas when he faces a challenge he does it with great determination. Everyone knows that every student should equip himself thoroughly if he wants to land into a good job which offers handsome salary. Presentation of skills skillfully in a test or before an interview board is an essential quality of job seeker. He should excel in both oral and written test.

'A sailor without direction
Knows no favorable wind"

The above proverb serves as a light house for a present generation of students. Unless a student knows where he stands, he cannot proceed further. Here comes the major role of a teacher who puts the students in right track by introducing innovation method of teaching. It is the duty of the teacher to evaluate a student before he proceeds to guide a student because evaluation is an integral part of the teaching process. It is nothing but measuring the achievements of the students. If the students are evaluated every now and then that will keep them to innovate many new dimensions in their learning. So that they can create an aristocratic and scholastic society. What they require is indomitable spirit which will induce them to come out with flying colours.

Pioneering approach of UGC

Every student possesses wonderful hidden qualities which ought to be brought out. It is the duty of the educational institutions to discover the hidden talents of the students. They can train such right students for right jobs. The foremost duty of the educational institution is to train students in communication skills, marketing skills, management skills, behavior skills and personality skills development. Thanks to U.G.C's plan which promotes the concept of core, optional, selective and supportive courses with a modular credit based approach. Introduction of new-value based subjects will provide more opportunities to students to interact with teachers and learn about subjects other than core subjects. Innovations of life-oriented and career-based subjects are introduced. So students are given lots of opportunities to learn about personality development motivation, learning the art of public speaking. On the part of students they must make lay while sun shines.

If students equip themselves in their core subjects along with other skills which are mentioned above, they can easily face international competition and encounter the world with much competence. They should have undaunted spirit and optimistic feeling to turn scars into stars. It is better to transform the whole system of education then to reform it. Instead of adding or removing a single policy let us remake the entire system. We strongly believe that significant change is unavoidable because the existing system of learning is crumbling under its own weight. We need the new – technologically sophisticated approaches for future generation of students. Words like 'innovate' and 'transform' and disrupt' have gained momentum in recent years but they often tend to over-simplify the process. Our current curriculum and the use of traditional teaching methods leave many students bored. We need more dynamic approaches to shift the century-old factory model of school. Students in many schools and colleges are treated like widgets (petty unknown things). New approaches and technology tools will make practioners job more efficient. But it remains out of reach for most.

A majority of people including students, parents and scholars are ready to say 'No' to our current education system but we have not yet invented the new system to which we all say 'yes'. So what we need is high investment which is essential to introduce capital programmes which foster innovation and enhance quality of education. City learning centers provide better facilities for digital technology whereas in rural areas these facilities are lacking use of libraries, museums, galleries and heritage sites will definitely provide scholarly study. The way the teachers are developed professionally, the school curriculum management and testing systems all in-termish with the design of schools to create the learning environment. Of course we are yet to learn about what makes effective learning. For advanced learning new pedagogic knowledge must be incorporated into our schools.

We need therefore to re-think not just the buildings in which learning is housed but every element that is required for learning environment-internal spaces, furniture, technology, lighting, storage systems, communication and determination to continue to provide innovative solutions. The main focus should be instead of creating the right building creating the right environment. The challenge for education is not only to provide access to information but to help people learn to think and to enable them to operate effectively within the rapidly changing world. The purpose of education should be to enable people to become effective learners, to be able to encounter new experiences unfamiliar ideas and changing conditions confidently and creatively.

Accessibility and Utilization of ICT

The differentiations in rural and urban location of any institution, the inequality and accessibility may contrast in a massive level. Socio-cultural and economical status among the higher education students may contrast at a giant manner, all other appropriate and narrowed features impacts the variations among the rural and urban students in all means and ways. This study aims to realize the causes and things which play a major role on it. Higher education plays a pivotal role in the development of a country, as it is viewed as a powerful means to build knowledge based society. In India, higher education imparted by universities is facing challenges in terms of Access, Equity and Quality. The Government of India has taken several initiatives during the Eleventh Five Year Plan period to increase access to higher education by adopting state specific strategies, enhancing the relevance of higher education through Curriculum reforms, Vocational programs, Networking, Information Technology adoption and Distance Education along with reforms in governance. The Indian Higher Education System has established itself as the largest system in the world in terms of number of institutions and third largest in terms of student enrollment (after China and USA). While several new institutions have emerged due to significant increase in private sector participation over the last few years, concerns remain regarding the quality of education being imparted to students. The main governing body at the tertiary level is the University Grants Commission, which enforces its standards, advises the government, and helps coordinate between the center and the state. Indian higher education is decentralized with separate councils responsible for the regulation of different institutions. The diagram below depicts the different councils of Higher Education functioning under Ministry of HRD, GOI.

Aim and Objectives

The prime aim of this study is to prepare a clear picture and collect the role of ICT in higher education sector in a right way. The following objectives were prepared to achieve the main aim of the study.

1. To find the factors influencing the accessibility of ICT among the higher education
2. To measure the level of awareness and utilization of ICT among the higher education
3. To assess and suggest measures to balance the barriers in accessibility and utilization of ICT

The uses of ICT is making major differences in the learning of students and teaching approaches. Schools in the Western World invested a lot for ICT infrastructures over the last 20 years, and students use computers more often and for a much larger range of applications (Volman, 2005). Several studies reveal that students using ICT facilities mostly show higher learning gains than those who do not use. Technology will play a bigger role in transforming higher education imparted by universities to the next level. The tools help to create a social, highly collaborative and personalized environment with innovative solutions that will enhance the way students learn, communicate & collaborate and study both on and off campus. Furthermore, the use of ICTs in education also shifts the learning approaches. As put by (Bransford, Brown, and Cocking, 1999) cited in Volman (2005), there is a common belief that the use of ICTs in education contributes to a more constructivist learning and an increase in activity and greater responsibility of students. This limits the role of the teacher to supporting, advising, and coaching students rather than merely transmitting knowledge. The gradual progress in using computers changes from learning about computers, to learning computers, and finally to learning with computers (Volman, 2005).

The recent ICT developments in higher education sectors mainly focus the urban learners at an immense level. This may cause various inequalities and disproportions on the basis of its geographical location. Use of ICT for promoting education and development has always been a part of policy and plan documents on education. At the moment, the decision makers at both central and state are favoring inclusion of new computer and internet based IT/ICT in education (adopting cloud based virtual classrooms/universities and media Learning initiatives). The Government of India has implemented several national as well as state specific schemes that run concurrent to large number of privately led IT initiatives at school and higher education levels. The following factors were influencing the accessibility and utilization in a drastic manner.

1. Socio-Economical status and background of the individual family
2. The generation gap
3. Regional gaps at the national level
4. Academic performance inequalities within educational institutions
5. Peer group enforcement
6. To maintain and update the contemporary technological advancements

Initiatives by the Government

The National Mission on Education through Information and Communication Technology (NMEICT) is envisaged as a centrally sponsored scheme to leverage the potential of IT/ICT, in teaching and learning process for the benefit of all the learners in Higher Education Institutions in any-time any-where mode. Content generation and connectivity along with provision for access devices for institutions and learners are the major components of the mission.

National Programme on Technology Enhanced Learning (NPTEL), a joint initiative of the IITs and IISc provides E-learning through online Web and Video courses in Engineering, Science and Humanities streams aiming to enhance the quality of Engineering education in the country by providing free online courseware. The National Knowledge Network (NKN) and Connected Digital has launched an initiative to cover 1,000 institutions besides providing digital campuses, video-conference classrooms, wireless hotspots, laptops/desktops to all students of professional/ science courses and Wi-Fi connectivity in hostels. A major development during the year has been the launch of Aakash – the low cost computing tablet on 5th October, 2011. An amount of Rs. 47.72 crore has been released to Indian Institute of Technology, Rajasthan, for the projects pertaining to acquisition and testing of low cost computing devices under the scheme of NMEICT.

This study tries to assess the standard and possess equilibrium between the future educational societies, in order to prepare an alternative solution to overcome the instability concerns by means of finding the suitable factors which created the underlying educational barrier. This study may provide a distinguished model for the forthcoming generations to perceive an appropriate assessment about the accessibility and utilization of Information and Communication Technology (ICT).

National Innovation System

Education is a complex social undertaking, and there is no easy way to analyze the many dimensions of the policies involved. Nonetheless, we can begin with the simple characterization of higher education as a process involving the allocation and use of available resources to achieve certain instructional, social and economic objectives. The first one is that these school resources and Academic achievement studies all test that the output of the educational process is closely related to school inputs. However, the added resources to schools in India actually can be ineffective as the market-valued cognitive skills such as mathematics and reading skills which one obtains from these school resources can be very low. Using micro datasets, the school resources literature has put a lot of efforts at studying the effects of class size, per pupil expenditure, teacher education and experience on the improvement of educational performance need for current knowledge innovation system for development of NIS.

In India as a case study, aims at understanding the national innovation system (NIS) in developing countries which are less successful in technological catching-up. In contrast to developed countries, the development level of India NIS does not link to its economic structural development level. In India to moves from agricultural to an increasingly industrial economy, an NIS remains weak and fragmented. The mismatch between the two affected India competitiveness and partially contributed to the recent economic crisis. Studies of NIS in countries like India should focus on factors contributing to the long-running perpetuation of weak and fragmented NIS. The ability to produce and use knowledge has become a major factor in development. In fact, this ability is critical to a nation's comparative advantage. Surging demand for secondary education in many parts of the world offers developing countries an invaluable opportunity to prepare a well-trained workforce can generate growth in a knowledge-driven economy.

Education for the Knowledge Economy (EKE) refers to the World Bank's work with developing countries to cultivate the highly skilled, flexible human capital needed to compete in global markets an endeavour that affects a country's entire education system. Bank support specifically seeks to help countries. Create a strong human capital base. Knowledge-driven growth requires education systems that impart higher-level skills to a greater share of the workforce. These systems must foster lifelong learning, particularly among existing workers who have not completed secondary or entered tertiary education. And they must offer recognized certificates through internally accredited institutions.

Build national innovation systems (NIS). A national innovation system is a well-articulated network of firms, research centers, universities, and think tanks that work together to take advantage of global knowledge assimilating and adapting it to local needs, thus creating new technology. Tertiary education systems figure prominently in such systems, serving not only as the backbone for high-level skills, but as centers of basic and applied research.

Innovation; National innovation system; Developing countries like India the concept of the national innovation system (NIS) has been gaining popularity as a core conceptual framework for analyzing technological change, which is considered to be an indispensable foundation of the long-term economic development of a nation. Most of the literature concentrates on analyzing the NIS in developed countries. Even though, many scholars from different academic disciplines have made a contribution to developing the NIS concept through various approaches, but only few studies focus on the NIS in developing countries their main focuses were on countries, such as Korea, Taiwan, Singapore, that have more aggressive policies and 'intensive technological learning', hence, to a certain extent, successfully catching-up with developed countries, This paper tries to supplement the studies of the NIS in developing countries by exploring India as a case study. It argues that the specific nature of the NIS and related problems in developing countries, which are less successful in terms of technological catching-up are different both from developed countries and 'learning intensive' developing countries. It highlights why the actors and linkages between them fail to produce 'learning intensive' catching-up. With a richer understanding, it may then be possible to develop policy recommendations that help to produce more systemic and effective NIS in such developing countries.

Create a Strong Human Capital Base

Knowledge-driven growth requires education systems that impart higher-level skills to a greater share of the workforce. These systems must foster lifelong learning, particularly among existing workers who have not completed higher secondary entered education. And they must offer recognized certificates through internally accredited institutions. National innovative system (NIS) in developing countries like India emergence of the NIS concepts, particularly in the information technology and technical based system of higher education, it can be traced back to the work of the National System of Innovation .NIS is the interactive system of existing institutions, private and public firms (either large or small), universities and government agencies, aiming at the production of science and technology within national borders. Interaction among these units may be technical, commercial, legal, social and financial as much as the goal of the interaction may be development, protection, financing or regulation of new science and technology While the study on NIS concept as a whole is still at the early stage, the study on NIS in developing countries is at an even more primitive stage. Most of research concentrate on how institutions and systems were built and shaped to produce 'intensive learning' which facilitated technological catching-up processes in newly industrializing economies in Asia, namely, India and Singapore. One of the most important factors behind the successes of these countries is embedded autonomy of their governments. These governments can formulate and implement economic policies that do not simply reflect of individual firms. However, they have sufficient and positive linkages with other the private sector. Surprisingly, there are only a few studies focusing on countries, like India which are less technologically successful in catching-up use empirical data, such as science and technology manpower, Research and development expenditure and educational figures, to analyze the relationships among social absorptive capability, NIS and economic performance by measuring and the concepts of NIS. The developing countries' are technological capability. They concluded that most critical element of any successful development strategy is the development of human resource. Only the social absorptive capability by itself, as measured by high technical human capital, is not sufficient to explain why some economies have performed much better than others. The macro and incentive environments, including the importance of a strong outward orientation of private sector on the innovation system, also affected the NIS in the latecomer economies. The effective utilization of foreign technology is more important than doing a lot of research and development in some Asian NIEs such as India and Singapore NIS by following the Oslo manual basis. The result illustrated that the Indian innovation system is not well organized, especially with respect to the macro-environment, innovation infrastructure, Research and development and technology transfer and innovativeness and technology capability in the industrial sector.

The higher education and academic achievement study does not directly indicate or highlight the uniqueness of Indian NIS. Other more applicable and conceptualized studies on NIS are they provide 'comprehensive' understanding and insights on NIS in developing countries. Historically, the technological and institutional properties necessary for modern growth were not developed within their systems. NIS in developing countries should be studied in the context of economic development .academic achievement and NIS in a developing country is specifically related to the country's development level. Therefore, it is important to connect level of NIS development with level of economic structural and institutional development. (c) Extraordinary 'intensive learning' of the countries like India and Singapore was the crucial factor for their successful catching-up, which required and was supported by the rapid development of their NIS. Studies on NIS in developing countries should pay high attention to purposeful strategic management for catching-up. As higher education system and school education system developed countries, capital accumulation, rather than intangible assets of knowledge and learning, is the main contribution to technical progress in developing countries. In particular, the manufacturing sector has grown considerably both in terms of growth of production and share of total export Indian NIEs by having its economic structure change from an agriculture-based economy to an economy in which the industrial (manufacturing in particular) sector has gain distinctive significance. Nonetheless, one cannot argue that Indian exports have turned to be more technological intensive, as the dividing categories do not reflect the sophistication of technological activities requiring producing goods, for example, those categorized as science-based exports might be only assembled locally, while their technologically sophisticated and high-value-added components are imported. However, this trend suggests a general change in the structure of the Indian economy need for fast modernization of school education system technological oriented and product oriented education.

Knowledge Transfer and Knowledge Exchange

On today's global world, generating new knowledge and turning it into new products and services is crucial to maintain and enhance the EU's competitiveness. Even more so, it is a precondition for sustaining the "European Way of Life". Innovation and excellence will positively impact on our lives in very different ways: through improved medicines, more efficient and sustainable energy resources, and with new technological solutions to protect our environment or to guarantee the security of the citizens. Transforming the results of scientific research into new commercial products is, however, a complex process involving a broad range of actors. We need to ensure that researchers and industry work closely together and maximize the social and economic benefits of new ideas. Knowledge creation is a dynamic process involving interactions at various organizational levels and it encompasses a community of individuals that enlarge, amplify, and disseminate their knowledge. It can be haphazard and idiosyncratic and should be viewed as a continuous process, rather than one with identifiable input-output phases. It may occur unintentionally and it may occur even if success cannot be assessed in terms of objective outcomes. Given its haphazard and idiosyncratic nature, firms may view resources committed to knowledge creation as extravagant and wasteful. The view here is that the ability to create knowledge and move it from one part of the organization to another is the basis for competitive advantage. While not all knowledge creation efforts will be successful, some will yield surprisingly important results. Also, not all knowledge creation efforts will have immediate performance payoffs. However, over the long term, successful knowledge creation should strengthen and reinforce a firm's competitive strategy.

The knowledge-based economy is based on the production, distribution and use of knowledge and information. It is affected by the increasing use of information technologies to increase the competitive advantage in the economy. The main objective of the industry cluster development and supply chain management is to maintain competitiveness of the each industry in the market by using available information/knowledge. Though, industry cluster and supply chain are not the same aspect. Industry cluster is more in the macro-economic level which focuses on collaboration between partners in the same industry. But, Supply chain is more in the micro-economic level which focuses on the information sharing between companies who are in the same production chain. But, there are some focal points between two aspects which will be explained in the next section. This paper examines interim knowledge transfers within strategic alliances. Using a new measure of changes in alliance partners' technological capabilities, based on the citation patterns of their patent portfolios, we analyze changes in the extent to which partner firms' technological resources 'overlap' as a result of alliance participation. This measure allows us to test hypotheses from the literature on interim knowledge transfer in alliances, with interesting results: we find support for some elements of this 'received wisdom'- equity arrangements promote greater knowledge transfer, and 'absorptive capacity' helps explain the extent of technological capability transfer, at least in some alliances. But the results also suggest limits to the 'capabilities acquisition' view of strategic alliances. Consistent with the argument that alliance activity can promote increased specialization, we find that the capabilities of partner firms become more divergent in a substantial subset of alliances.

Creating Path Collaborative Knowledge

There are four critical knowledge management processes used by firms to access and transform knowledge from an alliance context to a partner context: technology sharing; JV-parent interactions; personnel movement; and linkages between parent and alliance strategies. These processes create connections for individual managers through which they can communicate their alliance experiences to others and form the foundation for the integration of knowledge into the parent's collective knowledge base. As individuals interact through the various connections, the interactions become larger in scale and faster in speed as more and more actors in the organization become involved. This process has been described as a "spiral" of organizational knowledge creation. In the spiral, knowledge starts at the individual level, moves up to the group level, and then to the firm level. As the knowledge spirals upward in the organization, it may be enriched and extended as individuals interact with each other and with their organizations. Although the knowledge management processes are not complex or difficult to understand, the lack of complexity should not be associated with a lack of effectiveness. The creation of organizational knowledge requires the sharing and dissemination of individual experiences. Each process provides an avenue for JV parent managers to gain exposure to knowledge and ideas outside their traditional organizational boundaries. The processes deal with both operational and strategic knowledge and taken together, provide a comprehensive view as to how alliance knowledge can cross organizational boundaries and become the basis for knowledge creation.

Successful Knowledge Creation

Successful knowledge creation through alliances depends on two main elements. First, there are the organizational processes that firms can use to access and transform knowledge from an alliance context to a parent firm context. While these knowledge management processes are not complex, there was substantial variance in the extent to which firms in this study were actively seeking to exploit the knowledge potential of their JVs. Some parent managers were unable or unwilling to appreciate both the simplicity and the potential of these processes. Simple actions, such as visiting a JV and interacting with JV personnel, can be strong stimulants for learning. Despite the high cost of visits, the Japanese partner firms in this study were much more willing to send visitors to their JVs than were the American partners. The second element necessary for knowledge creation is an organizational climate that facilitates the effective implementation and utilization of the knowledge management processes (this incorporates the facilitating factors discussed above.). While a balance between the knowledge management processes and the facilitating factors is necessary, there is also the question as to which management processes are most important. Does a firm need to be good at all the processes to create knowledge or will an "unbalanced" approach to knowledge management work? The answer depends on the type of knowledge sought and the strategic value attached to JV knowledge. A firm seeking access to manufacturing process technology may use a very different approach than the firm interested specifically in product market positioning knowledge. The firm with a learning objective that covers a broad spectrum of knowledge will probably employ a broad knowledge creation strategy. No two firms will attach the same value to JV knowledge and, therefore, each firm will have to tailor its knowledge management strategy to its own objectives. Similarly, it is unlikely that all of the facilitating factors will be present in equal strength in any firm. The challenge is to develop an organizational climate that fosters knowledge creation and is consistent with collaborative objectives.

Knowledge Creation and Exchange

An issue that cannot be ignored is the cost of knowledge creation. The four knowledge management processes used by firms to access and transform alliance knowledge involve costs for the knowledge creating firm. Therefore, a decision to initiate knowledge creation efforts must be balanced with the cost of doing so. For example, visits and tours of JV facilities were identified as a simple and effective means for parent managers to interact with JV managers. While visits and tours can be effective, their cost cannot be dismissed. Given the uncertainty associated with any knowledge creation effort, it is not surprising that parent managers in this study raised questions about the value of visiting the JV plants. Nevertheless, Japanese firms appear to be more willing to make the investment in knowledge creation than American firms and also are willing to accept incremental developments of knowledge. As a result; Japanese firms may be in a better position to assess the cost-benefit tradeoff of knowledge creation processes. In contrast, American firms tend to seek knowledge in large discrete steps and there is often a reluctance to experiment and deviate from prevailing notions of what the company is about. Consistent with this perspective, a manager in this study suggested that Americans tend to look for "home runs" before new knowledge is considered worthwhile. The problem is that since potential projects are frequently evaluated against an ideal situation, many organizations fail to undertake any knowledge creation projects. This home run mentality, coupled with the failure to recognize the value of incremental learning, provides additional insights into why parent learning was low even when the potential for learning was high. Much of what could be learned from the JVs in this study was of an incremental nature and closely linked to the Japanese partner's business philosophy. A further issue associated with alliance knowledge is that partner firms may have to take steps to protect their core technologies. To protect themselves from the learning objectives of their partners, firms may have to be cautious in transferring their technologies to alliances. Firms can also institute measures to limit the transparency or openness of their skills to their partners. These measures include the establishment of gate keeping roles, limiting the number of partner personnel involved in active alliance management, and controlling key operational tasks in the alliance. A difficult question for any firm instituting knowledge creation structures and processes is: At what point has an optimal level of learning been reached? In other words, when does the cost of creating new knowledge exceed its benefit? Because knowledge creation and its benefits may be separated in time, or the benefits may be masked by intervening forces, assessing the true cost of knowledge creation efforts will never be easy. However, ignoring the cost entirely may lead to inefficient knowledge creation. Assuming the cost is prohibitive may mean no new knowledge is created.

Tacit and Explicit Knowledge

Organizational knowledge creation involves a continuous interplay between tacit and explicit knowledge. Tacit knowledge is hard to formalize, making it difficult to communicate or share with others. Tacit knowledge involves intangible factors embedded in personal beliefs, experiences, and values. Explicit knowledge is systematic and easily communicated in the form of hard data or codified procedures. Often there will be a strong tacit dimension associated with how to use and implement explicit knowledge. Table 1 shows the four knowledge management processes and the primary types of knowledge associated with each process. The table also provides examples to help clarify the tacit and explicit dimensions. Two of the knowledge management processes, JV-parent interactions and linkages between parent and alliance strategies, create the potential for both explicit and tacit knowledge to be created. Technology sharing provides access primarily to explicit knowledge. Personnel movement, while it could be associated with explicit knowledge, will be most effective as a means of gaining access to tacit knowledge.

In the cases studied, parent firms had put into place various mechanisms to gain access to JV manufacturing process and product technology. The most common approach was also the most straightforward-meetings between JV and parent managers. In one case, monthly meetings were held, with the location alternating between the JV and one of the American parent plants. In attendance at the meetings were plant managers, heads of quality control, R&D managers, the VP manufacturing at the American parent head office, and several senior JV managers. In addition, quarterly R&D meetings were held involving the JV and American parent. The manufacturing vice president of one of the American parent's said that "while he hated to admit it, the quality of the JV product was superior to that in the parent." As a result, he initiated a program with his plant managers about the need to improve quality and customer service.

Access to partner technology skills also occurred through direct linkages between Japanese and American partners. In two cases, there were regular visits by American parent personnel to Japanese parent facilities. Consistent with the argument that Western firms find it difficult to undertake activities not fitting prevailing notions of what the company is about," an American parent president expressed frustration at the lack of tangible output from these visits. Our engineers go to Japan and come back with some good ideas but nothing ever happens. They [the American engineers] are too protective of their technology and way of doing things. It drives me crazy when I visit a Japanese partner plant. They are doing the same things we are with one-third the employees. I tell our people here but they can't do it. Despite this frustration, the president recognized the value of the Japanese technology and decided to initiate some changes within the parent operation. To capitalize on the Japanese partner's fabrication knowledge and ability to operate with fewer equipment operators, the American president invited several Japanese engineers to the United States to train parent engineers. The Japanese engineers brought very detailed equipment designs that would allow the American firm to replicate their manufacturing process. When no visible progress was made on designing new equipment, the American president decided to contract the design and manufacturing of the equipment to the Japanese partner. An American engineer would be sent to Japan to learn about the equipment so it could be installed in the United States. In another case, the partners signed a very broad global technology agreement. Both partners agreed to be completely open in sharing both product and manufacturing technology. For example, the JV had developed a specific process technology that was considered proprietary (so proprietary, in fact that a section of the manufacturing line could be closed off behind dark curtains if necessary).

Personnel Movement

The rotation of personnel between the alliance and the parent can be a very effective means of "mobilizing" personal knowledge. Rotation helps members of an organization understand the business from a multiplicity of perspectives, which in turn makes knowledge more fluid and easier to put into practice.15 in this study, the rotation of interest, was a two way movement of personnel between the JV and parent. If there is only one-way movement, such as from the parent to the JV, this was not considered rotation. Interestingly, none of the cases studied had an explicit process of rotation between the JV and the parent. However, in four cases, there was an informal system of personnel movement between the organizations. For example, an American parent promoted a JV manager to a staff training position at parent HQ. Several engineers also were promoted. In four cases, senior managers were transferred to the JV when the JV was formed. The careers of these managers were considered closely linked to the American parent and not just the JV. In one JV, the Chief Operating Officer of the JV came from the American parent to act as mentor for the younger JV management. This manager will eventually return to the American parent. In another JV, two plant managers spent time in the JV and then returned to plant management positions in American parent plants. The chairman of the American parent in this case told one of the managers that he wanted him back in the American parent to "do some of the things he has learned here [in the JV". The attitude of the Japanese parent sometimes constrained rotation. In one case, the Japanese parent preferred that JV personnel not move to the American parent. The Japanese parent saw the JV as distinct and separate from the American parent. Despite this concern, the American parent has moved personnel from the JV to the parent. In another case, personnel were willing to move from the parent to the JV but less willing to return to the American parent. This prompted the American parent to ask its JV not to "poach" any more personnel from the parent.

Flexible Learning Objectives

The collaborative objectives of the JV partners are a key element in alliance knowledge creation. However, it is not enough to enter a JV with a learning objective. Initial learning objectives may have little impact on the effectiveness of knowledge creation efforts. This is not to suggest that learning objectives are unimportant. If learning objectives are associated with the formation of a JV, a parent firm may enter more actively into the search for knowledge. However, if the initial learning objective is not correctly focused and management is unwilling or unable to adjust the objective, knowledge management efforts may be ineffective. For example, in one case the American partner had a very explicit technology learning objective. However, this firm's knowledge management efforts were weak and inconsistent because the firm did not have a clear understanding of its partner's skills. While the partner was highly skilled in specific manufacturing technology areas, its success was also the result of skills in other areas such as customer management and scheduling. The American partner was unwilling to adjust its original, narrow technology learning objective. Rather than reorienting the learning objective, parent management saw the differences between the parent and the JV as irreconcilable. According to the president of the American partner, "the JV is in a different business than us. They do not have traditional customer relationships." In another JV, the situation was almost the reverse. The American parent was interested in forming a JV primarily to gain access to the Japanese transplant market. When negotiations to form the JV were started, American parent management made it clear that they were only willing to be involved if they managed the JV. According to the JV president, "we have a quality reputation which we should be able to carry over to the JV." But, after working together for several years, American parent management realized that alliance knowledge could be important to their firm and greater effort was made to gain access to the JV operations and JV partner knowledge. The American parent formed its JV with a weak learning objective that grew stronger with exposure to the JV partner. In several cases, the American firm did not have an initial learning objective until skill discrepancies became obvious and unavoidable. For example, an American firm that had prided itself on its high quality product status found its quality lacking once it formed its JV.

Initially, we thought there was nothing to learn from our partner. We thought we were better than anybody. When we first went to Japan we thought our partners wanted a JV so they could learn from us. We were shocked at what we saw on that first visit. We were amazed that they were even close to us, let alone much better. We realized that our production capabilities were nothing [compared with the Japanese firm]. We realized that we were not world class. Our partner was doing many things that we couldn't do.

As a starting point, a firm must have a learning objective. However, if the initial learning objective is based on an incorrect and inflexible assessment of partner competencies, learning and knowledge creation efforts may be ineffective. Ideally, as a firm builds a relationship with its partner, the learning objective will become more focused and ambiguity about the partner will disappear.

Creating path collaboration for successful knowledge transfer and knowledge exchange the most advanced and specialized forms of education and training available in modern societies. Their purpose can be defined in terms of providing society with the capacity for carrying out high quality research, and in terms of providing highly-qualified graduates with the skills and options to engage in their chosen careers. In both respects, social and individual requirements are changing. Today's attention to collaborative creating path collaboration for successful knowledge transfer and knowledge exchange education is one manifestation of these changes. A main objective of the project has been to build constructive dialogue with and among stakeholders engaged in collaborative education. By these means, the project aimed to expand the available knowledge of the range of issues involved, the nature and extent of collaborative programmes, employability perspectives and their relation to so-called transferable skills, and the role of institutional tracking.

Role of Educational Institution

The technical, Economic and social evolution has shaped people's way of living and thinking. The globalized markets, the technical and technological revolutions are transforming the modern economy into a "knowledge based society" in which new ways of organizing the work are governing the world, demanding a perpetual buildup of competences, a rapid spread of high performance technologies, solid knowledge and increasing responsibilities. In the society of the future, education will play the key part in the way of life specific to this education and knowledge-based society. Introducing in the educational system of new learning and teaching techniques is a prerequisite of national cultural success, as much as it is also a prerequisite of economic competitiveness. The real knowledge based society, as an expression of the globalized society, tries to connect the needs of human nature, ever growing and more and more diversified, with its own regeneration, coming up with ways of developing the inexhaustible resources - the human intelligence, the innovative spirit, the associative creativeness, etc.

Education has played and is still playing an important role in forming and training the individual throughout his existence. Several authors in their works underline the importance of education over the time. Otherwise other definition of education starting from three basic sources: nature, humans and objects. The spontaneous development of our organs and competences is education provided by nature. The day-to-day utilization of these competences is the education transmitted to us by other humans. The personal experience gained from the tools and things surrounding us, is the education provided by objects.

On a global level, education is regarded as a phenomenon, one of those activities that can favor communication through its very specific functions, as well as establishing close communication links between various countries, geographic areas and across various cultures. We cannot overlook education's role of forming and informing the individual, being a social phenomenon that in turns constitutes an important dimension of any philosophical approach of education. Education is not only about putting the individual in contact with values, but also raising him to the level of these values, than extending this process from the individual level to the society level, thus increasing its value and functionality. Education is a human right, since it leads to individual creativity, increases the participation to the economic, social, cultural activity in the society, contributing this way to the process of human development".

Education leads to lower incidence of health problems, reduced mortality and increased life expectancy. Health education, if included in the general education, tied to common organisms or other means of communication, can be more effective and less costly. In a world of evolution, of technological know-how, education plays an essential role. It is a top rank social institution that can contribute to increased democracy and equality, facilitating the rapport between man and nature. Thus, the developed countries of the world will rapidly evolve on the coordinates of a so-called knowledge based society, and the new direction of society will be towards knowledge and learning. Given this context, education stands as the basis for a society focused at the future, and knowledge becomes the key component of economic and social growth.

Economic Crisis

In the knowledge-based economy, the individuals need to be trained across the various levels specific to the professional forming system, adapting to the demands of the knowledge based society. The knowledge based economy and society have changed the political, economic, social and moral background of the world. The new society is a certainty and is one of organizations, where the primary resource is knowledge. A knowledge based society implies a large demand of overly-qualified workforce, forcing the population to learn how to operate with information and knowledge. Therefore, the development of the knowledge based society is dependent on the creation of knowledge, on its spreading via education and tuition and on its dissemination via communication and on its involvement in technological innovation. The outlook of the societies supporting knowledge-based economies is shaped by the human creative potential, which increases the importance of the innovative process and knowledge dissemination process in the modern economy.

The 21st century knowledge based society tends to expand to a global proportion. Acknowledging the rapid moral depreciation of knowledge and abilities, the modern society prepares to adopt a new approach to education in order for it to function as a life-long institution of learning. In the knowledge based economy, people need to learn before entering the labor market, while in school, passing through several levels of education, as well as afterwards, adapting through various sub-systems specific to the permanent education to the increasingly complex demands of the world's dynamics.

The mission of the educational system becomes a key component of change. The change is induced by several factors, the first of which must be the capability to innovate, the willingness to cooperate, to interconnect activities that are both competitive and high-performance oriented, in the sphere of knowledge, in industry and services, in the community life. The human intelligence and creativity need to be regarded as inexhaustible resources of learning and as means of integrating the human being in the labyrinth and paradox of the future world. Changing the way of thinking is affecting not just the emotional and conceptual level, but also the actions carried out in the economic background, with direct effects on the strategically important directions of the economic policies. If during the pre-industrial and society the focus was on the classic manufacturing factors, in the knowledge based economy new sides of the human factor need to be re-discovered, after previously being quantified only as residual factors, according to some authors.

The school of the future should provide a top rank and universal alphabetization, which assumes understanding the basic sciences, but also an increased dynamics of learning, the study of foreign languages, so that the individual may learn ever since the school age how to act efficiently later on after entering the labor market; Building the motivation to learn and adapt to the perpetual learning process in all individuals at all levels of the educational system; For this purpose, the new technologies can play a particularly important role, and the individual can advance in his path to knowledge to the point of having noticeable achievements. Providing the information and know-how, both as a substance and as a process is a priority generated by the new technologies; Surpassing the monopolistic condition of the school, applying a new axiom: the more educated a person gets, the more extra education they need, or at least the rerun of educational modules undertaken with unsatisfactory results in the past. This would prevent, for instance, having adults feeling overwhelmed by events.

If we consider the new educational challenges, than the new system of education needs to be an open one, conceived to ensure the equal training opportunity to all the members of society, so that the able and high-performing may have access to study in order to get a chance at social ascension, regardless of their origin, income and previous background. Furthermore, in a society of learning, often appears both the necessity of university graduates in particular to return systematically to the educational system and the necessity of any organization to continuously form its workforce, if superior results are expected to come from the work process. Learning must be a creative process, developing the capacity to solve problems.

Education can provide people not only with the best technological know-how, but also by training potential innovators, to create an advance in knowledge and create economic growth. A more education population leads in turn to a more developed society. Increasing the population's level of education will also create a more stable labor market, by decreasing overall unemployment. It is well known that well educated individuals have a higher participation rate on the labor market, and the extent of their active lifetime is generally superior to the one of lower educational level. According to the authors, the more time is allocated to an individual's education, the better that individual is likely to face the new challenges generated by the knowledge based economy and society. In this context, the investment in education becomes the most important investment of the society and of the organizations, with long lasting results, as "the ideas, the knowledge in general, can be used and reused forever, and grow in value as they are being utilized, this contributing to the success of society". The society based on information and knowledge assumes the intensive usage of information in all the domains of human activity and existence, with significant economic and social impact. The new information and communication technologies are used both on individual level and within organizations with high flexibility, resulting from the independence of human activity related to space and time.

Research Activity

A society of knowledge is one in which information, regarded as a sub-component of the processes of knowing and representing reality, of conceiving and communicating, inherent to the human action on a society and organizational level, represents power in the most general level of understanding. The informational revolution is not limited only to the ITC domain, but regards the very role of information plays in society; it has led to the expansion of the frontiers of knowledge, making a decisive mark on all the components of the global system, so that obtaining, owning and making use of knowledge would become the pinnacle of a society where education plays the main role, even when society itself is passing through a profound economic crisis. This research underlines the ways in which education remains the key element in the knowledge-based society, even if in today's economic crisis it is currently facing difficulties. According to the authors, this challenge could bring about a new configuration of the educational process in a new society of the future, with different sets of values.

To conclude the article, throughout the world, the roles of education and of its multiple benefits to the economic and social environment are well known, as education is recognized as being "the single most important path to development and to limiting poverty". The increasing extent of services in the economy, the pace of technological changes, the advanced level of information and knowledge, as well as the size of the industrial and social re-organizations, all give good arguments in favor of the knowledge based society. The main component of economic and social development becomes knowledge. In other words, the basis of the future society is education (perpetual, life-long educative process) and knowledge and information represent the key variables in the development of society. During the development process, the contribution of education and professional training are essential, their funding needs to be recognized as being of maximum importance and today's economic crisis demands identifying new funding mechanisms resulting from the partnership between the companies and the public sector.

The University Demarcates Itself

The common lexical definition of a "university" is that it is an institution for the advancement of several branched of higher learning". The university has assumed a very salient presence in contemporary society. Worldwide there are just over 17 000 universities. A higher education revolution is currently sweeping all over the world. This key feature of this revolution can be summarized by one word, namely "massification". Higher education enrolments worldwide has almost doubled in the first decade of the twenty-first century, from 99 527 915 in 2000 to 181 007 006 in 2010 (and have continued to surge, to reach 196 077 086 in 2012), while the global higher education gross enrolment ratio has grown by almost 50 percent in the same decade, from 19 percent in 2000 to 30 percent in 2010 (UNESCO, 2015). Large amounts of (precious) resources are poured into this higher education expansion project. Education constitutes the largest single item on the budget of most countries in the world. Almost without exception, higher education lays claim to a substantial part of the public education budget, being per student much more expensive than primary and secondary education. This differential increases as the *per capita* level of countries decrease. In a country such as Tanzania, where all children of primary school age are not even at school, much less all children of secondary school age, governmental expenditure per university student amounts to more than a thousand times governmental expenditure per primary school student. While this expenditure is justified in terms of the belief of the role of education (and higher education in particular) as panacea of all societal ills and particular as to the indispensible role of the university in the nascent knowledge economy (both these are unpacked later in this paper), there is likewise a chorus of voices critical about the university going up, especially in view of the rising specter of graduate unemployment.

This division of opinions can be graphically illustrated by two quotes. At the gates of the University of Granada (one of the oldest universities in Europe) the following is inscribed: "The world is held up by four pillars: The Wisdom of the Learned, the Justice of the Great, the Prayers of the Righteous and the Valour of the Brave." At the same time, popular British journalist and social commentator, Paul Johnson, is on record as describing the university as "the most overrated institution in modern society". The aim of this paper is to clarify the place of the university in early twenty-first century society. The paper commences with an overview of the university as it has evolved historically: its features and functions in society. The role of education in society and in particular in the imminent knowledge economy is outlined in the next section. Then it will show how the university as institution has come under pressure in recent times. The particularly acute problem of the university-employment mismatch is then focused upon, before a conclusion is offered as to the way forward for the university and its place in society.

The University: Historically Evolved Identity and Function

The history of the university can (arguably) be traced back to eleventh century Europe, the first universities then being the University of Paris, the University of Bologna and the University of Salerno (*cf.* Duggan, 1916). Of these three the University of Paris has the longest history. The cathedral school at the Notre Dame Church on an island on the river Seine, which runs through Paris, has the longest history of these three proto-universities. The big drawing card of the cathedral school in Paris was the reputation of two very competent teachers, Peter the Lombard, and his student Abelard. Students from all over Europe flocked to be taught by these two teachers. The school became overfull, to the extent that the bishop found it difficult to fulfill his ecclesiastical duties. He therefore asked the two teachers to take their students and to leave the cathedral and the island, and to continue with the education activities on the left bank of the Seine (which is up to today the university quarter of Paris). Once they were on the left bank, the students and masters were no longer under the direct supervision and control of the bishop, and freedom and independence of thought and speech developed. Soon tension built up between the bishops on the one hand, and on the other, the students and masters. When the bishop attempted to reassert his authority, the students and masters appealed to the pope (as head of the Roman Catholic Church). The pope feared he could lose this intellectual bastion in his (and Christendom's) battle against Islam, so he sided with the students and masters. In 1180 he issued a decree proclaiming the students and masters' independent from control of the bishop. This year 1180 is then taken as year one of the University of Paris. Thus the principle of autonomy (independence) from church and political authorities as a hallmark of a university came to be established. Other key features of a university, which distinguish it from a school were: 1.a university was for comparatively adult students, and engaged itself with advanced levels of education, 2. Students came from far (in the case of the medieval university students hailed from all over Europe) and not only from the immediate environment, 3.individual professors were the drawing card.

Soon the institution of the university spread to all over Europe. In 1167 the University of Oxford came into being as the first university in England, and in 1385 the University of Heidelberg as the first German university. After the Middle Ages the university receded in the background in Europe. Neither in the Renaissance nor in the life of figures of Eighteenth Century Europe such as Voltaire or Montesquieu did the university figure. The next major event in the evolution of the university was the founding of the University of Berlin in 1810, and the pioneering work of Wilhelm von Humboldt. After the humiliating defeat of the Prussian armies at the hand of Napoleon at Jena in 1806, the Prussian king looked for ways of restoring Prussia's greatness. He saw in education a means to that end, and for this purposes he founded the University of Berlin, as the pinnacle of the new Prussian education. Friedrich Wilhelm von Humboldt (1767-1835) was tasked to establish this university.

Berlin University was not intended to be a mere addition to the set of existing universities, but to embody a totally new conception of the university. The main emphasis was laid on scientific research rather than teaching and examining, and with this in view the professors was chosen for their capacity to make original contributions to the furtherance of learning (Boyd & King, 1975: 337). Secondly they granted absolute freedom in teaching and in research, confirming a principle set by the Medieval University, as explained above. The university, moreover, was, as its medieval counterpart, granted full autonomy to manage its own affairs, without any fear of interference by the state. The next milestone in the development of the modern university was the establishment of the "Land Grant Colleges" in the United States of America, following the Land Grant Act (or the Morrill Act) of 1862. The Morrill Acts funded educational institutions by granting federally controlled land to the states for them to sell to raise funds to establish and endow "land-grant" colleges. The mission of these institutions as set forth in the 1862 Act is to focus on the teaching of practical agriculture, science, military science and engineering. These institutions strengthened the nexus between community and university, and brought to the fore another function of the university, namely (community) service.

The modern university has six functions. The first of these is teaching. This function has been present ever since the days of the first universities of the late-Middle Ages. Teaching of a dual nature took place, namely a general academic grounding in basic disciplines, and secondly a more vocationally directed teaching, originally for the higher professions, but in recent times these have been expanded to the full round of lower professions and even beyond. The second function is that of research. Research too has a dual nature. Firstly basic (or "blue sky") research takes place, with the aim of pushing back the frontiers of knowledge. Secondly applied research takes place, using knowledge to solve practical problems experienced by society. These two basic functions, teaching and research are believed to exist in symbiosis and mutually reinforcing each other. Indeed, empirical research has shown that teaching proficiency and research productivity of academics are positively correlated (*cf.* Sutherland & Wolhuter, 2002).

A third function of the university is service. Of the above functions, *service* is perhaps the vaguest and least well circumscribed. Some definitions understand faculty *service* as "engagement", others as "out-reach", others as "service" (Shin. 2010: 175). Ward (2003) gives a thorough and clear explication of the range of activities which (could) fall under faculty service. These he classifies as internal and external service. Internal service could, in turn, be divided into on-campus and off-campus (discipline/scholarly field oriented) service:-on-campus service entails activities such as services to students, academic oversight, institutional governance and institutional support -faculty are also involved in service activities to their disciplines or scholarly fields through various associations, e.g. professional/scientific societies (such as membership committees, programme committees), or publication-related activities (e.g. serving on editorial boards or as reviewers) (Shin, 2010: 176) -external service is the way for higher education to put its expertise to use for various external stakeholders and can include consulting, service learning, community action-based research, community upliftment projects, participation in cultural activities and civic service. Service can be paid or unpaid, but the common factor among all service activities is that it is based on the expertise of faculty.

A fourth function of the university is to act as the conscience of society, to critique society (*cf.* Habermas, 1968: 3-4). This function assumes particular significance in an era where societies and governments are subscribing to the Creed of Human Rights, and where humankind are facing challenges and critical issues such as the eco-crisis, biotechnology or genetic manipulation. This university can fulfill this function only if it operates on a basis of complete autonomy, and not stand under the influence of government or any interest group in society. A fifth function of the university is the preservation, transmittance and promotions of culture, of the best and highest products of culture bestowed by and for humankind (*cf.* Wolhuter, 2012). This is most salient, but by no means limited to the objects of art, i.e. literature, language, painting.

A sixth and final function of the university is with regard to innovation. This pertains to innovation requiring high levels of expertise knowledge of a scholarly type. This is evident in the number of patents flowing from universities, and this function has assumed importance especially in the era of a knowledge society/economy which is currently dawning.

Expectations of and Regard for Education in Modern Society

The role of the university - as the top educational institution - in contemporary society should be viewed within the context of the surging expectations and regard for education harbored by modern society. After centuries and millennia of being at the fringe of society, and being part of the lives of but a tiny minority of people. Education moved to the centre of public and private life after the middle of the twentieth century.

The post-war decades ushered in a dynamic period for education, with the development of UNESCO (founded in 1945) and the slow inclusion of educational issues within institutions such as the World Bank and USAID. This post-war era, also a time of decolonization worldwide, focused considerable attention on the relationship of education to national development. The sociologist Talcott Parsons (1902-1979) could be regarded as the founder of structural-functionalism. Structural-functionalism views society as a harmoniously functioning whole. Every system (such as the economic system, political system, education etc.) performs a function and contributes to the smooth, successful functioning of society as a whole. Similarly, every institution (every school, family, church, enterprise, cultural organization, etc.) contributes to the successful functioning of society as a whole. Changes in one system or institution will inevitably lead to changes in all the others; indeed change could deliberately be planned in one system to effect desired changes in other. From there the ceiling less belief in the potential of education to induce any kind of change desired by society - economic growth, social mobility, eradication of unemployment, combat of crime or whatever, could be effected by just providing more education.

Modernization theory held that the developing countries needed economic, social and political development; and the fastest and cheapest way to effect these developments, would be to just supply the people in these countries with more education (Fägerlind & Saha, 1984: 49). Modernization became the most important theoretical framework in Comparative Education during the 1960s and early 1970s (Kelly *et al.*, 1982: 516).

The limitless belief in education, held not only by educationists, but also by politicians, financial, industrial and business leaders, developmental experts, newspaper editors and the public at large, explained above paved the way for a massive expansion of education worldwide during the decades following the Second-World War, reaching maximum momentum in the 1960s. This expansion is well explained in two classic publications in the field of Comparative Education, Philip Coombs' *the world education crisis: a systems approach* (1968) and *the world crisis in education: the view from the eighties* (1985).

Not the least was the explosion of higher education enrolments and gross higher education enrolment ratios. This surge of higher education enrolment enrolments and higher education enrolment ratios has picked up momentum since 1950 and is still showing no signs of abating. Indeed in the first decade of the twenty-first century enrolments have almost doubled while the global higher education gross enrolment ratio has grown by approximately 50 percent, to reach 30 percent in 2010. Several scholars have remarked that the world is currently experiencing a higher education revolution. Foremost is surely the UNESCO report on higher education, authored by renowned higher education scholar Philip Altbach and his co-authors (Altbach *et al.*, 2009). This revolution can be summarised by one key word, namely "massification" (Altbach, 2010). The past quarter of a century, since 1990. A global higher education has taken off; the signature feature of this revolution is massification. This revolution, this spectacular expansion of higher education, has been made possible by a combination of factors. These include higher levels of affluence (the global economic upsurge which put higher education within reach of ever more people), the information and communications technology revolution, and the wave of democratization (with its attendant Creed of Human Rights, making more and more people felt they are entitled to higher education) (*cf.* Wolhuter, 2011).

Global Higher Education Enrolments and Ratios, 1950-2010.

Year	Global Higher Education Enrolments (x000)	Gross Higher Education Enrolment Ratio (%)
1950	6 317	5
1960	11 174	8
1970	28 084	9
1980	51 037	12
1990	88 613	14
2000	99 511	19
2010	180 207	30

(Sources of data: UNESCO, 1971, 1977 1999, 2014) (1950 figures imputed from best available data on demographics and enrolments)

Two factors or trends in contemporary society have enhanced the importance attached to education. The first is the compelling force of globalization, creating what Friedman (2009) calls a flat world, that is, a world where whatever advantage a country or nation may have enjoyed in the past on strength of its geographical location or natural resources, have been wiped out by the information and communications technology revolution and other facets of globalization. All nations and national economies now compete in the fiercely competitive globalised world, where the main determinant of competitiveness is the quality (i.e. levels of skill, of education and training) of the nation's workforce.

The second trend is the rise of a knowledge society or knowledge economy that is an economy where the driving axis is the production and consumption of new knowledge (*cf.* World Bank, 2002). Historians of economic development divide economic history into a number of stages through which every society goes. The first stage is the stage of collection and hunting, that is when collection and hunting are the main and only activities constituting the economy of a society. The next stage is an agricultural economy, after the agricultural revolution, when animal husbandry and crop cultivation becomes the mainstay of an economy. That is followed by an industrial economy, after the industrial revolution. The economic basis of society now becomes manufacturing industries. The next phase is a service economy, when services become the main economic activity. A final stage, now dawning in the leading economies of the world, is that of a knowledge economy.

On the other Hand, The University Under Pressure

While the above paints a picture of the university assuming ever greater value and an indispensable place in contemporary society, and while this view is incessantly widely underscored by the media and by leaders in politics and industry alike, not to mention by individuals voting with their feet (as can be seen by swelling enrolment figures. And by the number of applicants to universities by far exceeding the number of available places), at the same time the university - at least the university in its historically evolved form - is coming under increasing pressure. These pressures can be divided into two main groups, namely doubts as to the societal elevating power of education, and secondly, changes in the form of the university forced by societal contextual forces.

The optimism which fired the massive expansion of the education in the 1960s turned to disillusionment and pessimism in the 1970s, when it became clear that the massive education expansion of the 1960s did not bring the expected results. By the early 1970s, educationist's policy makers and the public at large were disillusioned with the societal effects of education, and the massive educational expansion project, which took place worldwide since the early 1960s. For example, rather than promoting economic growth, the 1970s saw the specter of stagflation. Instead of eradicating unemployment, the educational expansion brought the new phenomenon of schooled unemployment (this very salient problem will be further unpacked in the next section). Jencks demonstrated on the basis of extensive empirical analysis in his book, *Inequality: a Reassessment of the Effect of Family and Schooling in America* (1972), that education was no major determinant of social mobility.

Secondly in times of the global policy regime of neo-liberal economics, the triple helix of university-government-industry relations have come under threat. The neo-liberal global policy regime dictates that government reduces spending on education, leaving education to the forces of the market (Rizvi & Lingard, 2010: 2). At the level of higher education this means Worldwide the share of the state in funding higher education is being downscaled, and students and industry are required to shoulder an ever increasing part of higher education costs. Private higher education institutions and corporate universities are becoming more prominent. One indicator of the extent of state support for higher education is per student public spending on higher education as a percentage of per capita Gross Domestic Product. On the global aggregate scale this has declined from 38.5 percent in 1998 to 34.5 percent in 2004 (World Bank, 2006: 22). Although the state is cutting its financial support to universities, it remains the largest single source of universities' income, and in return, in a time of neoliberal economics, is demanding accountability and a say in the running of universities.

This is not the end of the effect of the global neoliberal policy regime on universities. Under the influence of this regime, the principles of neo-liberal economics, such as the cult of efficiency, the profit-motive, performativity and quality control, have been carried into higher education. In this way the university, and the core work of academics, the unhindered quest for truth, has been seriously compromised. These have given rise to a cult of managerialism, placing a heavy administrative load (inevitably to the detriment of research and to work satisfaction) on academic staff.

The Intractable Problem of the Education-work Mismatch

While education disappointed on many counts those who advocated in the 1960s the expansion of education to attain modernization, economic growth, creation of social capital, stabilizing and entrenching a democratic culture, establishing a value system of respect for Human Rights, or whatever, probably none is as painful as the education-work mismatch; painful on individual as much as on societal levels. While there were few countries, if any, where in the 1960s unemployment among university graduates was a reality, actually even thinkable, the pace of higher education expansion in the 1960s simply outstripped the (even generally rapid) rates of economic growth at the time. While a pure projection of these two trends would have shown a looming danger of graduate unemployment sometime in the future, the 1973 oil crisis and the ensuing economic slump, especially the phenomenon of stagflation (of high inflation rates at the same time as high unemployment rates, something hitherto not experienced, and something economic theories, above all Keynesian economics could not explain, let alone find a way out of it), brought this problem to a head. Ever since graduate unemployment has been a problem in most of the world, although the severity of the problem has ebbed and flowed in step with phases of economic contraction and expansion.

It should be mentioned that generally, a person's chances of being unemployed decreases with a rise in level of education. In South Africa, for example, the unemployment rate among university graduates is 11 percent (for those with a post-graduate qualification this drops to 3 percent), among those with a tertiary education qualification below a university degree 16 percent, among those with twelve years of schooling completed 29 percent and among those with less than twelve years schooling completed 42 percent (Altbeker & Storme, 2013). Two remarks are however, immediately apt. While 11 percent is much lower than 42 percent, it still represents 1,21,000 people, and not only for the country (including the state which have invested public money into their education) but for each one personally (and for their families who have likewise sacrificed to afford them a university education) this is a painful reality. Secondly while substantially lower unemployed rates for graduates compared to non-graduates are the norm, it is by no means universal. In the MENA (Middle-East-

North-African) region, for example, the rate of unemployment among university graduates is twice as high as under secondary school graduates (Moreno, 2012).

In order to get the world of education in tandem with the world of work, a number of strategies have been attempted in various countries in the world. The most obvious strategy was to introduce vocational education, or the variant technical and vocational education. These range from the Secondary Modern Schools and Technical Schools in England in the twentieth century, to Sidney Marland's (Education Minister in the Nixon presidency in the United States of America in the early 1970s, in America Sidney Marland was nicknamed "the father of vocational education") initiatives in the United States of America. This strategy has drawn a number of criticisms over a long time. These include the relatively low prestige (seen as an option for less gifted students) this kind of education is hold compared to academic education, all over the world; the fact that students of school age, particularly those at the stage of beginning their secondary school cycle, are not yet ready to make life-binding vocational choices, the fact that tracer studies have shown a very poor correlation between type of vocational education received and final work done by students, and the fact that in a fast changing world, many of the occupations a generation from now we do not even know the names, let alone know how to educate workers for them.

A second a strategy was the introduction of polytechnic education (that is where students spend part of their school day on farms or in workshops). The prototype of this was the education system devised in the Union of the Socialist Soviet Republics by their first Minister of Education and wife of Vladimir Lenin, N.P.Krupskaya; although widely followed since then in twentieth century East Bloc, and countries in the Global South attracted to the Socialist model, for example such a system was introduced in Mali in Africa in 1962 or, on a more limited scale, immediately after independence in 1980, in Zimbabwe as the Business Education Partnership Agency (BEPAZ) project. It would, however, outrageous to suggest that such a scheme can solve all the challenges involve in aligning the world of education with the world of work.

Thirdly, a more extreme form was the transformation of schools into production units, such as, in Africa, in Benin in 1971, the Education for Self-Reliance in Tanzania in 1967, or the Brigades, a private initiative in Botswana. Of these the Brigades of Botswana had a success record; other projects such as Education for Self-Reliance in Tanzania failed miserably (*cf.* Wolhuter, 2004). It would in any case be equally outrageous to suggest that, in a modern diversified technologically advanced and rapidly developing and changing economy, that such a scheme can accomplish all the tasks in aligning the world of work with the world of education.

Fourth, National Youth Community Service Schemes were introduced in countries such as Botswana, Ethiopia, Ghana, Malawi, and Nigeria. It should be added that these initiatives generally were not very successful and that the governments found many of them impossible to implement (for reasons, *cf.* Durt, 1992).

A fifth strategy was for the state to make projections of human power needs, and to tailor the education system accordingly. This was tried in the erstwhile Soviet Union with GOSSPLAN making these projections and the education system used as a conveyor belt to deliver (*cf.* Wolhuter, 1996). Apart from the objection of the state assuming such a role of prescription and compulsion (in the economy, in the education system and in the lives of individuals), there is the problem of the difficulty and unreliability in projecting future human resources needs, as explained above. The dismal record of the Soviet experiment is in any case there for everyone to see (*cf.* Wolhuter, 1996).

A sixth strategy is the Dual Model of Vocational Education and Training, the prototype being in Germany (the system of *Duale Ausbildung*), whereby from the senior secondary phase, the education system and industry take co-responsibility for the vocational education and training of the student (*cf.* Wolhuter, 2003). However, a number of criticisms against this model should be stated. Firstly, while the model has worked reasonably successful thus far in Germany, all of the many attempts to export it to other countries, with the possible exception of Singapore, have failed (*cf.* Wolhuter, 2003). Secondly, even in Germany - where the specific context had proven to be very propitious for this model - it began to run into problems in the early years of the new millennium. These problems too related to finding space in industry willing to take in students, and to the fast changing nature of the labour place, rendering skills learned very quickly obsolete (*cf.* Wolhuter, 2003).

The best that can be offered from the many studies done, regarding tying the world of work with the world if education, is the fairly general lists of broad skills probably valuable in the near future, such as the SCANS list of the Ministry of Labour in the United States of America (*cf.* Hamilton, 1999: 12). The problem of getting the world of education and the world of work in tandem appears to be the Gordonian knot of education. No easy solution can be offered from what have been tried and what research report from all over the world. All that can be said is that further research and considerate experimentation are necessary. Furthermore a number of points should be made.

Firstly, it could be accepted that many tertiary education institutions in the world, with a decidedly vocational bent, such as the Community Colleges in the United States of America and beyond, the TAFE (Technical and Further Education Colleges in Australia) or the Institutes of Technology in India, and the like, certainly perform a necessary and valuable function, the University, considering its functions as an institution operating at the most advanced level and at the cutting-edge of knowledge, too is fulfilling an indispensible function in society. These functions can only be fulfilled on the basis of academic autonomy. Society, governments, industry and students should move away from a narrow instrumentalist conceptualisation of the university, and come to see that the aim of education is far more than securing a job and a high income. Then the value of the university and the outcomes of university education will be rightfully appreciated.

Bridging the Gap between Education and Work

Education and training need to be adapted and linked more closely to the world of work. To help put this into practice, the EU has developed the European Framework for Key Competences for Lifelong Learning, The EU supports the cooperation between national governments to modernize their higher education systems (the Bologna Process), and the Copenhagen Process which aims to improve the performance, quality and attractiveness of vocational education and training. Upgrading, adapting and widening the skills portfolio of individuals to create and fill the jobs of tomorrow is one of the greatest challenges facing Europe today. Everyone needs to step up and be more ambitious for their futures - individuals, private and public employers, the education sector and governments at all levels. Improving people's skills is a real 'win, win' for all - for the economy, for society, for employers and, of course, for individuals themselves. Another major challenge is to ensure that people have the right skills. Future demographic trends will add further pressure to tackle this challenge. Fewer and fewer young people will graduate from schools and universities, and the only growth of the labour force is likely to be amongst those aged over 50. The numbers of over-65s in relation to those aged 15-64 will increase from 26 % in 2008 to 38 % by 2030.

Our Vision for 2020

We want to see a Europe where citizens have more and better skills. Where people as well as organizations are able to make better informed choices about which education or training to invest in, depending on which jobs they have, would like to develop in, or apply for. Where education and training systems propose innovative and equitable approaches such as flexible learning pathways, and focus on developing essential skills as well as intellectual and job-specific skills. Danish society puts a high value on education which is traditionally seen as a crucial vehicle for development in all spheres of social and economic life. Large sums are spent on work-related adult learning, an important example being academically based masters programs. Yet, the actual effects of such educational investment in terms of improved workplace efficiency remain obscure both with respect to the organization and the individual.

In this article we present a theoretical framework for providing guidelines to the way educational institutions should interact with public and private workplaces. The aim is to improve the quality of their continuing efforts at skills development and professional training. Our main focus is on advanced masters programs where experienced managers and highly skilled specialists acquire new knowledge and methods in order to improve their own work practices and those of their organizations. Many resources are devoted to train professionals through such programs. In our role as professionals responsible for planning, developing and implementing masters programs, we regard continuous dialogue on result optimization for the participants and their workplaces as essential. Too often, theoretical perspectives encountered by students of masters programs prove difficult to translate into everyday, work-related practice. Our article aims to show how new ways of structuring relations between educational institutions and workplaces can enhance the probability that individual learning acquired in an educational setting will in fact lead to improved organizational performance.

Vocational Training and Education in Denmark

Vocational training and skills development have boomed during the last three decades. Concepts like organizational or lifelong learning have become part of everyday language. During this period, investment in vocational training has risen steadily. In 2004, the Danish Employers' Association issued a report that identified Denmark as the European Union country with the highest relative investment in this sector of education. Almost 5 billion Euros were earmarked for vocational training in Denmark during 2004. Yet, according to the same report, little is known about the effects of this substantial investment. A possible explanation for this empirical gap may be that Danish organizations and educational institutions are linked to each other by an unacknowledged pact of mutual non-interference.

Organizations hand over responsibility for continuous workplace training to external educational agents: "That's their job, let them deal with it!" Equally, educational institutions do not take a real interest in life as it is lived in society at large. Nor do they concern themselves with the peculiar logic underlying organizational decision making. Intellectually speaking, such real-life concerns may seem insufficiently challenging: "Our job is not to give them, more of the same", but to help them move beyond the limitations dictated by short-term, pragmatic or profit-related concerns."

Integration of Stakeholder Perspectives in Classroom and Curriculum

Traditional scholastic thinking views the classroom as a place specialized in the delivery of conceptual learning directed at students brains. When it comes to vocational training, learning through apprenticeship and supervised practice have typically been absent in university-based programs. In one advanced masters program for which we are jointly responsible, this pattern is challenged. In our program planning we operate with three learning arenas. Each learning arena is designed with a view to catering for the educational needs of one of the three stakeholder positions shown. The Auditorium is the learning arena where academic values are the main focus. A teacher's oral monologue (lecture) and teacher-student dialogues (discussion, joint reflection) play dominant roles. Auditorium is the academic institution's learning arena par excellence. In the Auditorium the teacher acts as a theoretical expert, challenging and expanding the student's knowledge in certain areas. In the said program however, we insist that Auditorium should not be considered a monolithic law-giver for what is deemed right and wrong in the two remaining learning arenas. Theoretical communication, dialogue and discussion take place in a multi-paradigmatic field of tension in which questions and answers are continually subjected to further discussion.

The Laboratory is the learning arena where the individual student viewed as embodied learner is the main focus. Structured training activities allow students to find out whether professional subject matters they've understood "with their heads" can be enacted by their bodies in real-life interaction with others. Personal experiences generated in Laboratory settings may be fed back and serve as arguments in Auditorium based theoretical exchanges: "This idea doesn't match what happened to me when...

Learning categories

Learning as a generic term covers a wide array of processes involving change and development. As common denominator, the term indicates that new patterns of interaction evolve between a learner and her surroundings. Following Illeris (2009), we distinguish between four different categories of learning: mechanical; adaptive; developmental; and transformative. Figure 3 illustrates our way of distinguishing between these categories.

According to Illeris (2009: 142) transformative learning processes equal "what could be termed personality changes or changes in the organization of the self". Such change may come about as an effect of cumulative life experiences: "Older and wiser". Participation in lengthy, formalized training programs may also trigger them. The individual's thinking about self, others, and the world has been altered in fundamental ways. The changes have become integrated in her way of being.

As educational planners and designers, we are bound to subscribe to an ambitious desire to make our contributions to such learning processes – thus living up to the classical maxim that, ideally, teaching should not just be "for school", but also "for life": "non scholae, sed vitae". At the same time, we do not consider learning processes of this kind an explicit target value for educational strategic planning. By including personal coaching as part of our teaching program we do, however, make it an option for students who feel so inclined to reflect upon the possible existential impact of their program participation. Developmental learning is also referred to as accommodative. It requires that the individual learner or community of practitioners somehow move beyond their existing, action-guiding mindsets. When situations or impulses baffle us, our efforts to come to terms with what is going on may lead to a restructuring of our current mindset. Mindset changes of this sort may have repercussions far beyond the situations that initially bring them about.

Practice-inspired Transfer

The concept of learning transfer became a research issue in the early twentieth century. As such it is a classic within experimental psychology. Owing to its very age, the terminology and concepts of this research field may have a somewhat *altmodisch* feel about them. The concept carries connotations of the maligned so-called "banking" concept of education:

We understand and describe ourselves, not only as teachers, but also as managers responsible for optimizing the ongoing production of learning. In the same vein, we invite the students to think of themselves as the educational organization's productive employees. We ask them for evaluative feedback on our way of managing and organizing the educational production line. We do not simply address them as individual learners but organize them in action learning teams that are meant to be jointly responsible for the fruitful learning activities of their members.

The first section discusses our efforts to engage students workplaces in actively supporting the learning process of their employees. The second section describes how we support the students in translating and transferring educational experiences back into workplace practice.

Learner Intentionality - getting the Workplace Involved in the Learning Process

Several researchers have shown interest in the relationship between trainees learning objectives before an educational intervention, and the learning outcome which eventually results from this. According to Kemerer (1991) students, when left to them, tend to couch their learning objectives in fairly general terms. This, however, seems to inhibit learning. Kemerer recommends that students be helped to establish immediate, concrete end goals for the desired learning program before they begin their training. Elliot & Dweck (1988) differentiates between two kinds of objectives reported by students.

Performance objectives. The learner focuses mainly on ensuring a positive evaluation of his or her performance. In formalized educational contexts this evaluation will be communicated through a grading system. Performance objectives imply that an external authority has laid down criteria for good performance and, hence, may judge whether, or to what extent, the learner satisfies these criteria. Typically, performance objectives receive retrospective evaluation at the end of an educational course. Therefore they cannot help the learner experiment with process improvements along the way.

Learning objectives. The learner engages in an ongoing process of self-observation with a view to developing experience-based quality standards in both personal and task related terms. The main focus is on improving performance in relation to new tasks. Compared to their performance objective counterparts, students guided by learning objectives become far more involved in self-evaluation of educational effects: "Have I acquired useful knowledge or skills?" Evaluation becomes an ongoing process allowing for continuous, personalized progress monitoring and self-correction.

Individual Coaching

Dialogues between student and relevant workplace representatives aim at creating an organizational interest and commitment in the student's learning process. Individual coaching is used as an educational tool intended to help students to translate (transfer) learning outcomes from the academic context to the organizational context of the workplace. Individual coaching is structured as a traditional coaching dialogue dealing with the student's professional role and personal challenges in relation to role enactment. Yet, the fact that it takes place between a student and a teacher adds special qualities to the traditional template. If the student chooses to talk about a concrete, current challenge at work (Practicum), the coach may invite the coached to explore this challenge from an educational perspective using the insights and experiences from the Auditorium and/or Laboratory. Such coaching practice may help the student link the three learning arenas that make up the masters program.

Finally, several MOC students have told us that, apart from the professional learning issues discussed so far, coaching has also functioned as a vehicle for their personal growth and development. Coaching sessions may be used to explore personal leadership style and to reflect on career opportunities, work-life balance or family-related issues. Thus, the eight coaching sessions offered to the student during the two year long educational program may provide a valuable contribution to the students existentially relevant transformational learning.

This corresponds to difficulties worldwide in recruiting students to the environmental sciences (Brasseur 2000). While there are many reasons for such difficulties, and legitimate concerns regarding current and future demand for graduates in the atmospheric sciences. It is widely understood that the atmosphere exhibits chaotic dynamics, a characteristic that imposes if niter limits on predictability, regardless of the adequacy of the prediction model (Lorenz 1963; Leith 1974). In practice, imperfections in the weather prediction models themselves, as well as errors in observations, contribute to the growth of the instabilities that ultimately limit forecast.

Simply put, students are not empty vessels waiting patiently to be filled with knowledge; new learning must connect with what students already know (Shulman 1999). To connect, it is important to employ teaching strategies that account for the range of student learning styles (see below) present in a given classroom (Knox 1986; Felder 1993; Felder.

Teaching and Knowledge Society

We wish our Guru to possess highly specialized knowledge that is as dear to us as life itself and which could be acquired through armless activities. We want him to have knowledge of sciences, speak cultivated tongue, know the meaning of the sastras) Researches), reflect deeply. And thereby be a highly competent and knowledgeable teacher "-Yajureveda 36/16.

Today as never before, meeting our society's challenges demands educational excellence. Reinvigorating the economy, achieving energy independence with alternative technologies and green jobs, and strengthening our health care system require a skilled populace that is ready for the critical challenges we face. There is widespread consensus, however, that our education systems are failing to adequately prepare all students with the essential 21st century knowledge and skills necessary to succeed in life, career and citizenship.

Determining the enabling structures, policies, and strategies that can best support 21st century knowledge and skills acquisition among teacher candidates is a first step toward creating the kind of environment that will promote this kind of learning. In the 21st century, all educators play a significant role in shaping the lives and careers of their students. When teaching and learning is at its best, our students, our communities; and our nation thrive the relationship between the reform of technical teaching and the quality of education offered by the school was generally looked at by the teachers from the point of view of the effects the latter had on the duration of the courses. Teachers are, by their nature, important facilitators in building social capital within their community and nation.

The last decade of this century has suddenly paced the country in a global context and atmosphere of greater communication, competition and cooperation. Till the day of independence, we imported from pin and having blade to cars and airplanes. Today we are able to lunch our own satellites'. It only point out that this country has the talent needed to achieve anything. What needs to be examined is whether this achievement is a natural result of the existing educational system and the contributions teachers have made or whether this is in spite of them. However, it in necessary in the present global context to find out whether the success in present day examinations is any guarantee that the person will also succeed in making a meaningful career as well as adapt to the change and challenges that will be forthcoming.

Teachers' role is not just limited to imparting information or instruction to the students in the classroom. He is an overall social model whom students imitate. He is also a model in the society for moral reasons. We saw that this was so historically and this should be so at any time in the history as well as at present or in future if the word education has to have its substantive meaning. In the recent past, the issue of accountability has been raised time and again. Especially, accountability of the teacher is discussed more often considering the critical position he occupies in the system. Teacher's role is defined in the statements of various committees, commissions and working groups. His responsibilities vis-à-vis those of the students, the society, the parents, the institution and so on are described. The teacher knows that his job is that of teaching, but often he does not know what it means to teach.

The teacher has to contribute to the understanding of the objectives of higher education, relevance or courses, flexibility in courses of study, openness of the system, up datedness of teaching materials and methods, examinations and a number of others academically supportive programmes besides presenting himself or herself as a model before students as well as the society at large. If the teacher initiates this process in the interest of his students, he will stay in the system. Otherwise, their strength which is dwindling in most of the colleges and subjects will further drop. Students will have to find an alternative system for their own survival and if they do so, it will be considered wise on their part. And if they actually have to do it someday, it will be judge otherwise of the teachers.

Let us visualize the working of the teachers at three levels the craft level. The technological level, the art or creativity level. Though the lowest level of functioning is the craft level, it does not imply that it is in any way less important than the others. The next higher level of functioning is the science-based technological level. There will be many branches of technology such as technology of arts education. The third and the highest level of a teacher's functioning goes beyond the craft and the science/technology levels and manifests itself in the work of a creative teacher. Such teachers are few.

The term 'knowledge society' has gained prevalence in recent years due to the revolutionary strides in technology and the rapid evolution of new systems for the gathering, transmission and application of information. A confluence of technologies-television, computers, networking, satellite communications and the internet-constitute the technological basis for the knowledge revolution. Their rapid proliferation over the past decade has made possible movement of information around the world at lightning speed. This dramatic acceleration in the development of information technologies; in the speed and extent of global knowledge accumulation, dissemination and exchange; in the blurring and transcendence of traditional boundaries between fields of knowledge; and in the emergence of new knowledge-based industries are defining characteristics of the knowledge revolution.

The concept of Knowledge Society includes also that of the learning society. The pace of knowledge generation and adoption is so rapid in the world of today that learning can no longer be confined to formative years of youth. All members of the population must continue to acquire knowledge throughout their adult lives in order to avail of the economic opportunities that rapid development makes possible. This requires the development of innovative delivery systems for dissemination of practically useful information on a continuous basis.

The knowledge revolution is not a fashion or a fad. However, in striving to adapt and respond to the opportunities generated by the knowledge revolution, two guiding principles should be kept in mind. First, efforts to spread the Knowledge Society should avoid as far as possible the empty hype and fads currently sweeping the world and concentrate rather on the real role of knowledge as a catalyst for development. Second, rather than blind imitation of other countries, India should seek to innovative new strategies and new applications of the knowledge revolution adapted to local needs, conditions and culture.

School Education and the "Knowledge Society"

The knowledge society has created a paradox for its schools: the more teachers try to teach their students, the less they seem to learn. Demands for more teaching come from many sources, among them those who expect schools to prepare students for knowledge-based globalized life. Simultaneously, much of the energy of the educational change community goes into efforts to understand and improve the performance of educational systems.

Family, community or nation social capital lead to cohesiveness, trust, supportiveness, and care for those students in these networks that, in turn, help them learn better in school and to possess higher expectations for their own thinking, behaviour and learning. These expectations, however, should reach beyond measurable academic knowledge. Students need to experience personal and social development and change as the most important outcome of schooling. "Being bored in school", Sharan and Chin Tan (2008, p. 4) explain, "means that students' learning is unproductive." School that does not stimulate desire to learn, need for learning, or curiosity to know more, is not able to generate productive learning required by the knowledge society.

Teaching in our insecure and complex world is influenced by two change forces that are more contradictory than complementary. Steering educational systems towards producing intended outcomes requires congruence between teaching for the knowledge society, and what educational reforms require from teachers and students. The high-demand features of modern schooling-learning together, creating new ideas, and learning to live with other people peacefully, best occur in an environment decidedly different from what our schools offer young people and their teachers today. Furthermore, treating ingenuity and diversity simultaneously in classrooms is a challenge to teachers. Schools will not be able to meet these expectations to educate their students for a knowledge society, unless they have:

1. Internal conditions that respect their professional intuition, knowledge and skills to craft best learning environments for their students;
2. A social context and necessary social capital in their community that provide encouraging and supportive conditions of and will to learning for their students; and
3. Adequate external norms and expectations that rely on responsibility and internal accountability to reach good learning for all students.

The knowledge society has three dimensions. First, it comprises an expanded scientific, technical, and educational sphere; second, it involves complex ways of processing and circulating knowledge and information in a service-based economy. Third, it entails basic changes in how corporate organizations function so that they enhance continuous innovation in products and services by creating systems, teams, and cultures that maximize the opportunities for mutual, spontaneous learning. The second and third aspects of the knowledge society depend on having sophisticated infrastructure of information and communication technology that make all this learning faster and easier.

The learning environment within an educator preparation program is a key component of any systemic reform initiative. The knowledge society is a learning society. Economic success and a culture of continuous innovation depend on the captivity of workers to keep learning themselves and fro one another. A knowledge economy turns into on machine power but on brain power-the power to think, learn, and innovate. We are moving into a 'learning economy" where the success of individuals, forms regions are countries will reflect, more than anything else their ability to learn. There speeding up of change reflects the rapid diffusion of information technology, the widening of the global marketplace and deregulation of and less stability in markets. The integration (or non-integration) of information and computer technology into high schools provides a striking example of the failure of ingenuity in educational change. At one level, the growth of computer technology in schools has been phenomenal.

Teaching for the Knowledge Society

Teachers must take their place again among society's most respected intellectuals'-moving beyond the citadel of the classroom to being and preparing their students to be, citizens of the world. They must do their best to ensure that their students promote and prosper from the private goods of the knowledge economy. They must also help their students committee to the vital public goods that cannot be taken care of by the corporate interests of the knowledge economy-a strong and vigorous civil society, developing the character that promotes involvement in the community, and cultivating the dispositions of sympathy and care for people in other nations and cultures that are at the heart of cosmopolitan identity. These are the challenges facing teachers in the knowledge society today and that are the focus of this book, which deals with the changing world as well as the changing worked of teaching.

Teaching for the knowledge society, involves cultivating these capacities in young people-developing deep cognitive learning, creativity, and ingenuity among students; drawing on research, working in networks and teams, and pursuing continuous professional learning as teachers; and promoting problem-solving, risk-taking, trust in the collaborative process, ability to cope with change and commitment to continuous improvement as organizations.

Teaching is practical; profession of all the jobs that are or aspire to be professions only teaching is expected to create the human skills and capacities that will enable individuals and organizations to survive and succeed in today's knowledge's society. Teachers are expected to build learning communities, create the knowledge society, and develop the capacities for innovation, flexibility and commitment to change that are essential to economic prosperity. At the same time, teachers are also expected to knowledge societies create, such as excessive consumerism, loss of community, and widening gaps between rich and poor, somehow, teachers must try to achieve these see ingle contradictory goals at the same time. This is their professional paradox; meanwhile, public expenditure, education, and welfare have been the first casualties of the slimmed-down state that knowledge economics have often required. Teacher's salaries and work conditions have been among the most expensive items at the top of the public-service causality list.

In general, as catalysts of successful knowledge societies, teachers must be able to build a special kind of professionalism. This cannot be the professionalism of old, in which teacher had the autonomy to teach in the ways they wished or that were most familiar to them. Teachers who are catalysts of the knowledge society must build a new professionalism where they.

1. Promote deep cognitive learning;
2. Learn to teach in ways they were not thought;
3. Commit to continuous professional learning;
4. Work and learn the collegial teams.
5. Treat parents as partners in learning;
6. Develop and draw on collective intelligence;
7. Build a capacity change and risk and
8. Foster trust in processes.

More and more governments, businesses, and educators and urging teaching the knowledge society commit themselves standards-based learning in which all students (not just a few) achieve high stands of cognitive learning; they also create knowledge, apply it opt unfamiliar problems, an communicate effectively to others instead of treating knowledge as something that students should simply member an regurgitate.

New approaches to learning necessitate new approaches to teaching. These include teaching that emphasizes high-order thinking's skills, met cognition (think gable thing) contractive approached learning and understanding, brain-based learning, cooperative learning strategies, multiple intelligences and different "habits of mind, "employing a wide range of assessment techniques, and using computer-based and other information technology that enables students to gain access to information independently.

Teaching for today's knowledge society is technically more complex and wide-ranging than teaching has ever been. It draws on a base of research and experience about effective teaching that is always changing and expanding. Today's teachers therefore need monitoring and reviewing their own professional learning. This includes but is not restricted to participating in face-to-face and virtual professional learning networks, adopting continuous professional –development.

Knowledge is only one input to the development process, but it is an absolutely essential one. Without adequate knowledge all the other essential inputs-land, infrastructure, factories, capital, technology, administrative and social organization-cannot yield full results. Enhancing knowledge generation, dissemination and application is the fastest, most cost-effective means of increasing the productivity of all these other resources and accelerating national development.

Development Depends on four Knowledge Processes

1. Knowledge generation and acquisition through scientific discovery, R&D and transfer of technology.
2. Knowledge adaptation through innovation to particular fields, needs and operating environments.
3. Knowledge dissemination through formal and informal channels from knowledge developers and adapters to those responsible for applying the knowledge in society.
4. Knowledge application through skilled action in fields, factories, classrooms, hospitals and every other field of activity to achieve practical results.

Education is the process of passing on to future generations in a concentrated and abridged form the essence of knowledge accumulated by past generations .Properly planned, educational input can contribute to increase the gross national product, enhance cultural richness, build greater receptivity to technology, and improve the quality and effectiveness of government. Education opens new horizons for the individual, releases new aspirations and develops new values. It strengthens competencies and develops commitment.

Education generates in an individual a critical outlook on social and political realities and sharpens the ability for self-examination, self-monitoring and self-criticism. During the last five decades India has gained valuable experience in all spheres and stages of education. The expectations of the people regarding education and the potentialities for future growth are better understood. But the present reality and future potential are separated by a wide gap in the level of social commitment, institutional credibility, quality of human and institutional resources, and efficiency of functioning. Contrary to expectations at the time of Independence, disparities in levels of education within the society are increasing. There is a visible loss of credibility of existing systems of imparting education in schools and institutions of higher learning. In addition, educational infrastructure is inadequate and even the effective utilization of existing infrastructure has not been ensured.

Teaching for the knowledge society, involves cultivating these capacities in young people-developing deep cognitive learning, creativity, and ingenuity among students; drawing on research, working in networks and teams, and pursuing continuous professional learning as teachers; and promoting problem-solving, risk-taking, trust in the collaborative process, ability to cope with change and commitment to continuous improvement as organizations.

Partnership towards Creating a Knowledge Economy

Embracing the knowledge economy: The time is very opportune for India to make its transition to the knowledge economy-an economy that creates, disseminates, and uses knowledge to enhance its growth and development. The knowledge economy is often taken to mean only high-technology industries or information and communication technologies (ICTs). It would be more appropriate, however, to use the concept more broadly to cover how any economy harnesses and uses new and existing knowledge to improve the productivity of agriculture, industry, and services and increase overall welfare. In India, great potential exists for increasing productivity by shifting labor from low productivity and subsistence activities in agriculture, informal industry, and informal service activities to more productive modern sectors, as well as to new knowledge-based activities-and in so doing, to reduce poverty and touch every member of society. India should continue to leverage its strengths to become a leader in knowledge creation and use. To get the greatest benefits from the knowledge revolution, the country needs to press on with the economic reform agenda that it put into motion more than a decade ago and continue to implement the various policy and institutional changes needed to accelerate growth.

Advantage India. India has many of the key ingredients for making this transition. It has a critical mass of skilled, English-speaking knowledge workers, especially in the sciences. It has awell-functioning democracy. Its domestic market is one of the world's largest. It has a large and impressive Diaspora, creating valuable knowledge linkages and networks. The list goes on: macroeconomic stability, a dynamic private sector, institutions of a free market economy, awell-developed financial sector, and a broad and diversified science and technology (S&T) infrastructure. In addition, the development of the ICT sector in recent years has been remarkable. India has created profitable niches in information technology (IT) and is becoming a global provider of software services. Building on these strengths, India can harness the benefits of the knowledge revolution to improve its economic performance and boost the welfare of its people.

Four Pillars

1. Strengthening the economic and institutional regime
2. Developing educated and skilled workers
3. Creating an efficient innovation system
4. Building a dynamic information infrastructure.

The following are some of the key issues that India needs to address in each of the four pillars to spur growth and innovation and, in so doing, increase economic and social welfare. Taking advantage of the knowledge revolution's potential hinges on effective economic incentives and institutions that promote and facilitate the redeployment of resources from less efficient to more efficient uses. This fundamental pillar of the knowledge economy provides the overall framework for directing the economy. Important elements of the economic and institutional regime include macroeconomic stability, competition, good regulatory policies, and legal rules and procedures conducive to entrepreneurship and risk taking. A key feature is the extent to which the legal system supports basic rules and property rights.

India's economic and institutional regime has several strengths: flourishing entrepreneurship and free enterprise; a strong infrastructure for supporting private enterprise; capital markets that operate with greater efficiency and transparency. India has other intrinsic advantages, such as macroeconomic stability, a large domestic market, and a large and relatively low-cost and skilled workforce. It also has a critical mass of well-educated workers in engineering and science.

Make in India

Make in India is an initiative of the Government of India, to encourage companies to manufacture their products in India. This will create a large number of employments within India. Universities and colleges should leverage these excellent opportunities to get their students involved. By making use of this initiative we can groom hundreds and thousands of younger generation students to become an entrepreneur. Innovation is a new idea. Next generation of our kids is very innovative. The availability of tools, infrastructure is huge and exploration of kids is going tremendous. Every university should have a Seed Innovation program to groom the students and bring their intellectual skills. Should have a tie up with industries based on the skills of the students. Seed Innovation program could bring more innovative ideas from students, industries and governments should invest financial aid to make the idea possible. This would help succeed the student's career as well many more startup companies can be formed to offer more employment opportunities for the current generation of students.

Education is the fundamental enabler of the knowledge economy. Well-educated and skilled people are essential for creating, sharing, disseminating, and using knowledge effectively. The knowledge economy of the twenty-first century demands a new set of new competencies, which includes not only ICT skills, but also such soft skills as problem solving, analytical skills, group learning, working in a team-based environment, and effective communication. Once required only of managers, these skills are now important for all workers. Fostering such skills requires an education system that is flexible; basic education should provide the foundation for learning, and secondary and tertiary education should develop core skills that encourage creative and critical thinking. In addition, it is necessary to develop an effective lifelong learning system to provide continuing education and skill upgrading to persons after they have left formal education in order to provide the changing skills necessary to be competitive in the new global economy.

A strong basic education system is a necessary precondition to underpinning India's efforts to enhance further the productivity and efficiency of its economy. Investments in basic education are thus fundamental for countries to improve the productivity and the quality of labor and deliver the manpower needed for their development efforts. India has made substantial progress in increasing literacy and increasing primary and secondary enrollments and overall education attainment but the country still accounts for one-quarter of the world's 104 million children out of school. The participation of girls in the 6- to 14-year-old age group in elementary education is low. And considerable gaps exist in access to secondary education, particularly for girls. But, the Indian leadership is very committed to increasing educational attainment. The national program for universal elementary education, Sarva Shiksha Abhiyan or Education for All, was initiated in 2001, and the constitution was amended in 2002 to make elementary education a fundamental right of every child. In addition, some private Indian companies, such as Tata are using advances in ICTs to deliver education more efficiently

India also possesses a large pool of highly educated and vocationally qualified people who are making their mark, domestically and globally, in science, engineering, IT, and research and development (R&D). But they make up only a small fraction of the population. To create a sustained cadre of "knowledge workers," India will need to develop a more relevant educational system and reorient classroom teaching and learning objectives, starting from primary school. The new system would focus on learning, rather than on schooling, and promote creativity. It would also improve the quality of tertiary education and provide opportunities for lifelong learning.

Tertiary education is critical for the construction of knowledge economies. India currently produces a solid core of knowledge workers in tertiary and scientific and technical education, although the country needs to do more to create a larger cadre of educated and agile workers who can adapt and use knowledge. Efforts have been put into establishing a top-quality university system that includes many world-class institutions of higher learning that are competitive and meritocratic, such as Indian Institutes of Technology (IITs), Indian Institutes of Management, Indian Institute of Science, and the Regional Engineering Colleges (RECs). Despite these efforts, not all publicly funded universities or other educational institutions in India have been able to maintain high-quality standards or keep pace with developments in knowledge and technology. Major steps are thus needed to ensure that India's institutions meet high-quality national (and if such services are exported, international) standards. Measures are also needed to enhance the quality and relevance of higher education so that the education system is more demand driven, quality conscious, and forward looking, especially to retain highly qualified people and meet the new and emerging needs of the economy.

In the area of scientific and technical education, even though India produces almost 200,000 scientists, engineers, and technicians a year, it has not been obtaining the full economic benefit from this skill base, because of the mismatch between education and the labor market. The professional workforce that is emerging from India's higher education system often cannot find suitable employment due to a growing gap between their knowledge and real practice and to limited job opportunities in their fields, coupled with low salaries. Many professionals also leave the country in search of better opportunities, which leads to brain drain. This calls for an urgent effort to promote policy and institutional reforms in scientific and technical education for both public and private institutions to improve the quality and skills of India's current and future pool of technical manpower.

Strengthening India's Education System

1. Improving the efficiency in the use of public resources in the education system, and making the education system as a whole more responsive to market needs, as well as ensuring expanded access to education that fosters critical thinking and learning skills for all, not just the elites.
2. Enhancing the quality of primary and secondary education, including tackling issues related to quality and relevance, with special emphasis on ameliorating teacher vacancies and absenteeism, reversing high dropout rates, and correcting inadequate teaching and learning materials and uneven levels of learning achievement. This is especially important for India to meet the goal of providing eight years of schooling for all children by 2010.
3. Ensuring consistency between the skills taught in primary and secondary education and the needs of the knowledge economy, introducing materials and methods to teach students "how to learn," rather than stressing occupation-specific knowledge.
4. Reforming the curriculum of tertiary education institutions to include skills and competencies for the knowledge economy

(communication skills, problem-solving skills, creativity, and teamwork) that also meet the needs of the private sector.

5. Raising the quality of all higher educational institutions, not just a few world-class ones (such as the IITs).
6. Improving the operating environment for education, especially higher education, which calls for a shift in the role of the government from managing the administrative aspects of higher education institutions to becoming an architect of education standards and regulations, including improving and monitoring the quality of academic programs, establishing accreditation standards and procedures, ensuring equity, and coordinating a system with multiple players and multiple pathways to learning.
7. Embracing the contribution of the private sector in education and training by relaxing bureaucratic hurdles and putting in place better accreditation systems for private providers of education and training.
8. Establishing partnerships between Indian and foreign universities to attract and retain high-quality staff and provide opportunities for students to receive internationally recognized credentials.
9. Increasing university-industry partnerships to ensure consistency between research and the needs of the economy. This will include reforming the university curriculum to include the development of skills and competencies that better meet the needs of the private sector.
10. Using ICTs to meet the double goals of expanding access and improving the quality of education.
11. Investing in flexible, cost-effective job training programs that are able to adapt quickly to new skill demands generated by changing markets and technologies, aligned with the needs of firms.
12. Develop a framework for lifelong learning, including programs intended to meet the learning needs of all, both within and outside the school system. This will also require greater coordination across the different government bodies responsible for various components of the education and training system and

development of procedures for recognition of what is learned in different parts of the system.

13. Making effective use of distance learning technologies to expand access and the quality of formal education and lifelong training.

Research and Development

Every year most of the Big Corporate as well MNCs is investing billions of dollars for research and developments. Universities and Industries should engage in a partnership agreement to have their research facility within university campus. This would help educate the students on the research subjects. Apply their theoretical knowledge into practical approach. So that they can explore the real time value of their university/college studies.

In addition, India's share of global patenting is small; therefore, despite having a strong R&D infrastructure, India is weak on turning its research into profitable applications. But, an increasing trend is discernible in the number of patents granted to companies by the Indian Patent Office, indicating greater awareness of the importance of knowledge and the value of protecting it through patents. Among Indian patents, it is the drugs and electronics industry that has shown a sharp increase in patenting in recent years. In addition, several Indian firms have registered their innovations with the United States Patent and Trademark Office (USPTO). The number of U.S. patent grants to the CSIR, for example, increased from just six in 1990–91 to 196 in 2003–04. This shows that the focus of research is shifting to patentable innovations, indicating better conceptualization of research. The recent amendments to the Indian Patent Act adopted in a move toward adhering to the intellectual property norms under Trade-Related Aspects of Intellectual Property Rights (TRIPS) has also boosted confidence among international players.

In India, some 70 percent of R&D is performed by the central and state governments, an additional 27 percent by enterprises (both public and private sector industries), and less than 3 percent by universities and other higher education institutions. In contrast, in most countries in the Organisation for Economic

Cooperation and Development (OECD), the private sector finances 50–60 percent of R&D, because it increasingly has the finance, knowledge, and personnel needed for technological innovation. Firms play an even bigger role in R&D in Ireland, Japan, Korea, and Sweden. Universities also undertake research to a much larger extent in developed countries and have stronger linkages with the corporate world.

India should thus take steps to improve its innovation system further, not only by taking advantage of new knowledge created at home, but also by tapping knowledge from abroad and disseminating it for greater economic and social development. It should also improve the efficiency of public R&D and increase private R&D, as well as encourage greater university-industry linkages.

Tapping into the growing stock of global knowledge more effectively and providing incentives for international technology transfer through trade, FDI, licensing, and personnel movements, along with informal means through imitation, reverse engineering, and spillovers.

1. Attracting FDI more effectively, given the importance of FDI in the generation and dissemination of global knowledge and the role that they can have in domestic R&D. This should include removing regulations on foreign investment and encouraging FDI R&D into the country.
2. Encouraging members of the Diaspora and renowned expatriates to contribute further to innovative activities by appointing them to the management boards of national research institutes, universities, and so on to facilitate the design of university programs that better suit corporate requirements.
3. Motivating scientists and engineers from India working in the United States and other developed countries to enter into alliances with multinational companies and establish firms or labs to undertake R&D on a contract basis in India.
4. Auditing and monitoring S&T efforts and institutional performance to identify what works well and then redeploying resources to programs that have a proven track record of success.

5. Using the savings to strengthen university-industry programs by means of matching grants and other initiatives, including encouraging academics to spend sabbaticals in relevant industries so that their research meets the needs of the productive sector.
6. Finding alternative sources of funding for R&D, especially as the government reduces its budgetary support for research programs. In some countries such as China, academic institutions are launching commercial ventures of their own or in collaboration with the corporate sector.
7. Allowing national research institutes to collaborate with domestic and foreign firms to forge closer links with industry. One way of encouraging scientists to work closely with industry and in so doing improving linkages between technology development and application would be to provide incentives such as bonuses and a share of royalties from products created through their research.
8. Paying adequate salaries and creating a proper working environment for scientists and engineers that provides them with access to capital equipment, instruments, and other infrastructure needed for R&D. Failure to compensate researchers adequately and lack of a supportive environment will only exacerbate the problem of brain drain.
9. Restructuring and modernizing universities and publicly funded R&D institutions by giving them flexibility, freedom of operation, and financial autonomy.
10. Increasing the intake of students into science and engineering, given the competition for recruitment of trained personnel; this may require adding colleges and universities (such as IITs or others modeled after them).
11. Developing entrepreneurial skills and management training for S&T professionals to encourage them to undertake business activities.
12. Encouraging the private sector to invest in R&D.
13. Strengthening R&D by companies so that they can have a more demand-driven and market-oriented approach with closer

collaboration among researchers, partners, and customers in developing new products and services that can be speedily brought to the market.

14. Developing communication and other infrastructure for R&D, and creating an attractive environment to motivate R&D investments, including favorable tax, and other incentives.
15. Establishing science and technology parks to encourage industry-university collaboration. Such parks might attract R&D work from both foreign and domestic firms if the parks are situated close to reputable academic institutions.
16. Encouraging venture capital, which can also be used as an incentive for commercialization of research?
17. Effectively enforcing and implementing IPR to create confidence among domestic and foreign innovators on protection of their innovations in the country.
18. Promoting a national fund to support grassroots innovators, with the aim of building a national register of innovators, converting innovations into viable business plans, and disseminating knowledge of indigenous innovations, especially for job creation.
19. Strengthening the emerging new model of reverse drug design to produce innovations in a more cost- effective way based on leveraging traditional knowledge with modern science and exploiting public- private partnerships.

In sum, India is well positioned to take advantage of the knowledge revolution to accelerate growth and competitiveness and improve the welfare of its citizens and should continue to leverage its strengths to become a leader in knowledge creation and use. In the twenty-first century, India will be judged by the extent to which it lays down the appropriate "rules of the game" that will enable it to marshal its human resources, strengths in innovation, and global niches in IT to improve overall economic and social development and transform itself into a knowledge-driven economy. Sustained and integrated implementation of the various policy measures in these domains would help to reposition India as a significant global economic power, so that it can rightfully take its place among the ranks of countries that are harnessing knowledge and technology for their overall economic development and social well-being.

Role of Educational Institutions in Generating Higher Knowledgeable Society

Excellence in education in most simple term implies the transformation of individuals and society to the higher levels of physical, intellectual, social, emotional, aesthetic, moral and spiritual attainments. It must enable students to prepare themselves not only for the job market but also for life. The erosion of human values in our society today has become a phenomenon. There is a maddening pursuit to accumulate wealth, power and status to the total exclusion of humanness in us. The only solution to this value crisis lies in Subjective education. "There is nothing on the earth equal in purity to wisdom. He who becomes perfected by yoga finds this of himself in his self on course of time." In twentieth century, the top reported offences in the schools and colleges were talking, chewing gum, making noise, running in halls, indecent behaviour, wearing improper clothing, looting cheating and not putting paper in waste baskets. By the beginning of 21st century, the offences have progressed to absenteeism, robbery, adultery, assault, burglary, arson, rowdiness, bombing, murder, rape, suicide, vandalism, extortions, drug abuse, gang warfare ect., Lack of values in individuals results in above offences and also leads to corruption, over-emphasis on materialism and ultimately to free-fall of the society and the nation as a whole.

In this context it is relevant to quote Dr. Sarvapalli Radhakrishnan, "Help the students to think rightly, make them to feel nobly, let them do rightly, above all let them posses the spirit of compassion (Karuna), universal love and brotherhood so that we can live together in a global village as brothers and sisters". He rightly says, "Education according to Indian tradition, is not merely a means of learning a living, nor is it only a nursery of thought or a school for citizenship. It is initiation into the life of spirit, a training of human souls in the pursuit of truth and the practice of virtue." According to Vendata, man's real nature is neither the body nor the mind but the self knows as the Atman. It represents the truest and deepest self of every individual his inner most self. Owing to beginning less ignorance known as Maya or avidya, the inner self remains veiled. Cognition removes a bit of this ignorance' then the self-manifests itself and its light reveals the object as knowledge. The knowledge is of two types; ordinary empirical knowledge and higher transcendental knowledge. In empirical knowledge, the removal of empirical ignorance takes place. This is the fundamental mental process taking place in education. Learning removes only empirical ignorance, but this enough to give us knowledge of the external world and bring out the talents and capacities inherent in individual minds. But this kind of empirical knowledge does not remove causal ignorance i.e., the ignorance of the true nature of the Atman. Only transcendental knowledge gained through value clarification can remove causal ignorance. When causal ignorance is removed, the Atman reveals or manifests itself in all its glory. This experience is known as self-realization which is the essential meaning and ultimate purpose of human life. The tapas, dana, arjavam, ahimsa, satyavachanam, self-renunciation, liberty, right dealing, non-injury to life and truthfulness are the cardinal virtues for self-realization.

Swamiji says, 'we want that education by which character is formed, strength of mind is increased, the intellect is expanded and by which one can stand on one's own feet'. According to him, education which makes the whole society happy with the happiness of individual and which produces a society which is constrained and fair in its relation with other societies is called right type of education. In spite of the marvels of science and technology, we live in a worried world under the dark shadow of fear of war and annihilation. In this scientific age, we have gained enough knowledge of our surrounding i.e. objective knowledge but we have lacked in the wisdom of life i.e. subjective knowledge. "He who has faith, who is absorbed, in wisdom and who has subdued his senses gains wisdom and having gained wisdom he attains quickly the supreme peace." (The Bhagvad Gita-IV: 39).

Faith is necessary for gaining wisdom. Faith is not blind belief. It is the aspiration of the soul to gain wisdom. It is the reflection in the empirical self of the wisdom that dwells in the deepest levels of our being. It faith is constant; it takes us to the realization of wisdom. Jnana as wisdom is free from doubts while intellectual knowledge where we depend on sense data, and logical inference, doubts and skepticism have their place. Wisdom is not acquired by these means we have to live it inwardly and grow into its reality. The way to it is through faith and self-control.

Valluvarhas said something similar as follows:

1. "Whatever be the apparent diversity of things, it is wisdom,
2. To analyse and perceive the basic truth of the matter."
3. A parallel in Sivakachinthamani (28, 45, 42.3) is as follows:
4. Wisdom is the ultimate and impregnable defence for protection against destruction;

It is also the fortress of inner strength against enemy onslaughts.

True Knowledge

1. "Once the triple evils of lust, anger and delusion are eliminated,
2. All sorrow will come to an end".
3. All the knowledge, acquired out of the five senses, will be of no avail,
4. If it is not accompanied by true understanding.
5. All our sorrows in this world stem from the fact that we seek to build our life on a set of evanescent and even false values. Only a life based on true values has the potential for ultimate deliverance.
6. The parallel message of the Tirukkural is as follows:
7. "The miseries of birth and life on earth arise out of the delusion,
8. of mistaking the worthless things, as of true value" (Tirukkural: Chapter: 36: 351).

Only a controlled mind can break out of the nets of delusion and concentrate on self alone severely, thus becoming steadfast in the same manner "as a lamb in a spot sheltered from the wind does not fickler".

1. When the disciplined mind is established in the self alone, liberated from all desires then is he said to be harmonized in yoga. Gita VI, 18.
2. Complete effacement of the ego is essential for the vision of truth. Every taint of individuality should disappear, if truth is to be known. There should be an elimination of all our prejudices and idiosyncrasies.
3. Valluvar says, "He who awareness the pride of ego and possessions, will directly attain Godliness". (Kural 35:3ab)
4. Exactly the same lines occur in an appropriate context in Gita (II, 11)
5. That man who lives devoid of longing, abandoning all desires, without sense of 'I' and 'mine' he attains peace.

Spirituality in education produces human beings with self reliance, tolerance and ethical values. Spirituality aims at awakening the inner human faculties which are dormant. Education and spirituality should go hand in hand. Throughout the world, peace will reach at all levels, only by Value-oriented Education. All true education must ultimately involve the spiritual growth from individuality (Vyaktitva) to personality (Vikasita Vyaktitva) through the process of clarification and assimilation of human values. Persons are individuals who transcend their organic individuality in conscious social participation. The fundamental importance of the spiritual and moral values of life must be recognized in any scheme of education.

Education, in Swamiji's view, aims in the unfoldment of the perfection already in man. Secular education (apara vidya) consisting of the knowledge of the external world and spiritual education (para vidya) consisting of the knowledge of the inner reality of man together constitute the science and technique of total human development. Thus, education is of two types. One should teach us how to make the living and other should teach us how to live.

Role of the Teachers in Generating Higher Knowledgeable Society

In an educational setup no other personality can have an influence more profoundly than that of a teacher. Everyone who recollects his own educational experience remembers teachers, not methods and techniques. It is often said that as is the teacher so is the child. In most of our sacred scriptures, the guru is seen as the preceptor, and the acharya. Teachers have always been hailed as pathfinders, who have generously shared their knowledge, skill and attitude with their disciples. Society, too, has always accorded the status of guide, facilitator, counselor, advisor, philosopher and mentor to teachers.

The Purity of behaviour is the sign of healthy heart. On the other hand, the impurity of behaviour is the sign of sick heart. Following are diseases of heart which may hamper the process of learning: Imposterity, Blasphemy, Arrogance, Prohibition, Falsehood, Back-biting, Ill-will, Dishonesty, Jealously and Greed. The Pedagogy should remove these impurities from the heart. Thus the system of teaching must begin with the process of purification of heart. The element which needs purification is the self refers to the individual's awareness of being a district social identity, a person separate from others. Human beings are not born with self- consciousness buy acquire an awareness of self as a result of early socialization.

Swamiji said, "Teach we, teach everyone his real nature. Call upon the sleeping soul and see hour it awakens. Power will come, glory will come, and goodness will come, when this sleeping soul is roused to self-conscious activity. Spiritual development of man is progressive manifestation of the purity, perfection, freedom and consciousness of the eternal soul. Through spiritual awakening, man becomes the embodiment of all virtues and moral values. He perceives the divine essence in all and his self-knowledge makes him realize his own identity with all. He experiences peace and integration within himself and radiates the same outsides. He becomes capable of expressing love and compassion. He will be concerned with the welfare of others everywhere and in every field of their life. Therefore, the teachers have to spend every ounce of his energy to educate children in achieving spiritual realization.

1. Let me recite a few lines of a great poetry from Josiah, Gilbert Holland written during the American war of Independence, which specially seems to be relevant for us at the present time:
2. God give us men! A time like this demands strong minds, great heart, true faith and ready hands.

   Men whom the lust of office does not kill;

   Men whom the spoils of office cannot buy.

   Men who can stand before a demagogue

   And damn his treacherous flatteries without winking!

Tall men, sun- crowned, who live above the fog in public duty and in private thinking.

Socrates says, “The nation is a good as its schools. The school is as good as its teachers”. The teachers have been considered conscience keepers of the society and admired by their students for their knowledge and human qualities. They are expected to observe their own code of ethics and lead a disciplined life. By so doing, they inspire several generations of learners with multiplier effect. They must learn to observe and practice the four pillars of education recommended by UNESCO Report on Education for 21st century for improving the quality of education. They are:

1. Learning to know (tools of comprehension)
2. Learning to do (to be able to interact with environment)
3. Learning to like together (participate and co-operate with others in all human activity) and
4. Learning to be (essential way of integrating the above aforesaid three)

The loss of values and decline in morality is apparent when we contrast these statements with the words of Pandit Nehru highlighting the role of a university in national life at the convocation address of Allahabad University in 1947, "A University stands for humanism, for tolerance, for reason, for adventure of ideas and for the search of truth. It stands for the onward march of the human race towards even higher objectives. If the universities discharge their duties adequately, then it is well with the nation and the people". In order to fulfill this vision the teachers should have commitment for the basic cultural values.

Issues in Higher Education of Present and Futuristic

In the present scenario of Education system, the Higher education system is complicated and significant one. Higher education institutions are large, complex, adaptive social systems like all other human organizations. Over the last decade, Higher Education around the world is facing a number of challenges and potential threats to effective learning and teaching support. In recent years considerable interest has focused on identifying those challenges, identifying opportunities and threats and proposing ways to address them. However, the relevant literature on higher education challenges is scattered over many textbooks, conferences and journals. This article provides an intelligible presentation of all those challenges found in the literature in a structured way. Also this study will identify how technology and data infrastructures could provide responses to address those challenges in a world where students are changing their learning styles, and the technologies to accommodate their changing needs.

Over the past decade, everywhere in the world the Higher Education has doubled in size. There are lots of changes in the Higher Education namely, students are changing, and their learning styles are changing as well as their demands is changing. At the same time, much more has been expected of institutions in terms of their wider engagement locally, regionally, nationally and globally. Universities need to prepare students for a more global future. Higher Education (HE) institutions around the world face the growing problem of relevance as they enter the twenty-first century. Higher Education facing a number of challenges and most contributions mention curriculum design, student retention, new technologies, quality of learning and teaching, widening participation, quality of research, funding and the necessity to improve governance and management as the most burning challenges. To provide the best service to the new students, higher education institutions need to change and hence, they need to response to the challenges.

Higher Education Challenges

Higher education is a large and complex system. Over the last decade, Higher Education around the world is facing a number of challenges. In recent years considerable interest has focused on identifying those challenges. We have found innumerable challenges mentioned in the literature, which are summarised below:

It has been argued that higher education Institutions should listen carefully to the changing needs and expectations of the society. The universities should be more responsive when offering new study programme or course. To act globally in a competitive environment, the Higher Education institutions must offer programs to students that will cover their needs and wishes and they can also provide interdisciplinary programs to meet the 21st century's higher education demands. Higher Education institutions need to reformat and reorganize courses, programs, and structures to increasingly sophisticated and knowledgeable students. As students are paying more, so their demands have increased in course and quality and higher education should respond their demands. So Higher Education Institutions require to redesign or align their curriculum to support today's' students to fit globally to ensure the quality of learning all institutions need to redesign of the curricula.

Students' Employability

Employability remains high on agenda for Higher Education Institutions in all over the world. People are seeking educational opportunities to survive in the world of work. As the financial burdens on students and graduates grow, they increasingly find gaining a degree as a necessary first step to starting their career hence employability is a major and growing concern. Higher skills significantly influence life chances and earning potential. Employability has been defined as a set of skills, knowledge and personal attributes that make an individual more likely to secure and be successful in their chosen occupation. Higher education should take steps to enhance student employability. The choice of degree subjects and its relevance to the employment market is affected to some extent and Higher Education institutions should respond to this by involving employers in course validation to ensure that academic standards meet employer requirements. Therefore, Higher Education Institutions should take necessary steps to address this issue immediately for the greater interest of students as well as for themselves.

Maintaining quality has the highest priority to any organization and it is mostly appropriate to the Higher Education institutions. Higher Education Institutions should care about the quality of learning and teaching because it is the only way to become recognized globally. To improve the quality of learning and teaching, Higher Education Institutions can enable access to learning and teaching material across institutions. Therefore, students/learners can get more information about their subject area to learn as well as teachers can have also more information to teach broadly in an area Higher Education institutions need to take extra care to maintain the quality of learning and teaching to ensure best possible student experience. The Government of Indi aims to ensure that all higher education (HE) student's benefit from a high-quality learning experience that fully meets their needs and the needs of society.

Information and Communication Technologies

The international mobility of information has exploded. It is an important complement to the mobility of students and teachers but does not and should not replace the mobility of people. The new information and communication technologies are enabling a far larger percent of students to have international contacts and access to information. Distance and time are no longer barriers.

Opportunities for distance and cross border delivery of educational programs are growing rapidly through the use of the new technologies. The key challenge for the universities is to determine how these emerging technologies can be used to enhance the learning process, extend its benefits, and bring international expertise together to solve shared problems in new and creative ways.

Changes in the Educational Model

New teaching and learning approaches that enable the development of critical and creative thinking should be integrated. The competencies common to all Higher-Education graduates should be determined and the corresponding expectations should be defined. In a knowledge society, Higher Education should transform us from disoriented projectiles into guided missiles adapting to variable circumstances, and constantly course-correcting. The idea is to teach people to learn quickly as they go along, with the capacity to change their mind and even renounce previous decisions if necessary. Teaching and learning must be more active, connected to real life, and designed with students and their unique qualities in mind.

The academic profession is in crisis almost everywhere. There is a rapid growth of part-time faculty members in many countries, and traditional tenure systems are under attack. The professoriate is being asked to do more with less, and student-teacher ratios, academic salaries, and morale have all deteriorated. The professoriate is being asked to adjust to new circumstances. Without a committed academic profession, the university cannot be an effective institution.

Issues such as the degradation of the environment, population growth, security, global warming, immigration, terrorism, human rights, and health epidemics are without borders, they require international collaboration and cooperation to find policies and strategies that will mitigate negative effects and lead to positive solutions. Multilateral government agencies, international nongovernmental organizations, national governments, the private sector and also the Higher Education sector all have a role to play at national and international levels in addressing these trends. The role that Higher Education plays in researching, teaching about, and analyzing these areas needs to be given greater attention and prominence.

A contemporary trend in Higher Education is increased recognition for the concept of lifelong learning as a benefit, not only for individuals but also for the collective good of a country. This trend constitutes a gradual but profound societal shift and will have a major impact on Higher Education providers. A strong emphasis on Lifelong Learning motivates individuals toward continuous learning and helps to equip them with the skills and knowledge to be contributing citizens at the local, national, and international levels.

To be the best in the world wide in research, Higher Education institutions need to strengthen their research capacity. In order to achieve this challenge Higher Education Institutions need to develop multidisciplinary centers bringing together many areas of expertise and building relationships between teams in universities and industries to well establish their research capacity. The government has increased funding for improving the quality of research. Also this will require a greater focus on world-class research and greater recognition of the potential benefits of research concentration in the key area.

One of the principal means of providing accountability for Higher Education Institutions and programmes is accreditation, the most critical part of quality assurance in higher education. It affects institutions' ability to attract students (home, international), research funding bodies or to attract interest from the business and private sectors. Accreditation is also specified as one of the major challenges In Higher Education. All accreditors make students' learning outcomes a central component in the accreditation reviews. Accreditation defined as a strong, meaningful assurance of academic quality in the Institutional and University level. To efficiently accredit Higher Education Institutions and programmes by professional bodies' institutions can make related information accessible to the accreditation bodies. As institutions information scattered across departments so institutions can integrate those information and then make it accessible for efficient accreditation.

Compete and Collaborating Globally in Research and Talent

There is global competition for talent in top students, researchers & lecturers .Institutions need to compete at a world-class level in teaching & research. Higher Education institutions need to maintain higher standard of research so that they can be recognized internationally and can compete with other Higher Education institutions by means of higher quality and higher standard of research. Today's' Higher Education Institutions have wide range of students from different regions and countries. Higher Education Institutions are increasingly recognizing that to gain public support and participation and to make higher standard of the institutions, they need to become more focused on student's retention. Higher Education Institutions need to focus on student retention with more effective student support.

Assessment is a key process in Higher Education. It provides how learners are assessed shapes their understanding of the curriculum and determines their ability to progress.

Access and equity remain central factors, but in the current policy context are sometimes ignored. While academic systems worldwide have expanded dramatically, there are problems of access and equity in many parts of the world. Gender, ethnicity, and social class remain serious issues. In many developing countries, higher education remains mainly an urban phenomenon, and one that is reserved largely for wealthier segments of society. Although women have made significant advances, access for women remains a serious problem in many parts of the world.

Accountability is a contemporary watchword in higher education. Demands by funding sources, mainly government, to measure academic productivity, control funding allocations, etc. is increasingly a central part of the debate on higher education.

Governance systems are being strained, sometimes to the breaking point. To meet the demands for accountability, universities are becoming "managerialized," with professional administrators gaining increasing control.

New approaches have brought "unprecedented competition" for traditional models of Higher Education. Universities arc looking for ways to provide a high quality of service and more technologically-enhanced learning opportunities, with massive open online courses (Moocs) at the forefront of the discussions to make the learning progressive.

Addressing of Plagiarism

Concern has recently increased in Higher Education system that the incidences of plagiarism may be rapidly increasing. Addressing of plagiarism is considered as the vital issues in Higher Education because many researchers try to adopt plagiarism as to finish their research work in short span time without having any knowledge related to title and fundamentals of research. The best-organized institution is worth nothing if it does not have a qualified teaching staff; an unqualified staff means poor teaching and unimaginative research. To teach the curriculum including employability skills successfully, universities need to develop the new capacities among their traditional teaching staff and new approaches to their teaching. Higher Education institutions will need to develop faculty and staff dedicated to engaging a diversity of learners with more complex learning needs. Higher Education Institutions can offer different types of training for their staff so that they can be up to date with current. Higher Education institutions are in serious financial crisis. Moreover, increased student fees, substitutions of loans for grants, diminishing subsidies to student facilities and so on form a financial barrier to perspective students Higher Education institutions' expenses have increased a lot than before. They have to maintain themselves with the limited budget. Hence, this becomes one of the major challenges in Higher Education now a day.

Group Formation for Learning and Teaching

In present Higher Education institutions where students come from different communities or different countries to study. Moreover in some cases students are not in the same place to study they stay in different place and learn through online regardless of time and place (virtual university). Hence to have efficient learning and teaching teachers often like to put students into groups to work together for any projects, to participate in different discussion forums, or even to make batches of students in order to study their performance on a certain task

Critical thinking has been recognized as an important aim of Higher Education institutions in the recent time. The process of critical thinking involves the careful acquisition and interpretation of information and use of it to reach a well-justified conclusion. Critical thinking is important, because it enables one to analyze, evaluate, explain, and restructure thinking. Higher Education institutions should give more emphasis on supporting their students in critical thinking and argumentation.

Universities are the most important mechanism we have for generating and preserving, disseminating and transforming knowledge into wider social and economic benefits. It is vital that universities use their knowledge capital to contribute to economic growth, both through the commercial application of the knowledge they generate and through preparing people for the world of modern work. Building new partnerships with business and industry will provide an important channel for generating the financial resources.

Higher Education Governance and Management

Higher education institutions' governing bodies are responsible for ensuring the effective management of the institution and for planning its future development. They are ultimately responsible for all the affairs of the institutions. Generally, they are responsible for approving institutional mission and the strategic plan, financial solvency, resourcing policy, employment and Human Resource (HR) policy and strategy, estates policy, senior appointments and remuneration, audit, legal compliance, determining educational character and mission and so on. They are facing challenges to effectively manage the institutions hence become one of the crucial challenges in Higher Education. To cope with this challenge, institutions need better leadership who will be able to provide academic freedom and will be able to make collective decision with the new requirements that is the necessity to make and implement important decisions in a timely manner.

Higher education institutions are clearly in the midst of rapid change in response to environmental, social, economic, technological, and political transformations sweeping the globe. As a result universities are facing a number of challenges and we identified those challenges in this paper. Over the last two decades, India has remarkably transformed its higher education landscape. It has created widespread access to low-cost high-quality university education for students of all levels. With well-planned expansion and a student-centric learning-driven model of education, India has not only bettered its enrolment numbers but has dramatically enhanced its learning outcomes. A differentiated three-tiered university system – where each tier has a distinct strategic objective – has enabled universities to build on their strengths and cater across different categories of educational needs. Further, with the effective use of technology, India has been able to resolve the longstanding tension between excellence and equity. India has also undertaken large-scale reforms to better faculty-student ratios by making teaching an attractive career path, expanding capacity for doctoral students at research universities and delinking educational qualifications from teaching eligibility.

21ST Century Global Market: The Need, the Gap and the Necessity

On the transition of open market economy, most of the countries face a huge challenge in creating a workforce that can either serve the domestic requirements or abroad. The days when each nation used to think only for their requirements of workforce for local or national market are gone. Now all the countries are going through a tough time in creating a global workforce for the global market which requires the nation to inculcate in the candidates an ever changing competence, skills and abilities related to specific discipline and work. Out of all the sectors, technical workforce plays a key role in the growth of a nation and hence this productive sector must be given priority compared to other sectors. The most common phenomenon as observed in today's engineering graduates is the lack of soft skills and communication skills in English which is considered most vital in the industrial recruitment. Though most other countries have already defined sector wise required skills and abilities and thereby have developed infrastructure and expertise for developing the global workforce, Bangladesh is still in a vulnerable state in such endeavor as most of its engineering university curricula do not take the necessary measure to develop soft skills and communication skills in English among the potential technical graduates. Hence this paper focuses on the potential gap between the students' needs and the gap between the industry requirements and the existing curriculum in engineering universities of Bangladesh.

Due to the rapid change and growth in the industrialization worldwide and due to the change in the requirements of industry and that of the corporate world, a rapid change has taken place in defining and designing the imparting of the right skills and abilities in the graduates of tomorrow. There are quite a many requirements of skills as defined today by various recruiting agencies worldwide and they do so keeping a close watch with the changing requirements of the industry. Technical skills, communication skills and soft skills are the vital prerequisites for today's graduates (Erling, Seargeant, Solly, Chowdhury, & Rahman, 2012). Since curriculum of higher education institutions are directly connected with providing the right skills and education to match the global requirement of job market, all these skills and requirements have to be incorporated in the curriculum of higher education sector.

Employability in Government vs Private Sectors

Like many other countries, the work environment and scope

in the government sector in Bangladesh is very limited and hence undergoing a process of rapid transformation in the context of globalization and technological change, leaving the majority of the workforce in the informal sector, composed of non-farm or off-farm rural subsistence activities and of work in family-run, urban micro-enterprises. The rapid expansion of informal sector is a resultant of the inability of the formal sector to generate adequate employment opportunities. In Bangladesh, the labour force is growing much faster than employment opportunities in the formal sector, and therefore, the problems of rising unemployment and underemployment remain high on the development agenda (Asian Development Bank, 2011). Hence to merge this gap between the public and private sector, the Government of Bangladesh has taken quite a many projects and MOUs in partnership with Asian Development Bank (ADB), European Commission (EC) and International Labour Organization (ILO) in ensuring the funding and infrastructure connected with manpower development and training of various sorts for employability in Bangladesh and abroad.

Bangladesh has been very consistent in maintaining a moderate annual GDP rate of 6% for the last six years, keeping the political turmoil and various types of natural disasters. This growth has generated new jobs in the service and manufacturing sectors. Remittances contribute about 10% of GDP. Despite these positive trends, the economy and employment face serious challenges. The economic base depends on garments and remittances. Half of the labor force is working in low skill agricultural activities. While unemployment is reported at 5% in 2009, underemployment is at 29% signifying a mismatch between the supply of skills and demand in the labor market (World Bank, 2010). 80% of the workforce is employed in the informal sector experiencing unproductive, uncertain, and unregulated underemployment. The economy needs to diversify and expand. With this increased GDP, there has been growth in the economic and employment sectors and thus millions of jobs created in the course of time. Hundreds of Multi-National Companies (MNC) has found Bangladesh as an ideal place for investment due to the cheap cost of labour, though political restlessness is one single concern for these investors in Bangladesh.

Advantages of Effective Communication Skills in Global Scenario

A competitive job market today needs effective communication skills in workplaces. Within that, increasingly under globalization, English as communication skills plays a crucial role in employment (Dustmann & Fabbr, 2003; Erling, et al, 2012; Kossoudji, 1988; Rivera-Batiz, 1990; Shields & Price, 2002; Tainer, 1988 as cited in Roshid and Chowdhury, 2013) all over the world. English is often a decisive factor in employment opportunities with higher earnings (Bleakley & Chin, 2004; Casale & Posel, 2011; Chiswick, 1991; Chiswick & Miller, 1995; Davila & Mora, 2000; Dustmann & Fabbr, 2003; Tainer, 1988) and in organisations aiming at higher productivity (Tainer, 1988). On the other hand, people who are incompetent in English face difficulty in finding jobs, especially well-paid jobs (Carliner, 2000; Leslie & Lindley, 2001). Lack of English fluency drives to earning losses (Dustmann & Fabbr, 2003; Leslie & Lindley, 2001). Proficiency in English therefore, is needed for employees to advance in both local and international companies and to improve their technical knowledge and skills. It provides a foundation for what has been called "process skills" - problem-solving and critical thinking skills under the broad category of 'soft skills' that are needed to cope with the rapidly changing environment of the global workplace, one where English plays an increasingly important role. However, most of the general and technical universities have taken into account this global change and have initiated revising their respective curriculum keeping the changing needs of the students in match with the industry and corporate world. The most unfortunate part is that everything in the curriculum has taken a new look except the English curriculum in the Government engineering universities in Bangladesh. Most of the recruitment notifications contain a compulsory punch line "Highly articulate with excellent presentation and ***communication skills in English***". This is common to 100% job notifications in the private sectors starting from X class job to any higher positions.

Skills Development and Bangladesh Chapter

Until recently there was no such skills development infrastructure in Bangladesh, or an agency to measure the employability score of the Bangladeshi graduates. Only recently, few research works have been conducted on the importance of developing technical human capital, identifying the gaps between industry requirements and existing university curriculum keeping the changing phenomena in the industrial sector across the globe. Though off late, Bangladesh Government has initiated quite a many highly prioritized national programs such as Skills Employment Project, (SEP), National Technical and Vocational Qualifications Framework (NTVQF), Technical and Vocational Education and Training (TVET). The National Educational Policy (NEP, 2010) and the National Skills Development Policy (NSDP, 2011) have been approved by the Government with a view to articulate the strategies to monitor, guide, implement and bringing in reforms in these projects keeping the national and global requirements in mind. The NTVQF, currently being implemented in Bangladesh was initiated in 2008 as one of the most important building blocks of the Technical and Vocational Education and Training (TVET) Reform Project, funded by the European Commission (EC) and implemented by the International Labour Organization (ILO) in collaboration with the Government of Bangladesh (Ministry of Education, 2011).

Bangladesh has a large economy based on private sector and an illiteracy rate of 65 per cent. Three quarters of the population is rural; about 31 per cent lives below the international poverty line. This means that every third person is struggling every day to survive. Bangladesh is highly dependent on the remittances migrant workers send back to the country (indeed, these constitute the largest source of foreign capital (Ministry of Education, 2011). Numerous government reports and industry bodies have called for improvements to the skill levels of Bangladeshi workers so that the value of these remittances will increase (BMET, 2008).

The technical and vocational education and training sector is beset by a number of difficulties. These include insufficient quality assurance; lack of autonomy for training centers to adapt courses to local needs; extremely rigid traditional school-based curricula and vocational standards; excessively long course durations; lack of continuing professional teacher training; lack of access to skills for underprivileged groups; lack of regulation and certification of informal apprenticeships; and insufficient recognition of existing skills and informal learning, preventing labour mobility. The government recognizes that these shortcomings lead to a serious wastage of skills in the economy (Ministry of Education, 2011).

At present, underprivileged youth and adults constitute the majority of the workforce in export-oriented industries (such as the garment business, light engineering, electronics, construction, services and transport), where they frequently underperform or remain underemployed because they lack the requisite skills (ILO/ Mia, 2010). This does not imply that these MNCs will stop outsourcing from Bangladesh; rather they will continue refilling the void with the potential non-native candidates and hence Bangladeshi graduates will lose their own ground. One such example is that all the CEO of the five mobile telecommunication subscribers in Bangladesh are mostly from India and Sri Lanka. The lack of required communication skills among our candidates is only to blame.

Hence, it is high time, all universities and very specifically the technical universities in Bangladesh must take necessary measures to accommodate all the necessary soft and communication skills in the existing English curriculum and also ensure the successful transaction of these components to make sure that Bangladeshi university graduates should not let the lucrative employment opportunities slip away from their grip; rather they should be empowered enough to grab such opportunities abroad. Therefore, reorientation of curriculum for tomorrow, vocational sing of curriculum from schools towards university, inculcating training in technology to match the existing demand of the market are some of the necessities and demands of today's employment market. In this endeavor, Bangladesh Government needs to develop strategic partnership with private sector to develop the required technical manpower and develop infrastructure for training soft and communication skills in English in an attempt to make the university graduates globally employable. Since the universities are struggling to match the demands of industry, there should be strategic partnership between university and industry as to fulfill their employment requirements in terms of hard and soft skills. Whatever the support and logistics are being received from the foreign donor agencies seems very temporary. Ultimately Bangladesh Government in partnership with private sector; more specially, the industries will have to carry forward this employability mission.

Expanding Knowledge Exchanges

A group of villagers heard that Goha was in the area and they went out to the countryside to meet him and ask him to speak to their village. Goha willingly agreed. When meeting with the villagers, he looked out at the waiting faces and then asked: "How many of you know what I am going to talk about?" No one raised their hand. Goha then said, "If you don't know what I am going to talk about, then there is no need for me to be here." Goha left the village and returned to his tent in the countryside. The next day a village delegation came to see Goha begging him to return to the village to speak. Again, Goha willingly agreed. The people from the village and surrounding country side came to hear him speak. Goha arrived and moved to the front of the assembled villagers. Goha asked the question again. "How many of you know what I am going to talk about?" Now, the villagers remembering the last time when asked this question, all raised their hand. Goha looked out and responded, "If everyone here knows what I am going to talk about, then there is no reason or need for me to talk." Goha returned to his tent outside the village. The villagers were disappointed and very determined to have him speak to them. A group of village elders approach Goha asking, "Won't you please come to speak to us." Again, Goha willingly agreed. The village was flowing with people from near and far. Goha amazed by the large group asked the question again, "How many of you know what I am going to talk about?" The people realizing the difficulty in getting Goha to speak had gotten together to discuss how they would respond if asked the question. With the question asked, 50% of the villagers raised their hand. Goha looked around and then asked, "How many of you don't know what I am going to speak about?" The remaining 50% raised their hand. Goha said, "Well then, the 50% that know what I am going to talk about need to tell the 50% who don't know what I am going to talk about." With that Goha left the village. The villagers did not approach Goha again to speak. Goha's story has meaning for my being here today. First, I am not going to ask you "Do you know what I am going to talk about?" Second, I suspect as Goha knew, what he had to say was not that important. So he knew to keep his presence short. Third, our being together is about sharing ideas, exchanging information, to know what we want to know, and developing answers to what we need to know. It is us participating in a knowledge exchange village.

Individuals, Societies, Organizations: Knowledge Exchanges

As teachers, we know that economic and social development is direct result of the quality of our teachers and schools. The levels of formal education are vital to, with and in developing our communities. We know that development is applying information to economic and social needs. As depicted in Figure 1, education serves individuals, societies and organizations within societies through formal and informal learning structures. How we communicate and behave between and among individuals, societies and organizations is changing at lightning speed.

What is changing in how we exchange and share information? What is this lightening speed? Here are examples of what is happening in the world of knowledge exchange paths.

This is an example of what occurs in my family which includes 25 children and grandchildren ranging in age from 50 to 2 years old. It is 10am Saturday morning in Spartanburg, South Carolina and I take a picture on my cell phone, post it on my Instagram with hash tags noting my word press blog which carries my art work and the name of a local art gallery. Meanwhile my granddaughter in Bloomington, Illinois notes a statement on Instagram with "Cool Beans". Friends in Cairo, Bangkok and Elizabethtown respond by clicking the "liked" bottom. My 10 year old grandson from Richmond, Virginia calls me on his iPad where we see each other in real time telling me that his sister, Lucia, saved her money to buy Skyrim and asked if I wanted to play Minecraft. At about the same time, I am asked by a friend to meet for coffee on Facebook Places. The Springfield, Illinois city events director where my daughter is a media manager notes she is hiring a social media marketing coordinator to publicize the city's activities by coordinating and cascading announcements with and among Instagram, snapshot, the city's blog, Twitter, Facebook and web sites. By the way, my wife and I went out for pizza that evening because of a Tweet posting "Buy 1 Pizza and Get the 2nd Pizza Free."

A final example from a Twitter posted as a result of an east coast snow storm this past February was a call for their community to help the elderly and sick. The posting read shovel it Forward, is asking anyone young, healthy and in possession of a shovel to consider shovelling out walks for the elderly or sick.

Social Media, Internet and Knowledge Exchanges

Our world, our societies, our local communities, our organizations are in the midst of a social media knowledge exchange revolution. It is present everywhere. It is huge and it is growing, adapting, ever changing into new and more dynamic forms. It is creating businesses and more important creating new ways of how we function, live out daily lives, how we process information, how we think. A revolution is here in information sharing, participation, collaboration, and learning. As Bullas noted, apparently there are 600 million more people that own a mobile phone compared to those who own a toothbrush. Some research reveals that there are 4.8 billion mobile users but only 4.2 billion people with a toothbrush. Does this mean that every mobile should be sold with a free toothbrush or should you need to produce your toothbrush before you are given possession of your new mobile phone to ensure that future personal close encounters are engaging and pleasant? Another interpretation of those statistics is that toothbrushes are too expensive.

Bullas offers further perspectives as to the magnitude of social media web demographics.

1. 72% of internet users are now active on social media
2. 18-29 year olds have an 89% usage
3. 71% of users access social media from a mobile device
4. Facebook has over 1.15 billion users
5. 23% of Facebook users login in at least 5 times per day
6. 47% of Americans say Facebook is their #1 influencer of purchases
7. 70% of marketers used Facebook to gain new customers
8. There are over 1 billion Google + accounts
9. Google + has over 359 million monthly active users
10. Google + is growing 33% per year
11. Twitter has over 550 million users
12. 34% of marketers use Twitter to generate leads
13. Instragram has over 150 million active users
14. 1.2 million blog posts per day
15. 67% of businesses say social media is their best source for advice on products and consumers

Jones noted that businesses are shifting from traditional marketing to social media marketing. It helps,

1. Manage and build brand reputation
2. Provides information, troubleshooting, user groups
3. Gets products and services closer to the customer
4. Offers creative and effective ways to learn
5. Features new and inexpensive ways to support clients

6. Is less expensive than traditional marketing
7. Offers ways to measure and track performance

As an example, the city of Charleston, South Carolina uses the following social media platforms to market their tourism.

The name Facebook, Twitter, Instagram, Google + are widely known. However, there are an ever increasing number of social media networks. The variety of alternatives reflects a revolution aimed at lifestyle markets, specialized services and products, and smaller takes on larger social media platforms. Social media availability is growing exponentially sharing, seeking and providing information to build market niches.

What do we know about social media and India in 2014? According to Nayak's research published in dazeinfo.com, the following were noted.

1. Of the 92 million Face book users in India, nearly 50% of them are between the ages of 18-24 years of age
2. By increasing internet penetration, Face book membership rises
3. In India, Face book is now the 2nd highest after the United States
4. Face book user demography is based on gender with 69.5 users being male and about 22 million female
5. Among teen agers 18-24, nearly 34 million of 37% of users are male and 11.6 million are female users
6. Among the teen age group 18-24, nearly 19 million users updated their status as engaged and 2.2 million indicated that they were in a relationship
7. More than 52% of Face book which is 48 million users did not mention their relationship status, e.g., single, engaged, married, in a relationship, etc.

Admittedly, current social media data profiles are difficult to obtain and substantiate given the nature of competitive private enterprises. In addition, platform transparency is difficult to obtain in terms of rolling and active membership, number of individual multiple daily hits, number of accounts by the same person, types and amounts of advertising revenues and the types and forms of social media platforms and adaptations being developed. Even with transparency and comparative data limitations, we cannot refute the tremendous social media impact on individuals, societies and organizations. In other words, given what is seen and experienced, social media is big and it is growing with different forms and different names leaving an unimaginable huge "fingerprint" on knowledge exchanges.

The issue of defining social media is complicated by its broad, colloquial use. For some, according to Garrity, social media is Facebook, Twitter, Myspace, etc. Others define social media more loosely in which users share and interact with prescribed content. According to Jones, "Social medial essentially is a category of online media where people are talking, participating, sharing, networking and bookmarking online. Most social media services encourage discussion, feedback, voting, comments and sharing of information from all interested parties." Social media provides a means to stay connected to sites, resources and people. It allows for and encourages recognition and participation. There are different types of social media including social news, social sharing, social professional networks and social bookmarking. These forms of internet communications have users creating online communities to share information, ideas, personal messages, pictures, and videos.

Social media is providing new ways in how we use the internet. Instead of using it as a tool to look up information or purchase merchandise, we are inserting ourselves into the web and using it to connect with other people. As Lu, Newman and Miller (2014) stated, "These digital locations have evolved from niche communication tools to common elements that promote public and private agendas, commerce, education, and transcend multiple social classes." This change has far reaching effects on creating a global collective intelligence and repositories of knowledge. The interactive worldwide web is the greatest information sharing tool in human history, with impact broader than the printing press in knowledge sharing.

Social media is dramatically changing the landscape and the ways in which we can provide participation and recognition. Our youth are growing up with fast response time and immediate availability of ideas, data, exchanges, pictures, videos. As youth embrace these dynamic forms of social interaction, our young people are changing their perceptions and expectations of learning. As we exchange information and opinions during this conference, we must remember that social media like education is meant to provide and direct offline behaviors. Commercial organizations want loyal purchasing customers, societies wants informed and participating citizens and we in education want future citizens and leaders to be productive and positive contributing members to their families and their communities.

One purpose of our conference is to explore, expand and refine our understanding of how we use knowledge exchanges with an understanding of how we learn. In order words, what can we learn from social media platforms for teaching and learning and how we can use this in teaching? A partial answer is to build upon what we as professional educators know as to how people learn. We typically learn effectively when,

1. We learn by doing

   We are actually involved in doing that which is to be learned

2. We learn with a purpose

   We are faced with a problem to be solved

   We are faced with a question to be answered

   We are faced with a task, e.g., an evaluation, a comparison, estimation

   We learn when we see the importance, i.e., when learning is personalized – is seen as important to the learner

3. We learn visually

4. We learn step-by-step

   We learn in increments that build upon each other

5. We learn by reinforcement

We learn by positive reinforcement of what is learned

The more closely the reinforcement, the more likely retention

Immediate reinforcement enables building upon correct responses

We learn by being successful in our learning

6. We learn by activities that lead us to arrive at answers on our own
7. We learn by using what has been learned

We learn by practicing/implementing what has been learned

1. We learn from each other

We learn from peers

We learn from self-help groups

2. We learn when there is a plan as to what is to be learned, how it is be learned and how we know that we have learned

An example of these learning attributes was illustrated recently when my wife and I moved to a new city, to a new home. My wife and I were invited to dinner with a group on the other side of the city. Since we have not ventured out much and since our GPS would not have the most recent road construction, Michael gave us directions over the telephone how to get there. We set out and quickly got lost. I stopped at a convenience store and ask the clerk how to get to the restaurant. The very nice store clerk stated "You cannot miss it. It is a well known restaurant. You go down this road for about 2 miles and take a right at the corner with a filling station on the left hand corner. Then go straight for about 2 miles pass the railroad tracks and at the first cross street after the overpass you should be able to see the restaurant on the left hand side across from the water tower". When I got back into the car, my wife asked "Any problems?" In which I responded "It's as clear as mud, but we are going in the right direction." A little further down the road, I was feeling at lost again wondering if I had missed a turn – was that corner? So I pulled over to the side of the road and asked a friendly face if they knew where the restaurant was located and if so I was headed in the right direction.

The kind person, said yes, but I missed the turn to the right. I should go to the next corner and take a right and then left and I should be going in the right direction. Eventually, after two more stops, we arrived at the restaurant in which the first question asked of us, did we have any problems in finding the restaurant. Of course, not wanting to appear that I could not follow directions, I said "No Problems" to which my wife smiled. This experience tells us about learning and the key attributes needed in learning. The key words in this learning experience were:

1. Personalized
2. Visualization
3. Problem centered
4. Reinforcement
5. Participation
6. Incremental learning
7. Repetition
8. Recognition

A Selfie Test

So let us do a quick Selfie Test with the following statements.

1. We learn better by doing. That is, if we learn a particular behavior or skill, we should — that behavior.

   A. Do

   B. Write

   C. Recognize

   D. Read About

   Answer: Do

2. It is not enough that we are actively involved. We must be actively involved doing that behavior which is to be learned. That which we do should be— as the behavior to be learned.

   A. Different

   B. Recognized

C. The Same

D. Listed

Answer: C

3. It is apparent that when we are given _____ we will learn more effectively.

A. A way to approach learning

B. A problem to solve

C. A narrative description

D. A motivator

Answer: B

4. Focusing on a problem to be solved by an answer is related to the need for us to be actively doing. Focusing on a problem allows us to engage in problem solving to determine which _____ is best.

A. Problem

B. Solution

C. Question

D. Answer

Answer: D

5. A factor which enhances retention is using what has been learned. Using what has been learned is accomplished through discussing its implications, through applying it in other situations, through basing further learning on it and by continuing to practice it. We should organize course material so that what is learned at one point is _____ in further learning.

A. Compared

B. Taught

C. Used

D. Related

Answer: C

6. There is agreement on the value of reinforcement following as closely after responses. Immediate reinforcement enables us to

build on correct responses. We should thus be concerned that good responses and performances are reinforced _____.

A. Frequently

B. Consistently

C. When Necessary

D. As Soon As Possible

Answer: D

7. We must make definite decisions about what behaviors will be reinforced. This requires that we establish objectives for learning. Which two of the following objectives best fit with the concept of doing?

A. Students will be able to interpret data

B. Students will be able to list data

C. Students will be able to identify teacher preferences

D. Students will be able to state problems

Answer: A and D

In examining social media exchanges and their platforms, much of what we know of how we learn is present and effectively used. Today, organizations are taking advantage of these learning attributes in their social media platforms. E-learning and learning management systems such as Moodle, Blackboard, Wise, etc. are employing instructional designs to deliver, involve, track, manage and reinforce learning. Typically, learning management systems are closed circuit platforms, i.e., restricted access to classes, so the idea of sharing content and reusing materials does not exist outside of the learning system.

Knowledge Exchange Questions

What would Goha suggest as to how we use our time during this conference? I think Goha would say, “It is not for me to decide. It is you that makes the difference. It is you that have the questions, the answers and the solutions.” I think Goha would say, we need to use this time together to explore how we can better build upon what we know and what we need to known. We have a very unique and precious opportunity to be together at this conference to exchange and develop our knowledge for improving our profession. As we gather, here are some questions to begin our journey for exchanging and growing in our knowledge.

1. Social media has become a growing part of our business and social life. How can we use social media learning attributes in our classrooms, e.g., in how we teach? How do we incorporate the learning episodes accessible in social media into our instructional plans? What do we need to do this?
2. As knowledge exchanges increasingly become a part of electronic communications, how does it advance student learning and if so how do we take advantage of it? How do we measure it? What are its limitations?
3. Are computer skills and knowledge exchanges new literacy skills? What role should formal education play in providing the necessary computer skills for students to navigate and use e-learning?
4. Let's ask our future teachers, what skills and knowledge do they think they need? How do we prepare them for a career 20 to 30 years from now?

I suggest that we exchange and share our insights over the next couple of days by writing down our questions, our comments, and our solutions in a journal or blog as a knowledge exchange path. Let's do some micro blogging in order to set an agenda to improve our profession. Again, I am delighted to be here and am looking forward to meeting you and to sharing thoughts with you on the needs of education and the role of our profession in providing education for our future. "How many of you know what I am going to talk about?" Please accept my very best wishes for an exciting and productive conference.

References

1. Anderson, Chris. What is Quality in Education?, Bizmanualz, July 15, 2009.
2. Abernathy, T. Coutts, J. Royce, D. Bartram, J. Kramer, D.

Chapesike, K. Gold, I. Marsh, L. (2001). Knowledge transfer: Looking beyond health (2000). Report on the conference held in Toronto, October 26-27, (2000).

3. Agarwal, Shailja and Mital, Monika (March 2009) "An Exploratory Study of Indian University Students' Use of Social Networking Web Sites: Implications for the Workplace," Business Communication Quarterly, pp.105-110.

4. Alhawary, F. A. & et al, (2011). Building a Knowledge Repository: Linking Jordanian Universities Elibrary in an integrated database system, International Journal of Business and Management, 6(4), 129-135.

5. Altbach, P.G., Reisberg, L. and Rumbley, L.E. 2009. *Trends in global higher education: Tracking an academic revolution.* Parys: UNESCO.

6. Anderson, R.C. Reeb, D.M. (2003). Founding-family ownership and firm performance: evidence from the S&P 500. The Journal of Finance, 58(3): 1301-1328.

7. Argote, L. Ingram, P. (2000). Knowledge transfer: a basis for competitive advantage in firms. Organizational Behavior and Human Decision Processes, 82(1): 150-169.

8. Arvanitis .S, Kubli .U, Woerter .M (2008). University-industry knowledge and technology transfer in Switzerland: What university scientists think about co-operation with private enterprises. Res. Policy, 37: 1865-1883.

9. Asian Development Bank, "Educational and National Development in Asia: Trends, Issues, Policies, and Strategies," Manila, Philippines: Asian Development Bank, 2001.

10. Atbach, P.G. 2010. Plenary paper on higher education reform worldwide. Annual Conference of Comparative and International Education Society (CIES). Palmer House Hilton, Chicago, VSA, 28 February – 5 March.

11. Barnes, T., Pashby, I. and Gibbons, A. (2002) "Effective University-Industry Interaction: A Multi-Case Evaluation of Collaborative Rand Projects". European Management Journal, 20 (3), 272- 275.

12. Barbolla.A & Corredera, J. (2009). Critical factors for success in university-industry research projects. Technology Analysis & Strategic Management, 21(5), 599-616.

13. Bergmark, U. (2007). Ethical learning through meetings with others. The International Journal of Learning, 14, 105-112.

14. Bismillah Khatoon bt Abdul Kader, "Malaysia's Experience in Training Teachers to Use ICT. In E. Meleisea (Ed.)," ICT in Teacher Education: Case Studies from the Asia-Pacific Region, Bangkok: UNESCO, pp 10-22, 2008.

15. Bozeman, B. (2000): Technological transfer and public policy: a review of research and theory. Research Policy 29(4-5): 627-655.

16. Brennenraedts, R.M.F., Bekkers, R., and Verspagen, B. (2006) 'The different channels of university- industry knowledge transfer: Empirical evidence from Biomedical Engineering', Eindhoven:Eindhoven Centre for Innovation Studies, The Netherlands

17. Brown .G & O'Brien T. (1981). University–industry links: Government as blacksmith. Technovation, 1, 85–95.

18. Bureau of Manpower Employment and Training (BMET). 2008. *National Forum on Improved Skills for Overseas Workers in Dhaka, Bangladesh.* Dhaka, Directorate of Technical Education (DTE), Government of Bangladesh.

19. Castel franchi, C. (2007). Six critical remarks on science and the construction of the knowledge society. *Journal of Science Communication,* 6(4), 1-3.

20. Central Board of Secondary Education (2003), Value Education, A Handbook for Teachers. New Delhi, CBSE.

21. Changsheng. C., Sannvya. L., Hong. W., and Zengzhao. C. (2011). Dual track teaching modal based on dual coding theory [J]. China Education Info, (3):52-55.

22. Cohen, W. M., Nelson, R. and Walsh, J (2002) 'Links and Impacts: the Influence of Public Research on Industrial R&D' Management Science, Vol. 48, No. 1, pp. 1-23

23. Colvin, J., Tobler, N., and Anderson, J.A. (2007). Productivity and multi-screen computer displays. Rocky Mountain Communication Review, 2(1), 31–53.

24. Commission of the European Communities (CEC) (2005) 'Mobilising the brainpower of Europe: enabling universities to make their full contribution to the Lisbon Strategy, COM(2005), 152 final, Brussels, 20.4.2005.

25. Coombs, P.H. 1985. *The world crisis in education: the view from the eighties.* New York: Oxford University Press.

26. Croissant, J. L.; Smith-Doerr, L. (2007): Organizational contexts of science: Boundaries and relationships between university and industry. In: J. Wajcman, E. Hackett, O. Amsterdamska and M. Lynch (Eds.): Handbook of science and technology studies. Cambridge MA, MIT Press: 691-718.

27. Davis D, Evans M, Jadad A, Perrier L, Rath D, Ryan D, et al. The case for knowledge translation: Shortening the journey from evidence to effect. BMJ 2003; 327:33–35.

28. Dr.Dandapani, S., (2000), *A Textbook of Advanced Educational Psychology,* Anmol Publications Pvt. Ltd., New Delhi – 110 002.

29. Drucker, P.F. (1969). *The age of discontinuity: Guidelines to our changing society.* New York, NY: Harper & Row.

30. Erling, E, J., Seargeant, P., Solly, M., Chowdhury, Q, M. and Rahman, S. (2012). Attitudes to English as a language for International development in rural Bangladesh. *The Open University Publications,* British Council, UK.

31. Etzkowitz, H. and Leydesdorff, L. (2000) 'The dynamic of innovation: from National Systems and "Mode 2" to triple Helix of university-industry-government relations'. Research Policy, 29, 109-123.

32. Evers, H. (2003) Transition towards a Knowledge Society: Malaysia and Indonesia in Comparative Perspective. Comparative Sociology, 2, 1, 355-373.

33. European Union/International Labour Organization / Government of Bangladesh. (2009). *Bangladesh Skills*

Development Policy. Final Draft. Decent Work. Dhaka, Government of Bangladesh and ILO.

34. Ewell, P.T. 1998. National trends in assessing student learning. *J. Engr. Education* 87, No. 2:107-113.
35. Fontaine, C.; Haarman, A. and Schmid, S.: The stakeholder theory. 2006, http://www.edalys.fr/documents/Stakeholders%20theory.pdf.
36. Fothergill, A. (2000). Knowledge transfer between researchers and practitioners. Natural Hazards Review, May, 91-98.
37. Freeman, R.E.: The politics of stakeholders theory: some future directions. Business Ethics Quarterly 4(4), 409-422., 1994.
38. Friedman, T.L. 2009. *Hot, Flat & Crowded: Why the world needs a green revolution- and how we can renew our global future.* London: Penguin.
39. Graham ID, Harrison MB, Logan J, and the KT Theories Research Group. A review of planned change (knowledge translation) models, frameworks and theories. Presented at the JBI International Convention, Adelaide, Australia, Nov. 28-30, 2005.
40. Gross, M. (2010). *Ignorance and Surprise: Science, Society, and Ecological Design.* Cambridge, MA: MIT Press.
41. Guillermo Kelley-Salinas (2000) - Different Educational Inequalities: ICT an option to close the gaps - Latin American Institute of Educational Communication (ILCE), Mexico - pp. 21-36.
42. Habermas, J. 1968. *Toward a rational society: Student protest, science and politics.* Boston: Beacon Press.
43. Hamilton SF 1999. Germany and the United States in Comparative Perspective. *International Journal of Sociology*, 20:3-20
44. Hare, H. (2007). Survey of ICT and Education in Africa: Ethiopia Country Report (ICT in Education in Ethiopia).
45. Hargreaves, A. 2003. Teaching in the knowledge society: education in the age of insecurity. New York: Teachers College Press.

46. Harmon, B., Ardishvili, A., Cardozo, R., Elder, T., Leuthold, J., Parshall, J., Raghian, M. and Smith,D., (1997) 'Mapping the University Technology Transfer Process' Journal of Business Venturing,12, pp. 423-434

47. Harvey, P.L. (2010). Applying social systems thinking and community informatics thinking in education. In Rudestam, K.E., & Schoenholtz-Read, J. (Eds.), 91-128. *Handbook of online learning*. Thousand Oaks, CA: Sage Publications.

48. Huberman, M. (1990). "Linkage between researchers and practitionners: A qualitative study." American Educational Research Journal 27(2): 363-391.

49. Huling-Austin, J. A systhesis of research on teacher induction programs and practices; paper presented to the Annual Meeting of the American Educational Research Association, New Orleans LA, April 5-9, 1988.

50. Gail B. West (1999), "Teaching and Technology in Higher Education: Changes And Challenges," Journal article of Adult Learning, vol. 10, Issue: 4, pp. 16, 26.

51. Geisler, E. (2003): Benchmarking inter-organisational technology cooperation: the link between infrastructure and sustained performance. International Journal of Technology Management 25(8): 675-702.

52. Innerarity, D. (2012). Power and knowledge: The politics of the knowledge society, *European Journal of Social Theory, 16*(1), 3-16.

53. International Labour Organization. /Mia, A. (2010). *Qualifications Frameworks: Implementation and Impact. Background Case Study on Bangladesh.* Skills and Employability Department, Geneva, ILO.

54. International Labour Organization. (2013). *Bangladesh: Skills Vision 2016.* Dhaka, Ministry of Education and ILO. http://www.moedu.gov.bd (Accessed 14 August 2013.)

55. J.B. Quinn, The Intelligent Enterprise (New York, NY: Free Press, 1992). 2. The notion of the learning organization is explored in

detail in P.M. Senge, The Fifth Discipline: The Art and Practice of the Learning Organization (New York, NY: Doubleday, 1990)

56. Johnson, D.W., Skon, L. & Johnson, R. (1980). Effects of cooperative, competitive and individualistic conditions on children's problem solving performance. *American Educational Research Journal 17,* 83 - 94.

57. Johnson, W. H. A. and Johnston, D. A. (2004) 'Organisational knowledge creating processes and the performance of university-industry collaborative R and D projects'. International Journal of Technology Management, 27 (1), 93-114.

58. Katz, J. S. and Martin, B. R. (1997) 'What is research collaboration', Research Policy, 26, 1-18.

59. Kelly, G.P., Altbach, P.G. and Arnove, R.F. 1982. Trends in Comparative Education. In: Altbach, P.G., Arnove, R.F. and Kelly, G.P. (eds). *Comparative Education.* New York: Macmillan.

60. Kittl, C. & Edegger,F. & Petrovic,O. 2009. Learning by pervasive gaming an empirical study in distributed learning environments. In H.Rue & D. Parsons (Eds), Innovative mobile learning. New York: Information Science Reference. 61-62.

61. Kozma, R.B, (2005).National policies that connect ICT-based education reform to economic and social development. An interdisciplinary journal of humans in ICT environment 1(2) 117-156.

62. Landry, R. and Amara, N. (1998) 'The impact of transaction costs on the institutional structuration of collaborative academic research'. Research Policy, 27, 901-913.

63. Lavis, J., Ross, S., McLeod, C., Gildner, A. (2003b). Measuring the impact of health research. Journal of Health Service Research Policy, 8 (3), 165-170.

64. Ledward, B.C. and Hirata, D.: An Overview of 21st Century Skills. Kamehameha Schools Research & Evaluation, Honolulu, 2011.

65. Lewis, S., Pea R., and Rosen, J. (2010) "Beyond participation to co-creation of meaning: mobile social media in generative learning communities," Social Science Information, (49)3 pp.351-369.

66. Lomas, J. (2000). Using 'linkage and exchange' to move research into policy at a Canadian foundation. Essay. Health Affairs, 19 (3).

67. Mariæ, I.; Barišiæ, P. and Jurjeviæ, I.: Knowledge and skills needed in knowledge economy. In Hunjak, T.; Lovrenèiæ, S. and Tomièiæ, S., eds.: Proceedings of 23rd International Conference "Central European Conference of Information and Intelligent Systems". Faculty of Organization and Informatics – University of Zagreb, Vara•din, pp.181-185, 2012.

68. Moreno, J. 2012. Plenary address at the 2012 Bi-Annual Conference of CESE (Comparative Education Society in Europe), University of Salamanca, Salamanca, Spain, June 2012.

69. Newman, R. E. and Michael T. Miller, M. T., (2014) "Connecting Secondary Media Skills: Recommendations for Administrators," in Educational Leadership and Administration: Teaching and Program Development, (25) pp. 54-64, ISSN: 1532-0723.

70. Paavola, S. & Hakkarainen, K. (2005). The knowledge creation metaphor: An emergent epistemological approach to learning. Science & Education, 14, 535-557.

71. Prabhu.G.(1999). Implementing university–industry joint product innovation projects. Technovation, 19, 495-505.

72. Ramírez Córcoles, Y.; Santos Peñalver, J. and Tejada Ponce (2011). Á Intellectual capital in Spanish public universities: stakeholders' information needs. Journal of Intellectual Capital.Vol.12 (3), 356-376.

73. Reagans, R., B. McEvily. 2003. Network Structure and Knowledge Transfer: The Effects of Cohesion and Range, Administrative Science Quarterly, 48, pp. 240-267

74. Roshid, M, M. and Chowdhury, R. (2013). English language proficiency and employment: A case study of Bangladeshi graduates in Australian employment market. Mevlana International Journal of Education an (MIJE), 3 (1) pp. 68-81.

75. Shin, J.C. 2010. Scholarship of Service: faculty perceptions, workloads and reward systems. In: Research Institute for Higher

Education, Hiroshima University. *The Changing Academic Profession in International and Quantitative Perspectives: A focus on teaching & research activities.* Hiroshima: Research Institute for Higher Education, Hiroshima University: 173-190.

76. Singh, N., Lehnert, K., and Bostick, K. (September/October 2012) "Global Social Media Usage: Insights into Reaching Consumers Worldwide," Thunderbird International Business Review, (54) pp. 683-700.

77. Steyn, G M. (n.d.). Harnessing the power of knowledge in higher education. Education, 124(4), p.627.

78. Sutherland, L. and Wolhuter, C.C. 2002. Do good researchers make good teachers. *Perspectives in Education* 20(3):77-83.

79. Szulanski, G. (2000). "The process of knowledge transfer: A diachronic analysis of stickiness."Organizational Behavior and Human Decision Processes 82(3), pp. 9-27

80. Taneja, V.R., (1974), *Educational Thought and Practice,* Sterling Publishers Pvt. Ltd., New Delhi – 110 016.

81. Tsai CM (2009). The knowledge diffusion model associated with innovative knowledge. Exp. Sys. Appl., 36: 11323-11331.

82. Tayebeh .A et al (2011). Factors affecting on collaboration of industry with University African Journal of Business Management Vol. 5(32), pp. 12401-12407,(14) December, 2011.

83. Vallima, J. & Hoffman, D. (2008). Knowledge society discourse and higher education. *Higher Education, 56*(3), 265-285.

84. van Weert, T. J. (2006). Education of the twenty-first century: New professionalism in lifelong learning, knowledge development and knowledge sharing. *Education and Information Technologies, 11*(3), 217-237.

85. Volman M. (2005). Variety of roles for a new type of teacher. Educational technology and the teacher profession. Teacher and Teacher Education, 21, 15-31.

86. United Nations Educational, Scientific and Cultural Organization (2005). Toward knowledge societies. *UNESCO World Report.* Conde-sur-Noireau, France: Imprimerie Corlet.

87. Ward, K. 2003. Faculty Service Roles and the Scholarship of Engagement. In: *ASHE-ERIC Higher Education Report*, volume 29, number 5. San Francisco: Jossey Bass.

88. Watson, D.M. (2001). Pedagogy before Technology: Re-thinking the Relationship between ICT and Teaching. Education and Information Technologies, 6, 4, 251-266.

89. Wolhuter, C.C. 1996. Whatever happened to education in the erstwhile Union of the Socialist Soviet Republics *Paidonomia* 19(1): 21-33.

90. Wolhuter, C.C. 2003. Die beoogde stelsel van tweeledige beroepsonderwys en –opleiding in Suid-Afrika: potensiaalbepaling vanuit 'n vergelykende perspektief. *Suid-Afrikaanse Tydskrif vir Opvoedkunde*, 23(2): 145-15.

91. Wolhuter, C.C. 2004. Education in Tanzania: Attempting to create an education system for a Sub-Saharan African country. *SA-eDUC* 1(2): 72-94.

92. Wolhuter, C.C. 2012. 'n Wêreldklasuniversiteit in Suid-Afrika: ideaal, wenslik, haalbaar, werklikheid, hersenskim? *LitNet Akademies* 9(2): 284-308.

93. World Bank. 2002. *Constructing knowledge societies: New challenges for tertiary education.* Washington DC: World Bank.

94. Yousef, A. B. and Dahamini, M. (2008). The Economics of E-Learning: The Impact of ICT on Student Performance in Higher Education: Direct Effects, Indirect Effects and Organizational Change.